GCSE

Chemistry
CLASSBOOK

Bob McDuell

Every effort has been made to trace copyright holders and to obtain their permission for the use of copyright material. The author and publisher will gladly receive information enabling them to rectify any error or omission in subsequent editions.

First published 1997

Contains material from GCSE Science Classbook first published 1996

Letts Educational
Aldine House
Aldine Place
London W12 8AW
0181 740 2266

Text: © Bob McDuell

Design and illustrations © BPP (Letts Educational) Ltd 1997

Design, page layout and illustrations: Ken Vail Graphic Design

All our rights reserved. No part of this publication may be reproduced, stored in a retrieval system, or transmitted, in any form or by any means, electronic, mechanical, photocopying, recording or otherwise, without prior permission of Letts Educational.

British Library Cataloguing-in-Publication Data

A CIP record for this book is available from the British Library

ISBN 1 85758 566 6

Printed and bound in Great Britain by Caledonian International Book Manufacturing Ltd, Glasgow

Letts Educational is the trading name of
BPP (Letts Educational) Ltd

Acknowledgements

The author and publisher are grateful to the following for permission to reproduce photographs:

The Ancient Art & Architecture Collection 24.6; Bruce Coleman Limited 8.4; 21.2; 23.2 (conglomerate); 24.2; 25.3; 35.4; 47.1; Eye Ubiquitous Picture Library B5.3; Ford Motor Company 41.2; Geoscience Features Picture Library A3.3 (bottom); B6.2; 23.2 (limestone and sandstone); 23.3; 23.5; 25.1; High Peak Borough Council 24.3; Holt Studios International 50.3; ICI Plc. 50.1; Image Select 32.2; Bob McDuell 18.2; B4.2; Milepost 921/2 Picture Library 19.2; Oxford Scientific Films Limited A3.3 (top right); C4.2; 47.2; Rex Features Limited 35.5; Science Photo Library A1.2; 3.1; 8.1; A3.3 (top left); 14.1; B4.1; 22.4; 23.1; 24.4; 32.1; 34.1; 35.1; 35.2; 35.3; C1.2; C1.3; 44.1; 45.2; C5.2; 46.1; United Distillers 10; Wilson/Biss Lancaster Plc. 6.6.

CONTENTS

Introduction — 1
Materials and their properties — 2

A Classifying materials

- **1** Materials — 4
- **2** Solids, liquids and gases — 6
- **A1** Handling and identifying gases — 8
- **3** Structure of the atom — 10
- **4** Ionic bonding — 12
- **5** Covalent bonding — 14
- **6** Structure — 16
- **7** Elements, mixtures and compounds — 18
- **8** Separating mixtures – 1 — 20
- **9** Separating mixtures – 2 — 22
- **10** Separating mixtures – 3 — 24
- **11** Separating mixtures – 4 — 26
- **A2** Structure of metals — 28
- **A3** Alloys — 30

B Changing materials

- **12** Solubility — 32
- **13** Change — 34
- **14** Crude oil and its refining — 36
- **15** Uses of alkanes — 38
- **16** Cracking hydrocarbons — 40
- **B1** Fuels — 42
- **17** Addition polymerisation — 44
- **B2** Condensation polymerisation — 46
- **18** Ethanol — 48
- **B3** The chemistry of food — 50
- **B4** The carbon cycle — 52
- **19** Reactivity series — 54
- **20** Stability of compounds — 56
- **B5** Corrosion of metals – 1 — 58
- **B6** Corrosion of metals – 2 — 60
- **21** Extraction of metals – 1 — 62
- **22** Extraction of metals – 2 — 64
- **23** Types of rock — 66
- **24** Uses of rocks — 68
- **25** The rock cycle — 70
- **26** Plate tectonics — 72
- **27** Chemical equations — 74
- **28** The mole — 76
- **29** Chemical formulae by experiment — 78
- **30** Calculations from equations — 80
- **31** Concentration calculations — 82
- **B7** Electrochemistry – 1 — 84
- **B8** Electrochemistry – 2 — 86

C Patterns of behaviour

32 The Periodic Table	88	
33 Structure of the Periodic Table	90	
34 The alkali metals	92	
35 Noble gases	94	
36 The halogens – 1	96	
37 The halogens – 2	98	
38 Rates of chemical reactions – 1	100	
39 Rates of chemical reactions – 2	102	
40 Rates of chemical reactions – 3	104	
41 Rates of chemical reactions – 4	106	
42 Enzymes	108	
C1 Air	110	
43 Reversible reactions and equilibrium	112	
44 The Haber process	114	
45 The Contact process	116	
C2 Water	118	
C3 Testing for ions	120	
C4 Calcium carbonate	122	
C5 Hard water	124	
C6 Soaps and soapless detergents	126	
46 Acids and alkalis	128	
47 Neutralisation	130	
48 Salt formation – 1	132	
49 Salt formation – 2	134	
50 Fertilisers	136	

Index 138

INTRODUCTION

This Letts GCSE Chemistry classbook has been specially compiled for the new GCSE syllabuses. It is closely linked to the National Curriculum and will help you to master the key concepts in Key Stage 4 Science, and to refresh your memory of the important topics from Key Stage 3.

The book is also suitable as part of your study towards all Double Science syllabuses. You will also need to study from the companion GCSE Biology classbook and GCSE Physics classbook.

The book is divided into three sections, labelled A, B and C:

- **A** Classifying materials
- **B** Changing materials
- **C** Patterns of behaviour

It has also been split into 67 topics called 'units'. Some of these units are numbered separately and are prefixed by a section letter. For example, in section A there are units 1, 2, 3 to 11 and units A1, A2 and A3.

If you are doing Chemistry you will need to study all of the numbered units and some of the lettered units. If you are doing Double Science you do not have to study any units prefixed with a letter. Your teacher will give you guidance on which units to study.

Each unit covers two pages and begins with a list of questions which will introduce you to ideas in that unit. Each is clearly written and illustrated, and there are questions for you to think about which will help you to understand the ideas involved.

It is very important to do regular homework in support of your work at school. We have therefore produced a homework book to accompany this classbook which contains a wide variety of questions, very closely linked to the content of this book. It also has topic summaries to remind you of the key points from the classbook, and a glossary so that you can find out the meaning of any important scientific terms. The homework book will provide a valuable way to practise and reinforce what you learn in class.

We hope that this classbook and the homework book will help you to progress in GCSE Chemistry or GCSE Science. Both the books have been written by an experienced examiner and teacher, very much with exam success in mind. But as well as helping you to achieve your desired grade, we hope that these books will give you an insight into the enjoyment of Chemistry and Science, which is vital to an understanding of the modern world.

Materials and their properties

This GCSE course is written in three sections. Each of the sections builds upon topics you have studied at Key Stage 3. Some of the content is common to GCSE Science courses and extension material is included in all three sections.

Throughout your course you should try to write chemical equations. Usually these will be balanced symbol equations but they will also include ionic equations. Ionic equations often give a clearer insight into what is actually happening in terms of electron transfer.

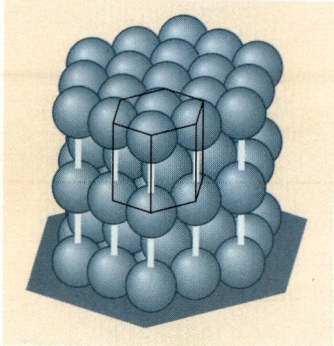

Section A, **Classifying materials** extends your understanding of matter being made up of particles and the way particles are arranged in solids, liquids and gases. It also introduces you to a model of the structure of atoms involving protons, neutrons and electrons.

The section introduces the ways in which atoms are joined or bonded together. Ionic and covalent bonding are two important methods of bonding. Bonding in different ways can lead to different structures, including molecular and giant structures. Many properties of materials can be explained in terms of their atomic, ionic or molecular structures.

The structure of pure metals based upon close-packing of atoms is considered in detail and also the structure of mixtures of metals, called alloys.

Section B is **Changing materials**. This involves an understanding of chemical change.

Crude oil is a valuable resource and this section extends your knowledge of how crude oil was formed in the Earth, how it is refined by fractional distillation, and how it is used to make many valuable materials including polymers (plastics). Polymers are divided into addition and condensation polymers. Polymers are also classified as thermoplastic or thermosetting according to the way they change on heating. The section also deals with other fuels, including fossil fuels and renewable fuels.

Metal ores are also important resources in the Earth. This section deals with the methods used to extract a metal from its ores, including electrolysis and reduction. The method used to extract a metal from its ores is related to the position of the metal in the reactivity series. The corrosion of metals is also linked to the position of the metal in the reactivity series.

The chemistry of food is also considered in this section. Food includes chemicals called carbohydrates, fats, proteins, vitamins and minerals.

This section also extends your knowledge and understanding of rocks and how the three types of rocks – igneous, sedimentary and metamorphic – can be formed, and how one type of rock is converted into another. The theory of plate tectonics is also studied. This explains many observations about the formation, deformation and recycling of rocks.

Underpinning this section is an introduction to aspects of quantitative chemistry – chemical calculations. These involve the introduction of the concept of the mole. Chemical calculations are very important in GCSE Chemistry including calculations based upon titrations.

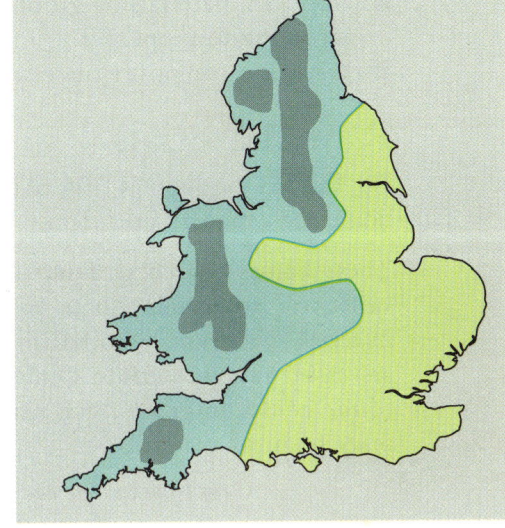

Section C is **Patterns of behaviour**. In this section a systematic approach to Chemistry is introduced. Much of this section is based upon the Periodic Table (page 91). You will study families of similar elements including alkali metals, halogens, noble gases and the transition metals. You will find out how the properties of elements are dependent on the position of the elements in the Periodic Table.

You will be aware that chemical reactions proceed at varying rates. In this section you will study factors which affect the rate of reaction. You will attempt to use simple models to explain why rates of reaction are affected by temperature, concentration etc. You will study the effects of biological catalysts called enzymes and the conditions under which they operate. Many important processes, e.g. fermentation, are controlled by enzyme processes.

Most reactions convert reactants entirely into products. However, in some reactions 100% conversion is impossible because the products react to produce the reactants again. These are called reversible reactions. You will study reversible reactions and how they can lead to the setting up of an equilibrium. You will also study industrial processes where controlling equilibrium conditions is essential for the economic production of a chemical. These include the production of ammonia and sulphuric acid.

Water is an extremely good solvent dissolving a wide range of substances. In this section you will study some of the properties of water. The unique solvent properties of water lead to problems of hardness of water and the economic problems of washing with soaps and detergents.

Finally in this section you will look at the changes in energy in chemical reactions. You will be aware that reactions are often accompanied by changes in temperature. Reactions may be exothermic (energy given out to the surroundings) or endothermic (energy taken in from the surroundings). In this section energy changes are related to changes in bonding which occur during reactions.

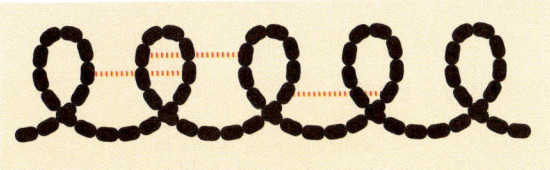

1 Materials

In this unit you will learn the answers to these questions:
- What are materials?
- What is a property?
- How can materials be grouped according to properties?
- What is a composite material?

Raw materials

Fig 1 shows two houses – an old stone house and a modern brick house.

These houses have been built using a variety of **materials**. Some of these materials are naturally occurring and are called **raw materials**. Other parts of the houses are made using materials made from raw materials.

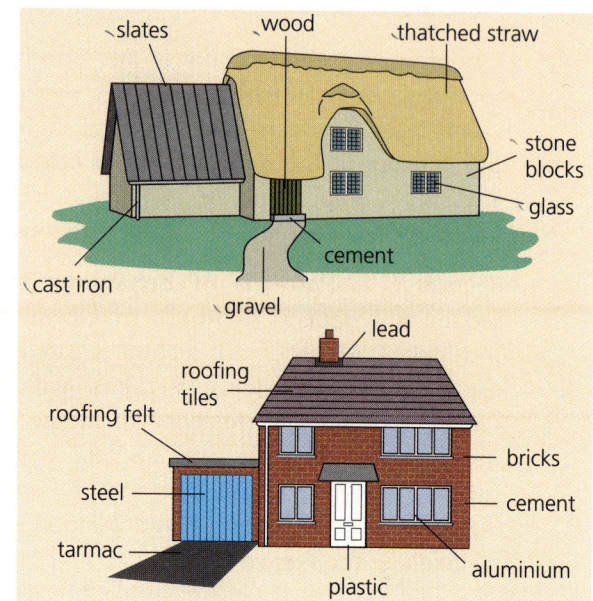

Fig 1 The building materials used in two different houses

Raw materials	Manufactured materials
thatched straw	cement
stone blocks	glass
wood	cast iron
slates	
gravel	

The table contains materials used to make the old stone house.

Q1 Which parts of the modern house are made of:
 a) raw materials *roof, walls, door, roof of gradge, path*
 b) materials manufactured from raw materials? *door step, windows, pipes.*

Q2 What do you notice about the materials used to make a modern house rather than an older house? Suggest a reason for the difference. *most of the materials are Manufactured materials.*

We use a particular material because it has an advantage over other possible materials. It is said to have a special **property**.

Properties of glass include:

- it is hard;
- it breaks easily (it is brittle);
- it has a high melting point;
- it does not react with chemicals.

None of these properties explain why glass is used for windows. The main reason is because it has the property of being transparent, i.e. light passes though it.

The properties of a material may make the material either suitable or unsuitable for a particular purpose.

Materials can be classed into five major groups according to their properties. These groups are:

    metals   plastics   ceramics (pottery)   glasses   fibres

The table on the next page summarises the main properties of these five materials.

A Classifying materials

Material group	Example of material	Typical properties of group	Raw material used
metals	iron, steel, lead, copper, brass	hard, strong, high density, good conductors of heat and electricity, malleable (can be beaten into thin sheets), ductile (can be drawn into fine wires), usually burn on heating, high melting points	metal ores in Earth's crust
plastics	poly(ethene), polystyrene, rubber	flexible, low density, easily moulded, poor conductors of heat and electricity, often transparent, melt and often burn on heating	crude oil, sap of rubber trees
ceramics (pottery)	china, concrete, bricks, tiles	hard, brittle, medium density, very high melting point, non-conductors of heat and electricity, very unreactive, do not burn	clay, sand and other minerals
glasses	Pyrex, lead crystal, soft soda glass	same properties as ceramics, often transparent	sand, limestone and other minerals
fibres	cotton, wool, paper, nylon, polyester	flexible, low density, may burn on heating, long stringy strands	natural fibres from plants and animals, crude oil

Q3 The table shows some of the properties of glass, copper, aluminium and stainless steel. Use the properties of materials from above to complete the table. (Copper, aluminium and stainless steel are metals.)

Q4 Why is glass unsuitable for making a saucepan?

Q5 The handle of a saucepan is usually made of plastic or wood. Suggest one property of the material used for the handle which is important.

Property	Glass	Copper	Aluminium	Stainless steel
good conductor of heat				
high density	✓	✓	✗	✓
high melting point				
shiny	✗	✓	✗	✓
reacts with an alkali	✗	✗	✓	✗

When choosing a material for a particular purpose it is important to make sure it has the best properties. Properties can be:

1 Physical properties, e.g. hardness, strength, melting point, conductivity of heat and electricity, density, transparency.

2 Chemical properties, e.g. does it burn, react with water, corrode, etc.

The relative costs of materials must also be considered.

Composite materials

Often a material has some properties which make it suitable for a particular use but other properties which are not very suitable. Composite materials (or composites) are made of two or more materials which produce a material more suitable for the job than either of the materials separately.

For example, car windscreens can be made of toughened glass or plastic. However, toughened glass still shatters and plastic is too soft and scratches easily. Laminated glass consists of a 'sandwich' of plastic between two thin sheets of glass. It provides a material which does not easily shatter and does not scratch easily.

Other composites include fibreglass and carbon fibre.

2 Solids, liquids and gases

In this unit you will learn the answers to these questions:
- What are states of matter?
- How are particles arranged in solids, liquids and gases?
- How do particles move in solids, liquids and gases?
- What is diffusion?

States of matter

All substances can exist in three states of matter depending upon temperature and pressure. These three states of matter are:

solid   liquid   gas

Water, for example, can exist as:
- ice (solid) below 0°C;
- water (liquid) between 0°C and 100°C;
- steam (gas) above 100°C.

Property	Solid	Liquid	Gas
volume	definite	definite	fills the whole container
shape	definite	takes up the shape of the bottom of the container	takes up the shape of the whole container
density	high	medium	low
ease of flow	does not flow unless powdered	flows easily	flows easily
expansion on heating	low	medium	high
compression	very low	low	high
movement of particles	very slow	medium	fast-moving particles

The properties of solids, liquids and gases are summarised in the table.

Changes of state

When water is heated to 100°C it starts to **boil** and water (liquid) turns to a gas. When steam is cooled, it **condenses** and forms liquid water. When liquid water is cooled to 0°C, the water **freezes** and forms ice. When ice warms up it **melts** and forms liquid water. Steam (or water vapour) in the air can turn directly into solid ice. This happens in a freezer where rapid cooling of water vapour produces ice directly by a process of **sublimation**.

The changes of state of matter are summarised in Fig 1.

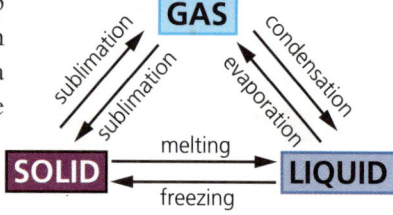

Fig 1 Changes in the state of matter

Substances are made up of particles

All solids, liquids and gases are made up of particles. Fig 2 shows simple representations of the arrangements of particles in solids, liquids and gases.

In a solid the particles are closely packed together. The arrangement of particles is usually regular. The particles are vibrating.

In a liquid the particles are not as closely packed as in a solid and the arrangement is not regular.

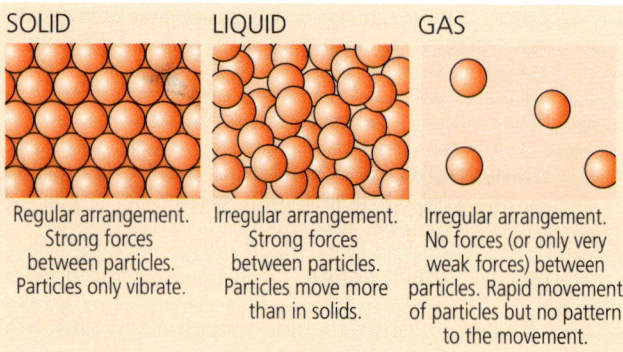

Fig 2 Arrangements of particles in solids, liquids and gases

A Classifying materials

In a gas the particles are not regularly arranged. They are widely spaced and are moving in all directions. This movement is called **random movement**. The particles in a gas collide with each other and also with the walls of the container. Fig 3 shows two samples of gas. In Fig 3a there are more particles than in Fig 3b. The particles in Fig 3a will make more collisions with the walls of the container, so this gas is said to be at a higher pressure than the gas in Fig 3b.

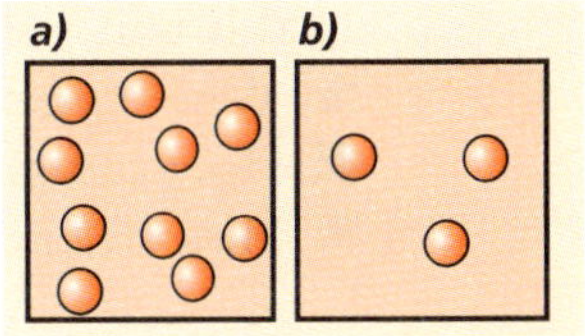

Fig 3 The gas in **a)** is at a higher pressure than the gas in **b)**

Diffusion

The smell of a perfume can spread very quickly through a room. The perfume is made up of millions of tiny particles and these spread out to fill the whole room. This process is called **diffusion**.

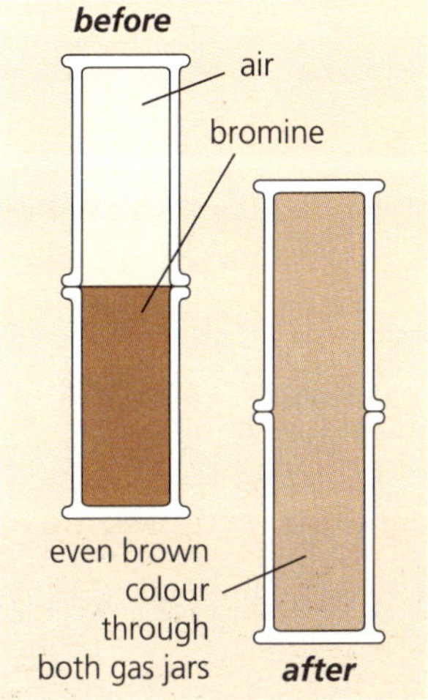

Diffusion is the movement of the particles of a gas to fill all of the available space. Diffusion can be demonstrated in the laboratory using bromine (Fig 4). A gas jar filled with air is placed above a gas jar filled with brown bromine vapour. After a few minutes the gases are thoroughly mixed and both gas jars look the same. The bromine particles have spread out to fill both gas jars.

Most examples of diffusion occur with gases. Diffusion does take place in liquids, but more slowly. This is because particles are moving much more slowly in liquids than in gases.

Fig 4 Diffusion of bromine in air

If a crystal of purple potassium manganate(VII) is placed in water, the crystal dissolves and the pink colour spreads evenly through the water. Without stirring, this can take several hours.

Diffusion is possible in solids, but it is very slow indeed.

Comparing the rates of diffusion of gases

Fig 5 shows a horizontal glass tube which is completely dry. At the same time, pads of cotton wool soaked in concentrated hydrochloric acid and ammonia solution are placed at opposite ends of the tube. Ammonia and hydrogen chloride gases pass along the tube towards each other. When they meet, they form a white solid ring of ammonium chloride.

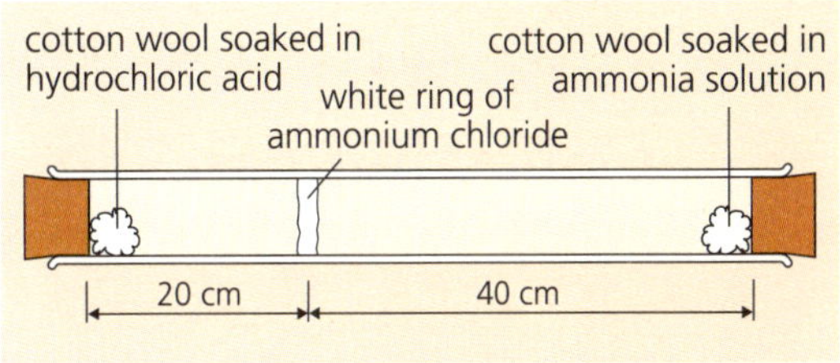

Fig 5 Comparing the rates of diffusion of ammonia and hydrogen chloride

ammonia + hydrogen chloride ➡ ammonium chloride
NH_3 (g) + HCl (g) ➡ NH_4Cl (s)

If the particles of the two gases move at the same speed, you would expect the ring to be formed exactly in the middle of the tube.

The particles are moving fast but the ring takes about five minutes to form.

Q1 What does the diagram tell us about the relative speeds of movement of ammonia and hydrogen chloride particles?

Q2 Why does the ring take five minutes to form?

A1 Handling and identifying gases

In this unit you will learn the answers to these questions:
- Why do gases cause problems when they are stored and transferred?
- How can gases be collected?
- How can common gases be identified using simple tests?

In Unit 2 we considered properties of solids, liquids and gases. Gases are more difficult to handle than solids or liquids. This is because they diffuse rapidly and expand to fill all of the available space. It is particularly difficult when gases are colourless as they cannot be seen.

Handling gases

Fig 1 shows how a gas in a test tube A can be transferred to test tube B, which was filled with water. As the gas enters B, it replaces the water in the test tube.

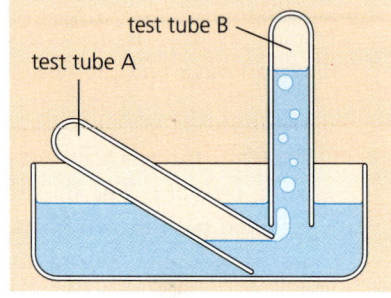

Fig 1 Transferring a gas

> **Q1** What would happen if the gas in test tube A was:
> a) very soluble in water;   b) slightly soluble in water?

Fig 2 Blue cylinders of carbon dioxide gas

Gases are usually stored in cylinders under a very high pressure. Gases in cylinders can also be stored as liquids. Gas is released from the cylinder through a valve. The valve often has a pressure gauge to show the pressure of the gas in the cylinder. The colour of a cylinder shows which gas is in the cylinder (Fig 2). For example, hydrogen gas is always in a red cylinder.

> **Q2** Why should the fire brigade know which gases are stored in a factory, and where the gas cylinders are kept?
>
> **Q3** The weight of the empty cylinder is stamped on the outside of a cylinder. How is it possible to work out how much gas is in a cylinder?

Collecting gases in the laboratory

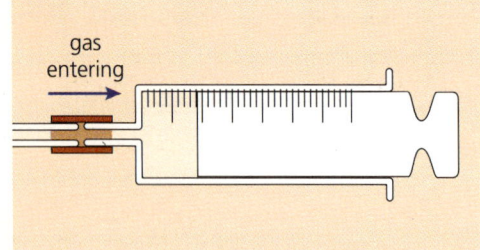

Small volumes of a gas can be collected in the laboratory using a gas syringe (Fig 3). Other methods of collecting a gas depend upon the properties of the gas.

Fig 3 A gas syringe is used to collect small volumes of a gas

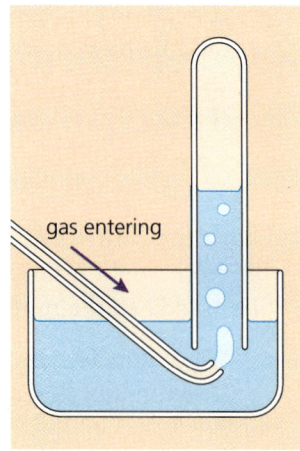

Fig 4 shows how a gas can be collected over water. This method is suitable when the gas being collected is not appreciably soluble in water and when it is not crucial that the gas collected is completely dry.

Fig 4 Collecting a gas over water

8

A Classifying materials

In the past scientists often collected gases over mercury instead of water. This had advantages because gases are not soluble in mercury. However, mercury vapour is very poisonous and mercury is very expensive.

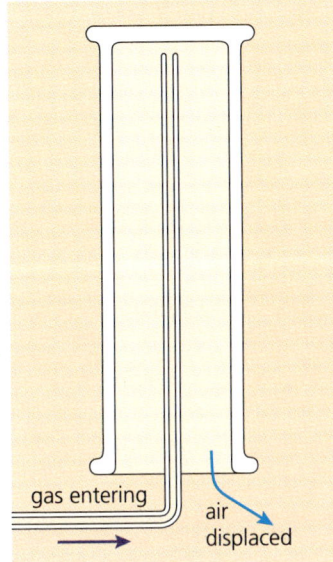

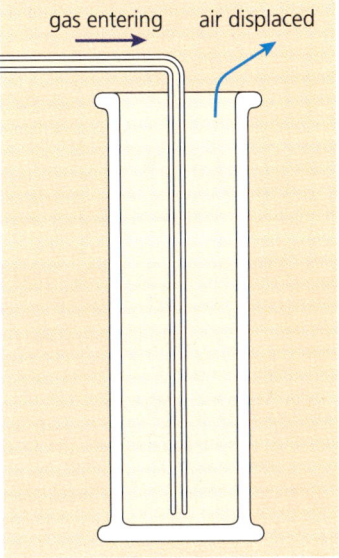

Fig 5 shows a gas being collected by **upward delivery**. A gas can only be collected by upward delivery if it is much less dense than air. As the gas fills the gas jar, air is pushed out downwards. The alternative name for this method of gas collection is **downward displacement of air**.

Fig 6 shows a gas being collected by **downward delivery**. A gas collected by downward delivery (or **upward displacement of air**) must be much denser than air.

Fig 5 Collecting a gas by upward delivery

Fig 6 Collecting a gas by downward delivery

Tests for common gases

Very often it is necessary to test and identify a gas produced in a chemical reaction. The table gives some properties of common gases.

Gas	Colour	Solubility in cold water	Smell	Test with moist litmus	Test with lighted splint	Other tests
hydrogen	colourless	insoluble	✗	✗	squeaky pop – splint extinguished	
oxygen	colourless	almost insoluble	✗	✗	relights glowing splint	
nitrogen	colourless	insoluble	✗	✗	extinguished	
chlorine	greenish-yellow	slightly soluble	✔	blue to red, then bleaches	extinguished	
hydrogen chloride	colourless	very soluble	✔	blue to red	extinguished	white fumes with ammonia
carbon dioxide	colourless	slightly soluble	✗	little change	extinguished	turns limewater milky
ammonia	colourless	very soluble	✔	red to blue	extinguished	white fumes with hydrogen chloride
sulphur dioxide	colourless	quite soluble	✔	blue to red	extinguished	turns potassium dichromate green

Q4 Use the table to identify the following gases.
  a) Gas A is a colourless gas which extinguishes a lighted splint and turns limewater milky.
  b) Gas B is a colourless gas which is very soluble in water and turns red litmus blue.
  c) Gas C is a colourless gas which turns blue litmus red and is very soluble in water.

3 Structure of the atom

In this unit you will learn the answers to these questions:
- What are atoms made up from?
- What is the difference between atomic number and mass number?
- How many protons, neutrons and electrons are there in an atom?
- What are isotopes?

Atoms

Every substance is made up from very tiny particles called **atoms**. Atoms are extremely small. A cube of iron (2 cm×2 cm×2 cm) contains about 600 000 000 000 000 000 000 000 atoms of iron. Each atom has a diameter of about 0.000 000 1 mm and a mass of about 0.000 000 000 000 000 000 000 09 g.

Despite their very small size, the idea of atoms as basic particles from which substances are made up is not a recent one. It was first suggested over 2000 years ago by the Greek thinker Democritus. The idea was revolutionary and was not accepted at the time. John Dalton revived the idea in 1808 and this became the basis of modern atomic theory. Dalton thought of atoms as being similar to snooker balls – hard, solid and impossible to divide. We now know that atoms can be subdivided.

Atoms cannot be seen through ordinary microscopes, which can only distinguish objects about 0.001 mm or larger. Powerful **electron microscopes** have now been developed which can magnify up to two million times. Using an electron microscope, it is possible to see groups of atoms or large single atoms.

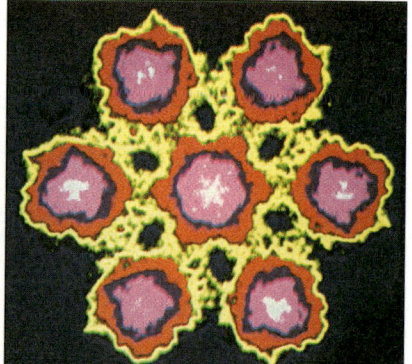

Fig 1 Electron micrograph of uranium atoms in a crystal

Protons, neutrons and electrons

All atoms are made up from three basic particles:

protons, **neutrons** and **electrons**

An iron atom is different from a copper atom because it contains different numbers of these particles.

A **proton** (p)   is a small, positively charged particle. Its mass is 1 a.m.u. (1 atomic mass unit).

An **electron** (e) is much smaller than the other particles. Two thousand electrons have the same mass as one proton or neutron. The masses of electrons can be ignored. An electron has a single negative charge.

A **neutron** (n)   is a particle which has the same mass as a proton (1 a.m.u.) but has no charge – it is neutral.

All atoms are **neutral**, i.e. there is no overall positive or negative charge.

> **Q1** What does this tell you about the numbers of protons and electrons in any atom?

A Classifying materials

When an atom gains or loses electrons it forms a charged **ion**. An ion does not contain equal numbers of protons and electrons. Note that it is electrons which are lost or gained because they are on the outside of the atom.

Atomic number (Z) and **mass number** (A) are two 'vital statistics' for any atom. The atomic number is the number of protons in an atom. It is also the number of electrons in an atom. The mass number is the total number of protons and neutrons in an atom.

A phosphorus atom has an atomic number of 15 and a mass number of 31. It can be represented as $^{31}_{15}P$. It contains 15 protons, 15 electrons and 16 neutrons. The number of neutrons is the difference between the mass number and the atomic number.

Q2 Lithium has an atomic number of 3 and a mass number of 7. How many protons, electrons and neutrons are there in a lithium atom?

Arrangement of protons, neutrons and electrons

In any atom the protons and neutrons are tightly packed together in the **nucleus** (Fig 2). The nucleus is positively charged.

The electrons move around the nucleus at high speeds in certain **shells** or **energy levels**. Each shell can only contain up to a fixed maximum number of electrons (Fig 3).

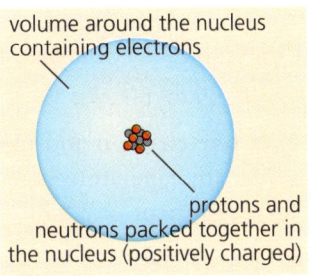

Fig 2 Arrangement of protons, neutrons and electrons in an atom

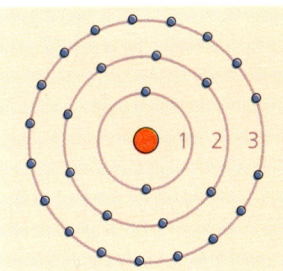

Fig 3 Maximum number of electrons in shells 1, 2 and 3

Fig 4 shows simple representations of some atoms.

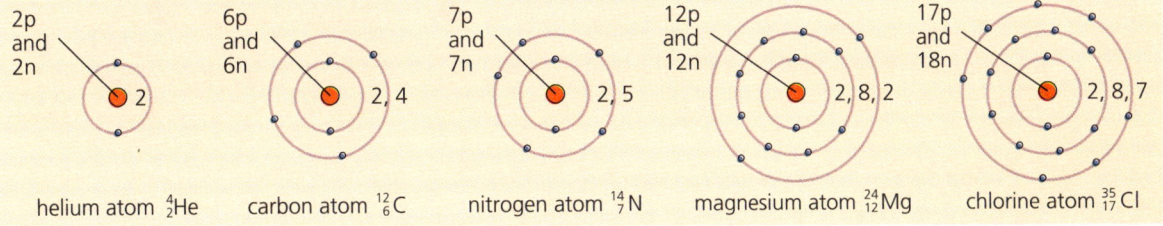

helium atom ^4_2He carbon atom $^{12}_6C$ nitrogen atom $^{14}_7N$ magnesium atom $^{24}_{12}Mg$ chlorine atom $^{35}_{17}Cl$

Fig 4 Simple diagrams of some atoms

Isotopes

Atoms of the same element containing different numbers of neutrons but, of course, the same number of protons and electrons are called **isotopes**. For example, there are three isotopes of hydrogen (Fig 5):
- normal hydrogen atom, ^1_1H (1 proton, 1 electron, 0 neutrons);
- heavy hydrogen atom (deuterium), ^2_1H (1 proton, 1 electron, 1 neutron);
- radioactive hydrogen atom (tritium), ^3_1H (1 proton, 1 electron, 2 neutrons).

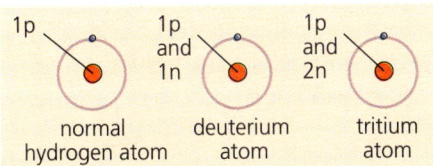

All three atoms are hydrogen atoms because they contain one proton and one electron. The three isotopes of hydrogen have the same chemical properties but slightly different physical properties.

Fig 5 The three isotopes of hydrogen

11

4 Ionic bonding

In this unit you will learn the answers to these questions:
- What is ionic bonding?
- What properties will ionic compounds have?

Ionic bonding is one way of joining atoms together. It usually involves the combining of a metal atom with a non-metal atom.

The common example of ionic bonding is sodium chloride. The arrangement of electrons in sodium and chlorine atoms is:

    Na 2, 8, 1   Cl 2, 8, 7

To understand how sodium and chlorine atoms bond, you must first understand a little about **noble gases** (see Unit 35). Noble gases have very stable electron arrangements, and atoms of other elements gain and lose electrons in order to achieve similar electron arrangements. (The noble gases are helium, neon, argon, krypton, xenon and radon.)

A sodium atom has one more electron than the noble gas neon. A chlorine atom has one less electron than the noble gas argon.

The sodium atom loses one electron and forms a sodium ion, Na^+, with an electron arrangement of 2, 8. The chlorine atom gains one electron and forms a chloride ion, Cl^-, with an electron arrangement of 2,8,8.

$$Na\ atom \rightarrow Na^+\ ion + e^-$$
$$Cl\ atom + e^- \rightarrow Cl^-\ ion$$

The sodium and chloride ions are held together by strong electrostatic forces. This can be summarised by Fig 1.

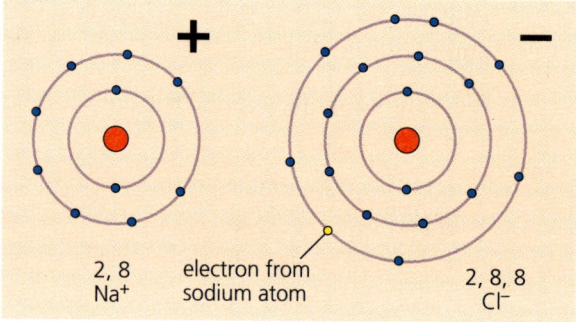

2, 8 Na^+ electron from sodium atom   2, 8, 8 Cl^-

Fig 1 Electron arrangements of Na^+ and Cl^-

Another example of ionic bonding is magnesium oxide. The electron arrangements of magnesium and oxygen atoms are:

    Mg 2, 8, 2   O 2, 6

Two electrons are lost by each magnesium atom and two electrons are gained by each oxygen atom.

$$Mg \rightarrow Mg^{2+} + 2e^-$$
$$O + 2e^- \rightarrow O^{2-}$$

Both magnesium ions and oxide ions have the same electron arrangement as neon, i.e. 2, 8 (with full outer electron shells). Again, strong electrostatic forces hold the ions together.

A Classifying materials

Properties of ionic compounds

Compounds containing ionic bonds usually have high melting and boiling points. At room temperature they are usually crystalline solids. The ions are held together in a **lattice**. Fig 2 shows a sodium chloride lattice. This is a cubic arrangement of sodium and chloride ions. Each sodium ion in the lattice is surrounded by six chloride ions and each chloride ion in the structure is surrounded by six sodium ions. The high melting point is due to the very strong electrostatic forces between these ions. Ionic compounds do not conduct electricity when solid but do conduct when molten or in aqueous solution.

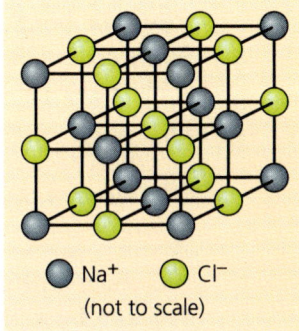

Na⁺   Cl⁻
(not to scale)

Fig 2 Sodium chloride lattice

Q1 Lithium and nitrogen form a compound Li_3N.
  a) What are the electron arrangements in lithium and nitrogen atoms?
  b) Assuming that the bonding is ionic, what changes take place when lithium and nitrogen combine?
  c) Why would you expect lithium nitride to have a different crystal lattice structure from sodium chloride or magnesium oxide?

Substances containing ionic bonding usually dissolve in water to form a solution which conducts electricity. These substances do not usually dissolve in organic solvents such as hexane or methylbenzene.

Q2 Why is the melting point of magnesium oxide much greater than the melting point of sodium chloride?

Crystal structure

The regular arrangement of ions in a lattice of sodium chloride will lead to the formation of a **crystal**. Crystalline structures are evidence of the regular arrangement of particles. There are seven basic crystal shapes. These are shown in Fig 3.

Q3 What crystal shapes do
  a) sugar
  b) salt (sodium chloride) have?

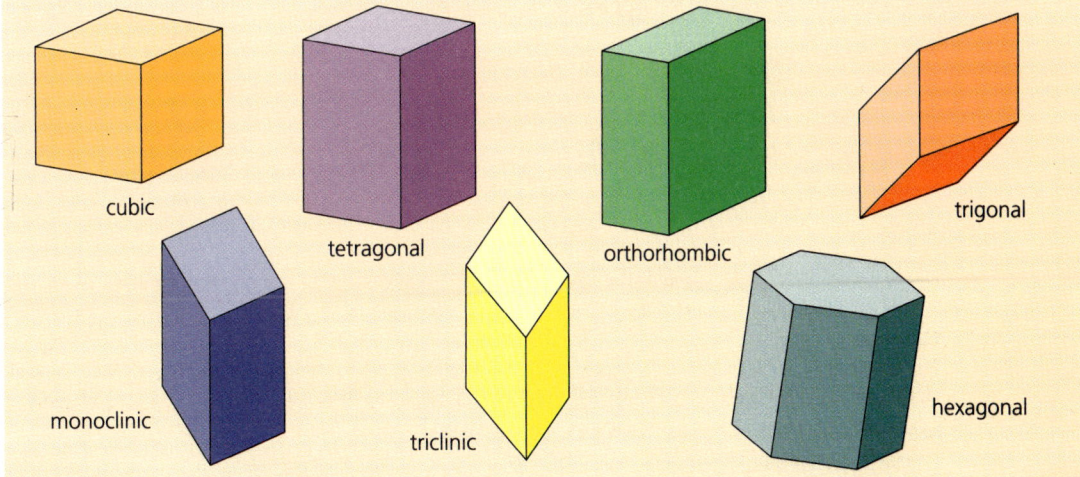

Fig 3 The seven basic crystal shapes

5 Covalent bonding

In this unit you will learn the answers to these questions:
- What is covalent bonding?
- What properties do compounds containing covalent bonding have?

Covalent bonding is a way of joining atoms together which involves the **sharing of electrons** between two atoms. It is particularly used to join **non-metal atoms** together.

For example, two hydrogen atoms join together with a **single covalent bond**. Each hydrogen atom has a single electron. The two electrons, one from each atom, form an electron pair which joins the two hydrogen atoms together.

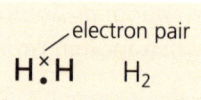

The electrons are shared so as to give each atom a full outer shell.

The electron pair is usually represented as a single bond by a single line.

Another example of covalent bonding is a chlorine molecule, where two chlorine atoms are bonded together by a single covalent bond. There are now eight electrons associated with each chlorine atom.

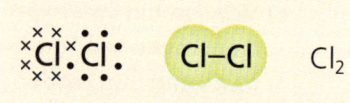

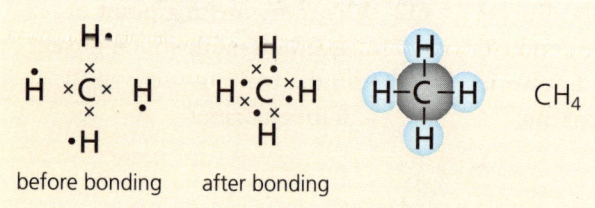

Methane is a compound of carbon and hydrogen with each molecule containing four single covalent bonds. In each bond one electron comes from the carbon atom and one from the hydrogen atom. The pair of electrons is then shared.

Other examples of molecules containing single covalent bonds include:

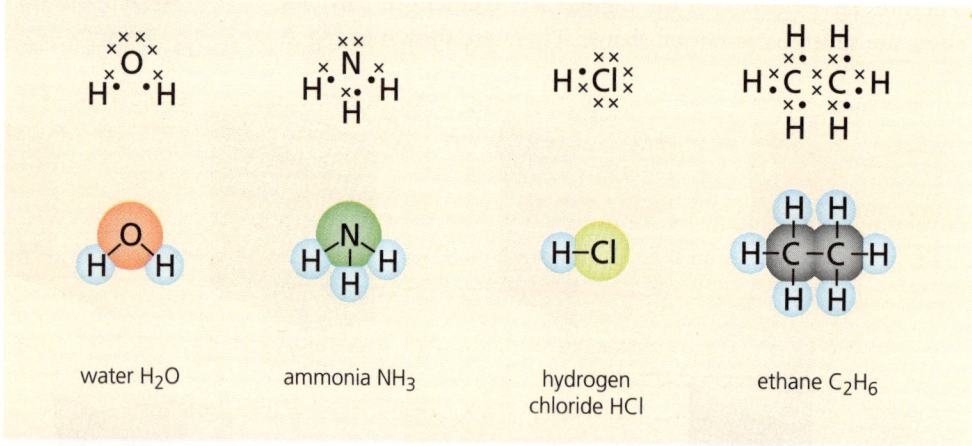

> **Q1** Draw diagrams to show the arrangement of electrons in molecules of hydrogen bromide, HBr, and phosphorus trichloride, PCl$_3$. Use the Periodic Table on page 91 to help you.

A Classifying materials

Oxygen, O_2, is an example of covalent bonding containing a **double covalent bond**. Here each oxygen atom gives two electrons and two covalent bonds are formed, each containing two electrons.

Other molecules containing double covalent bonds are carbon dioxide and ethene.

The double bond is represented by two lines.

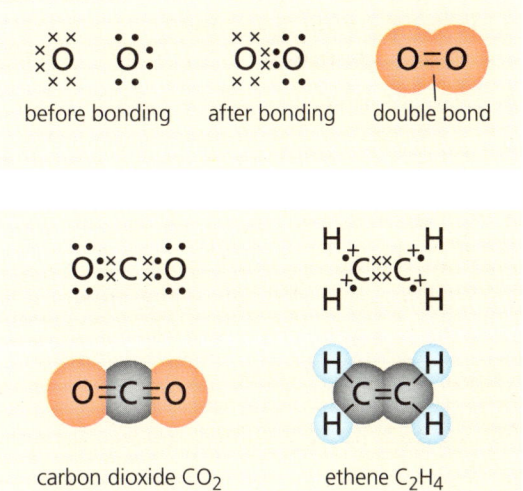

carbon dioxide CO_2 ethene C_2H_4

A nitrogen molecule contains two nitrogen atoms bonded together with a **triple covalent bond**. Each nitrogen atom gives three electrons and three covalent bonds are formed.

Another example of a compound containing a triple covalent bond is ethyne.

The triple bond is represented by three lines.

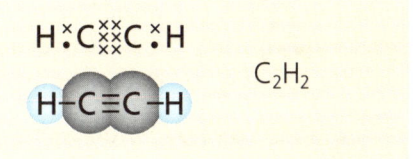

C_2H_2

Properties of substances containing covalent bonds

In all of the examples of covalent bonding, small, separate molecules are produced. It is possible for covalent bonding to produce large structures. These are considered in Unit 6.

Covalent bonds have a definite direction which give covalent molecules a definite shape. For example, water is a bent molecule with an angle of approximately 104° between the bonds and not a straight line as might be expected.

A compound consisting of small molecules containing covalent bonding will have a low melting point and a low boiling point. They are frequently gases or low boiling point liquids or solids. They are usually insoluble in water but soluble in organic solvents.

> **Q2** Using a simple particle model (Unit 2), explain why the boiling point of hydrogen, H_2, is much lower than the boiling point of oxygen, O_2.

15

6 Structure

In this unit you will learn the answers to these questions:
■ What are giant structures?
■ What is allotropy?
■ How are properties of substances related to structure?

Molecular structures and giant structures

The table shows some of the properties of iodine, silicon(IV) oxide, sodium chloride, and iron.

Substance	Melting point/°C	Boiling point/°C	Electrical conductivity when solid	Electrical conductivity when molten	Type of structure
iodine	114	183	none	none	molecular structure
silicon(IV) oxide	1610	2230	none	none	giant structure of atoms
sodium chloride	808	1465	none	good	giant structure of ions
iron	1540	3000	good	good	giant structure of atoms (metal structure)

When iodine crystals are heated they melt at a low temperature and form a dark-coloured liquid. On further heating the liquid boils and a purple vapour is produced. This consists of I_2 molecules. Iodine crystals (Fig 1) are in a **molecular structure** made up of iodine molecules regularly arranged and joined together by weak forces. Gentle heating breaks down the forces between the molecules without breaking the forces within the molecules.

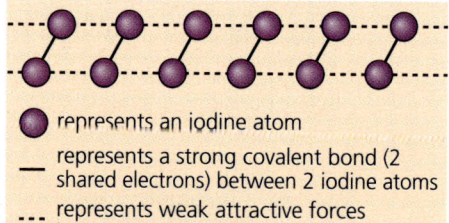

Fig 1 *Iodine crystals*

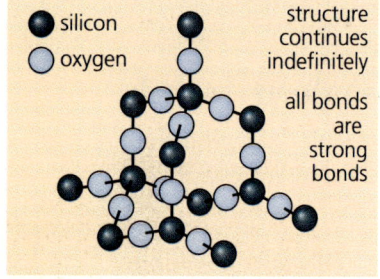

Fig 2 *Silicon(IV) oxide*

In contrast, heating silicon(IV) oxide produces no change until a high temperature is reached. This is because the atoms of silicon and oxygen are all bonded together to form one large molecule or **giant structure**. This is shown in Fig 2. Molten silicon(IV) oxide does not conduct electricity.

Sodium chloride consists of a **giant structure of ions** (Fig 2, Unit 4). When solid, the ions are not free to move and so electricity is not conducted through the crystal. When heated to a high temperature, the molten sodium chloride conducts electricity because there are **free ions**. When an electric current passes, free ions move through the melt and carry the charge.

Iron consists of a closely packed **giant structure of atoms** with electrons free to move through the structure to give good electrical conductivity. Fig 3 shows a layer of close packed atoms in iron. The sea of free electrons carry the electrical charge through a metal.

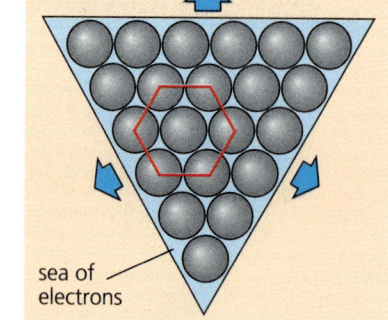

Fig 3 *Part of an iron layer*

A Classifying materials

Forms of carbon

Diamond and **graphite** are two forms of carbon with different properties and different structures. Different forms of the same element, in the same physical state, are called **allotropes**. Fig 4 shows the arrangement of atoms in diamond and graphite.

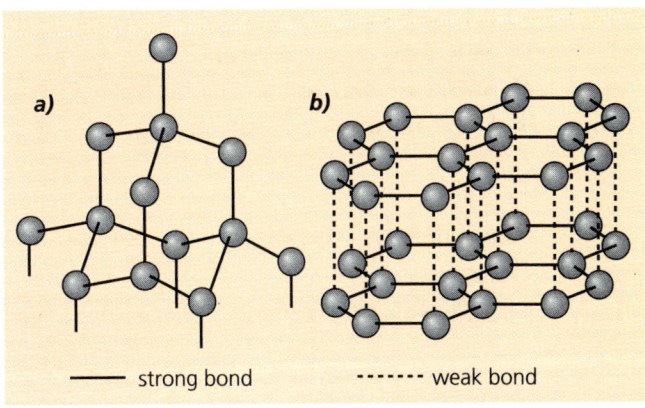

—— strong bond   ------ weak bond

Fig 4 Arrangement of atoms in **a)** diamond and **b)** graphite

Diamonds were formed in the Earth when carbon was subjected to tremendous pressures as the Earth cooled. The arrangement of carbon atoms is tetrahedral. Each carbon atom is attached to four other carbon atoms. All of the bonds are strong so it is difficult to break up the structure.

Graphite has a layer structure. Although the bonds within each layer are very strong, the forces between the layers are very weak. Graphite is soft because the layers slide easily over each other. Graphite, unlike diamond, is a good conductor of electricity as electrons move easily though the structure.

A chance discovery in 1985 led to the identification of a new allotrope of carbon. In fact, a new family of closed carbon clusters has been identified and called **fullerenes**. Two fullerenes, C_{60} and C_{70}, can be prepared by electrically evaporating carbon electrodes in helium gas at low pressure. They dissolve in benzene to produce a red solution.

Q1 Why is it important to evaporate carbon in helium rather than air?

Q2 Refer to Unit 11. Suggest a method for separating the different fullerenes dissolved in benzene.

Fig 5 shows C_{60} – sometimes called buckminsterfullerene after R. Buckminster Fuller, the American who designed the geodesic dome that resembles the structure of fullerene.

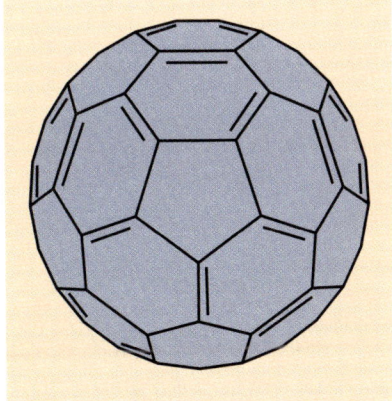

Fig 5 Buckminsterfullerene (C_{60})

Carbon fibre is a new material which is stronger and less dense than steel. It can be used for golf clubs, tennis rackets and bicycle frames. Carbon fibre is formed by partial decomposition of fibres. The structure consists of graphite layers arranged along the fibre to give strength.

Fig 6 A carbon fibre tennis racket

7 Elements, mixtures and compounds

In this unit you will learn the answers to these questions:
- What are elements?
- What are the differences between mixtures and compounds?
- How are compounds named?

Elements

Pure substances which cannot be split up into simpler substances are called **elements**. There are over 100 known elements, with 92 occurring naturally. Each element can be represented by a **symbol**, e.g. O for oxygen, Ca for calcium, Fe for iron, Mg for magnesium.

Q1 Use the Periodic Table on page 91 to identify the elements represented by the following symbols.

H; S; Na; Cl; P; K; Sb; Mn; Pb; Au; Ag; Hg.

Most of the elements are metals. There are 22 non-metallic elements.

Elements are composed of **atoms**. All atoms of the same element contain the same number of protons. A lump of sulphur is made up from sulphur atoms and a lump of carbon is made up from carbon atoms. Fig 1 shows a simple representation of atoms in sulphur and in carbon.

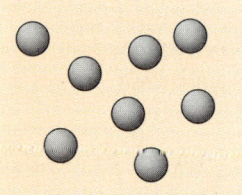
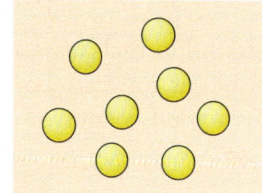

Key  carbon  sulphur

Fig 1 Atoms in the elements carbon and sulphur

Mixtures

Many substances exist as mixtures of other pure substances.

1 Air is a mixture of gases.

2 Universal Indicator is a mixture of simple indicators.

3 Sea water is a mixture of substances dissolved in water.

4 Crude oil is a mixture of hydrocarbons.

Fig 2 shows a simple representation of the atoms in two mixtures of carbon and sulphur.

You will notice that the atoms of carbon and sulphur are not joined and the proportions of the two elements in the two mixtures are different.

a) 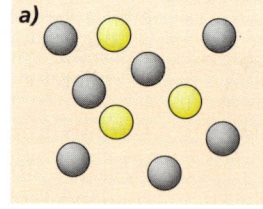 b)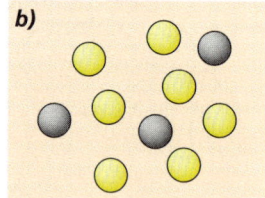

Fig 2 Mixtures of carbon and sulphur atoms

Q2 Which mixture *a)* or *b)* contains the greater proportion of carbon?

The properties of a mixture are always the same as the properties of the substances which make up the mixture. Sea water tastes salty because of the salt it contains.

A pure substance has a definite melting point. An impure substance (i.e. a mixture of substances) melts at a lower temperature and over a range of temperature. Butter is a mixture and it melts in a frying pan over a range of temperature.

A Classifying materials

Compounds

Compounds are pure substances made from two or more elements joined together. Some compounds may be split up or **decomposed** by heat (Fig 3) or electricity (Fig 4).

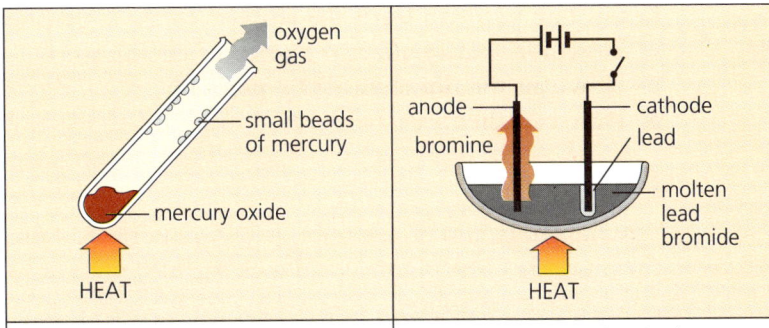

Fig 3 Thermal decomposition: heating mercury oxide splits mercury oxide into mercury and oxygen

Fig 4 Electrolysis: molten lead bromide is split up into lead and bromine by electrolysis

Joining elements together involves a **chemical reaction** called **synthesis**, e.g. heating a mixture of iron and sulphur forms a compound called iron sulphide. Fig 5 shows the change which occurs when iron sulphide is formed.

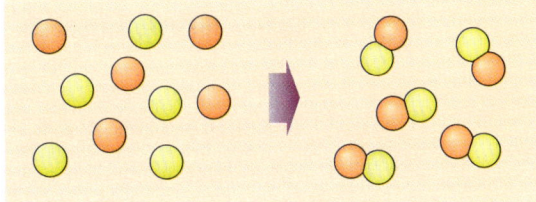

Fig 5 The synthesis of iron sulphide

The composition of a compound is fixed. For example, iron sulphide contains 7 parts of iron and 4 parts of sulphur by mass. You will notice that one iron atom is combined with one sulphur atom. For this reason the **formula** of iron sulphide is written as FeS.

The table compares the properties of a mixture and a compound.

Q3 Hydrogen and oxygen combine together to form water, H_2O. In both hydrogen gas and oxygen gas the atoms are in pairs, i.e. H_2 and O_2.

Draw diagrams to show particles in
a) hydrogen gas; b) oxygen gas; c) a mixture of hydrogen and oxygen; d) steam.

Mixture	Compound
Proportions of different elements can be altered	Different elements have to be present in fixed proportions
Elements can be separated by simple methods	Difficult to separate into its constituent elements
Properties of the mixture are the same as the properties of the elements making it up	Properties of the compound are different from the properties of the elements making it up
No energy change when a mixture is made	Energy is usually evolved or absorbed when a compound is formed

Rules for the naming of compounds

1 Compounds ending in **–ide** contain two elements.
E.g. copper(II) oxide is a compound of copper and oxygen
(Exceptions include sodium hydroxide – sodium, hydrogen and oxygen.)

2 Compounds ending in **–ate** or **–ite** contain oxygen. There is a greater proportion of oxygen in the compound ending in –ate.
E.g. sodium sulphate Na_2SO_4 sodium sulphite Na_2SO_3

8 Separating mixtures – 1

In this unit you will learn the answers to these questions:
- How does purity affect the price of chemicals?
- How can sodium chloride be purified?
- How can chemicals be purified using other solvents?

Purity

Separating mixtures of substances is very important in producing pure chemicals. Pure chemicals are essential for certain uses, e.g. medical uses, food production.

Below is information from a chemical catalogue about three grades of sodium chloride:
1 Technical grade,
2 General purpose reagent grade (GPR),
3 Analytical grade (Analar).

Sodium chloride technical	
3 kg	£5.50

Sodium chloride GPR	
Minimum purity	99.5%
Maximum limits of impurities	
Loss on drying at 105°C	1.0%
Sulphate	0.02%
Ammonia	0.002%
Iron	0.002%
Lead	0.0005%
Potassium	0.02%
1 kg	£4.10

Sodium chloride 'Analar'	
Minimum purity	99.8%
Maximum limits of impurities	
Water insoluble matter	0.003%
Bromide	0.005%
Ferrocyanide	0.00001%
Iodide	0.001%
Nitrogen compounds	0.0005%
Phosphate	0.0005%
Sulphate	0.002%
Barium	0.001%
Calcium	0.002%
Copper	0.0002%
Iron	0.0002%
Lead	0.0002%
Magnesium	0.002%
Potassium	0.005%
500 g	£3.40

Q1 Compare the prices of 3 kg of each grade of sodium chloride.

Q2 What is the minimum purity of GPR sodium chloride?

Q3 As the purity increases, the cost _____.

Uses of salt (sodium chloride)

The table gives some uses of sodium chloride.

Uses of sodium chloride
1 De-icing roads
2 Flavouring food
3 Preservative for butter, meat and fish
4 Making sodium carbonate industrially
5 Making sodium hydroxide, chlorine and hydrogen industrially
6 Salting out soap in the soapmaking process

Q4 Which of the uses in the table require pure sodium chloride?

A Classifying materials

Making pure sodium chloride

Sodium chloride is found in rock salt which consists of salt crystals mixed with insoluble materials such as sandstone. It can be mined as solid rock salt or mined by **solution mining** (Fig 2). A hole is drilled down to the salt deposits, cold water is pumped down to the deposits and salt solution (brine) is pumped back to the surface.

Fig 1 *Electron micrograph of pure sodium chloride*

Q5 Why can salt be mined by solution mining but coal cannot?

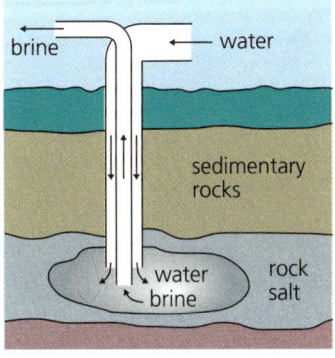

Fig 2 Solution mining

Salt can be purified by a series of processes. These are summarised in Fig 3.

Fig 3 Purification of rock salt

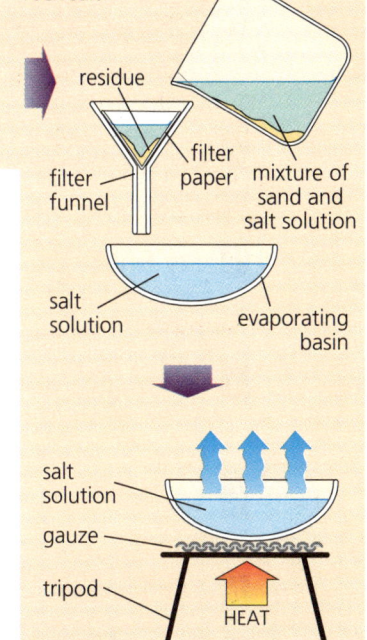

The salt produced by these processes will not be completely pure as it may still contain some of the soluble impurities.

Q6 Give two ways in which the dissolving of sodium chloride is speeded up in this experiment.

Q7 In the evaporation of sodium chloride solution, the solution starts to spit. Suggest two ways of slowing down the rate of evaporation, apart from removing the flame or turning down the gas.

Q8 Using the data in the table from the chemical catalogue, suggest likely impurities in the salt produced from rock salt.

Although water is a very good solvent which dissolves a wide range of substances, other solvents may be used in the purification of substances. Ethanol (meths), propanone and hexane are three **organic solvents** which can be used to purify substances.

In many places in the world, salt is produced from sea water. The photograph shows salt being produced in Brazil.

Q9 What is the source of energy used in this process?

Q10 Why are large, shallow lakes better than small, deep lakes for producing salt in this way?

9 Separating mixtures – 2

In this unit you will learn the answers to these questions:
- What is distillation?
- What are miscible and immiscible liquids?
- How would you separate miscible liquids?

Separating a liquid from a solid

Water can be obtained from a solution of a solid in water by the process of **distillation**.

For example, water can be obtained from a salt solution by distillation. Fig 1 shows a simple distillation apparatus which can be used to obtain pure water from a salt solution.

The following points should be remembered about simple distillation.

Fig 1 Distillation apparatus

1. Distillation consists of boiling followed by condensation.
2. Only steam leaves the flask. The solid salt remains in the flask.
3. The bulb of the thermometer should be alongside the exit to the condenser. The maximum temperature on the thermometer during the experiment should be 100°C – the boiling point of water.
4. The condenser is used for the efficient condensation of the steam. The cooling water should enter at the bottom of the condenser and leave at the top. The condenser must slope downward.
5. There should not be a stopper in the receiver, i.e the receiver should be open at the top.
6. The liquid collected in the receiver is called the **distillate**.

Separating mixtures of liquids

When two liquids are poured into the same container they may:

1. not mix but form two separate layers,
2. mix completely and form a single layer.

When the two liquids form separate layers they are said to be **immiscible** and when they mix completely and form a single layer they are said to be **miscible**.

An example of two immiscible liquids is glycerol and water. The table gives the densities of these two immiscible liquids.

Liquid	Density in g/cm^3
water	1.00
glycerol	1.26

A Classifying materials

Fig 2 shows the two liquids, glycerol and water, in a beaker. There are two layers with glycerol, the denser liquid, forming the lower layer. Immiscible liquids are best separated with a separating funnel (see Fig 3).

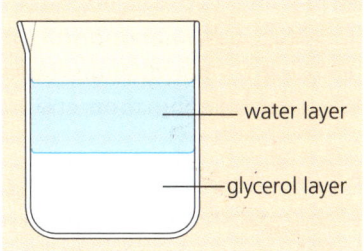

Fig 2 *Glycerol and water*

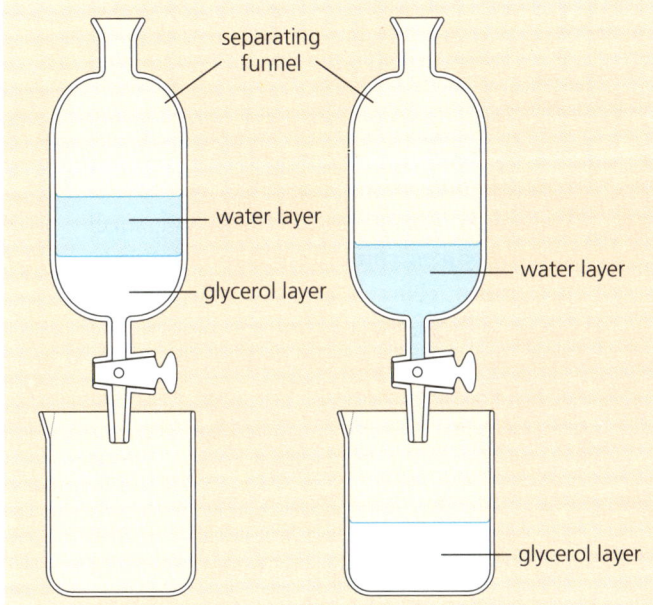

Fig 3 *Separating liquids with a separating funnel*

When two immiscible liquids are shaken together, an **emulsion** may be formed. An emulsion consists of small droplets of one liquid spread through the other liquid. Fig 4 shows an emulsion of oil-in-water viewed through a microscope. Droplets of oil are distributed through the water layer. Milk is an example of an oil-in-water emulsion.

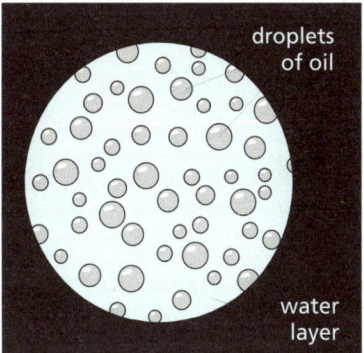

Fig 4 *An oil-in-water emulsion as seen through a microscope*

> **Q1** What would happen if a water-soluble dye was added to an oil-in-water emulsion?
>
> **Q2** Butter is a water-in-oil emulsion. What is a water-in-oil emulsion?

An **emulsifying agent** is added to an emulsion to stop the emulsion separating into two layers – an oil layer and a water layer.

> **Q3** Put the six statements below into the correct order so that they describe the method used to separate glycerol and water.
> **A** Put a second beaker under the separating funnel.
> **B** Put the mixture of water and glycerol into a separating funnel.
> **C** Leave the liquids to settle out into two layers.
> **D** Open the tap and allow the water to run into a beaker.
> **E** Remove the stopper from the separating funnel.
> **F** Open the tap and allow the glycerol to run into a beaker.

Miscible liquids can be separated by **fractional distillation** (see Unit 10).

10 Separating mixtures – 3

In this unit you will learn the answers to these questions:
- What is fractional distillation?
- What do petrol and whisky have in common?
- What is sublimation and how can it be used to separate substances?

Fractional distillation

Fractional distillation can be used to separate two or more liquids that have *different boiling points*. For example, hexane (boiling point 69°C) and methylbenzene (boiling point 111°C) can be separated by fractional distillation.

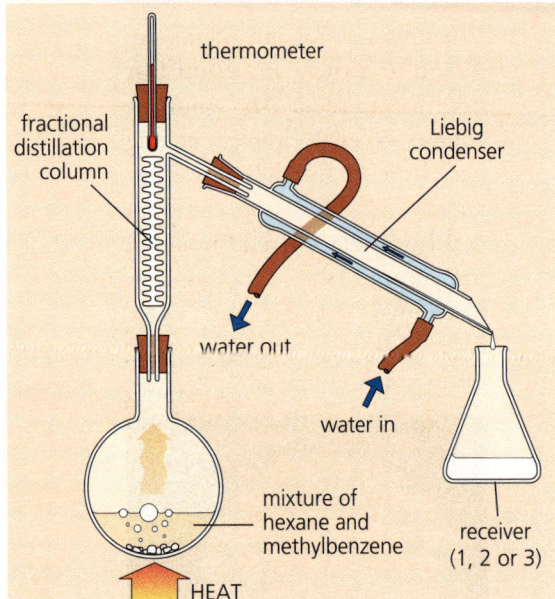

The apparatus in Fig 1 can be used for fractional distillation. The mixture to be separated is placed in the flask and small pieces of broken china are put into the flask. The broken china helps to ensure smooth boiling without the mixture 'bumping'. The flask is then slowly heated with receiver 1 in place. The hexane, with the lower boiling point, starts to boil first and the vapour passes up the fractional distillation column. Any methylbenzene that vaporises condenses in the column and the liquid drops back into the flask. The temperature shown by the thermometer remains below 69°C and only the hexane distils over. The liquid collected in the first receiver is called the **first fraction**. It consists almost entirely of hexane.

Fig 1 Fractional distillation

When the temperature reaches 70°C, receiver 2 is put in place. It is removed when the temperature rises to 110°C. The second fraction (liquid boiling between 70°C and 111°C) is collected. Receiver 3 is then put in place and a third fraction (liquid boiling above 111°C) is collected, which consists largely of methylbenzene.

Fractional distillation is used in the refining of crude oil (Unit 14).

Q1 Why are fractions 1 and 3 large, but fraction 2 very small?

Whisky production

Whisky is a spirit produced by the fractional distillation of a mixture of ethanol (boiling point 78°C) and water (boiling point 100°C).

Barley is malted by soaking the seeds in water and allowing them to germinate in a warm, damp atmosphere. When the barley has germinated, further growth is stopped by drying the barley in a peat-fired oven. The peat smoke gives much flavour to the whisky. The malt is then ground into a fine powder and the powder is mixed with warm water to produce a sugary solution called 'wort'. This process is called **mashing**.

A Classifying materials

The wort is mixed with yeast and **fermentation** takes place (see Unit 18). This turns the sugar into ethanol. The resulting mixture of ethanol and water is then distilled twice in copper fractional distillation vessels called **stills**. The stills are usually heated internally by steam-filled pipes. The resulting concentrated ethanol solution is stored in oak casks for years to mature. During the maturing process the whisky absorbs colouring and flavour from the casks.

Mashing

Fermentation

Maturation

Q2 During the fermentation froth is seen. What is produced to cause this froth?

Sublimation

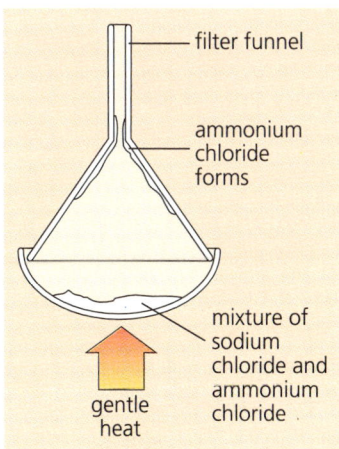

Fig 2

A mixture of sodium chloride and ammonium chloride can be separated using differences which occur on heating. Gentle heating of sodium chloride produces no change but gentle heating of ammonium chloride causes it to split up (or **dissociate**) into two gases, ammonia and hydrogen chloride. These gases recombine to form ammonium chloride on cooling.

If a mixture of sodium chloride and ammonium chloride is heated in the apparatus in Fig 2, the sodium chloride remains in the evaporating basin and the ammonium chloride re-forms after **sublimation** on the cool walls of the funnel. Iodine can also be separated from mixtures by sublimation.

25

11 Separating mixtures – 4

In this unit you will learn the answers to these questions:
- What is chromatography?
- How can chromatography be used to identify substances present in a mixture?

Chromatography

Chromatography is a method which can be used to separate mixtures of substances dissolved in a solvent. It was first carried out in 1903 by the Russian biologist Mikhail Tswett. He used a glass column packed with powdered chalk to separate plant pigments. A solution of plant pigments dissolved in petrol was poured through the column (Fig 1). The different dyes separated out and different bands were formed. These bands formed because the different dyes passed through the column at different rates.

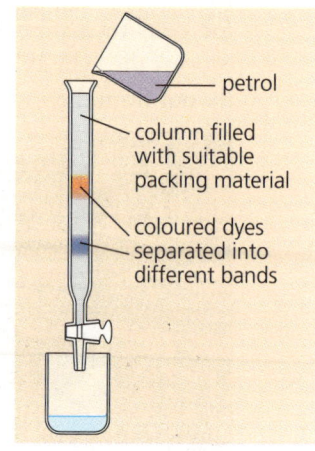

Fig 1 Column chromatography to separate plant dyes

Paper chromatography

In 1944 scientists showed that paper could be used to identify the components in a mixture and separate small quantities of these materials.

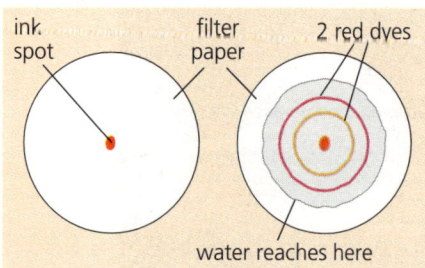

Fig 2 Simple paper chromatography with red ink

The dyes that are present in a red ink can be separated by simple **paper chromatography**. A spot of the red ink is dropped onto the centre of a filter paper circle (Fig 2). The ink is left to dry. Drops of water are then dropped onto the centre of the ink spot using a teat pipette. If this is done slowly and carefully the ink blot gets larger. The different dyes present in the ink spread out at different rates. Each dye forms a separate ring. In Fig 2 it can be seen that the red ink contains two red dyes.

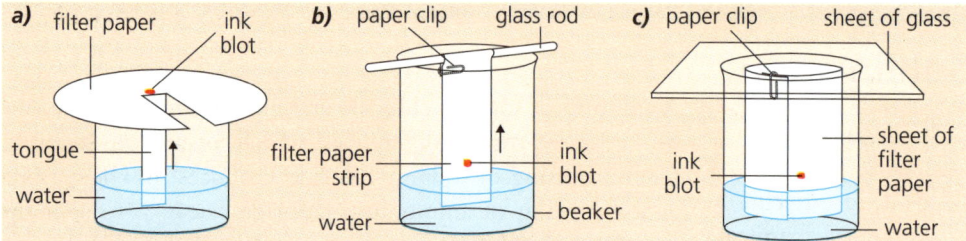

Fig 3 Three alternative ways of carrying out paper chromatography

Fig 3 shows three alternative ways of carrying out paper chromatography. In **a)** a filter paper is used with a small 'tongue' cut out. The 'tongue' dips into water in the beaker. The water slowly rises up the 'tongue', reaches the blot on the filter paper and the blot spreads out as before. In **b)** and **c)** the separation of dyes takes place on a strip or sheet of filter paper. In each case the water (or solvent) moves upwards and the dyes separate to form spots on the filter paper. Each dye present forms a separate spot. This type of chromatography is called ascending paper chromatography and the resulting strip or sheet of filter paper is called a **chromatogram**.

A Classifying materials

Identifying the dyes present in a sample

Fig 4 shows a chromatogram for a blue ink and also for three separate pure dyes – a pale blue dye, a dark blue dye and a purple dye. From these results we can conclude that:

1 the pale blue, dark blue and purple dyes are not split up as they each produce only a single spot on the chromatogram;

2 the blue ink is made up from a mixture of pale blue and purple dyes. The chromatogram for the blue ink shows two spots in the same positions on the chromatogram as the spots for pale blue and purple dyes.

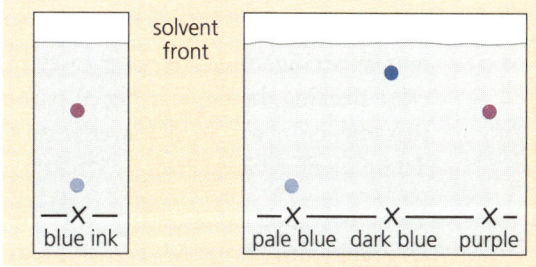

Fig 4 Paper chromatography of blue ink and three dyes

Q1 Fig 5 shows a chromatogram of the colour from orange squash and five possible dyes which could be used as colouring.

  a) Why is the spot for A further up the paper than B, C or D?
  b) Which dye or dyes are present in the colouring in the orange squash?

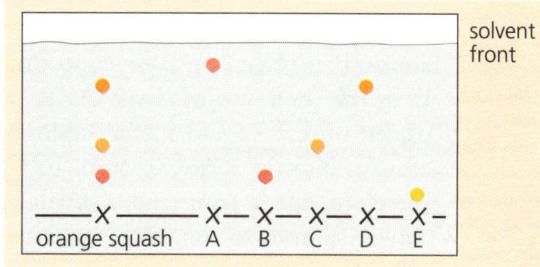

Fig 5 Chromatography of orange squash

Uses of paper chromatography

Paper chromatography is used to identify the colouring in coloured solutions, e.g. squashes, felt pens. In these cases the solvent is water.

2 Amino acids are colourless. Mixtures of amino acids can be separated by paper chromatography. The chromatogram is sprayed with a developing chemical called ninhydrin. The amino acids then show up as bluish spots.

3 A child suffering from phenylketonuria ('PKU') produces chemicals called ketones in its urine. Paper chromatography can be used to identify the presence of ketones in urine.

Q2 Ballpen ink is not soluble in water but is soluble in ethanol. How should you modify the method for paper chromatography if you wished to find the dyes present in a ballpen ink?

Q3 Fruit juices contain amino acids. It is illegal to add other amino acids to fruit juices to act as sweeteners. How would you try to show that amino acids had not been added?

Gas–liquid chromatography

Gas–liquid chromatography is a technique widely used in industry to identify substances present in a mixture. In 1952 Martin and James showed that this method was useful for separating small quantities of volatile materials. A small sample is injected into a stream of carrier gas. The different substances pass through the gas column at different rates.

A2 Structure of metals

In this unit you will learn the answers to these questions:
- How are atoms arranged in metals?
- How can the properties of pure metals be explained by the arrangement of atoms in a metal?

All solid metals are crystalline, which means that the atoms composing them are in a regular arrangement. In most cases the arrangement of atoms in metals is based upon close packing. In Unit 6 (Fig 3) part of a layer of iron atoms is shown. You will notice that any atom within the layer is surrounded by six other atoms in a regular hexagon. These identical layers can be stacked up in two ways.

You may find that using models will help you to understand the different arrangements.

Hexagonal close-packed structure

In a hexagonal close-packed structure the second layer of atoms, B is placed on layer A, so that the atoms of layer B fit into the hollows of layer A. A third layer of atoms is placed on top of and in the hollows of layer B, so that each atom is directly above an atom in layer A. The third layer is, therefore, an A layer and a further B layer can be placed above it, and so on. The structure built up is therefore called an ABABAB arrangement and is shown in Fig 1. This arrangement is known as the **hexagonal close-packed** (or **hcp**) crystal structure. Examples of metals having this structure are magnesium and zinc.

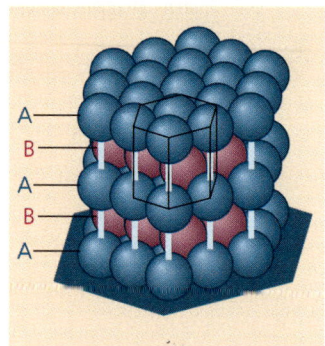

Fig 1 Arrangement of atoms in hexagonal close-packed crystal structure

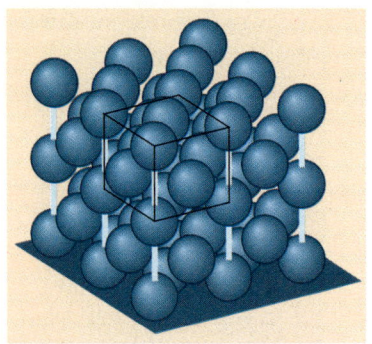

Fig 2 Arrangement of atoms in face-centred cubic crystal structure

Face-centred cubic structure

An alternative method of stacking the close-packed layers of atoms is shown in Fig 2. When a third layer of atoms is placed on the hollows in layer B, it can be placed in a different way so that the centres of the atoms in the third layer are above the holes in the first layer. The fourth is immediately above the first, and the fifth is immediately above the second, and so on. For this reason the arrangement is called the ABCABCABC structure. This structure is called the **face-centred cubic** crystal structure. Metals having this structure include aluminium, copper and lead.

Both structures put the maximum number of atoms possible into a given volume. The atoms fill 75% of the available volume. These structures explain why metals have high densities.

Q1 How many atoms are in contact with any atom within the structures shown in Figs 1 and 2?

In Unit 34 there are data about the alkali metals. You will notice that the densities of alkali metals are low. The atoms in alkali metals are less closely packed. They fill approximately 68% of the available volume.

A Classifying materials

Fig 3 shows the arrangement of atoms in an alkali metal. This is called **body-centred cubic** structure. Each atom is surrounded by eight other atoms.

Metals can change structure according to conditions. For example, nickel has hexagonal close packing at lower temperatures, and this changes to face-centred cubic structure at higher temperatures.

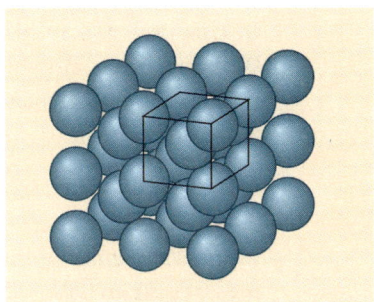

Fig 3 Body-centred cubic arrangement of atoms in an alkali metal

Faults within a metal structure

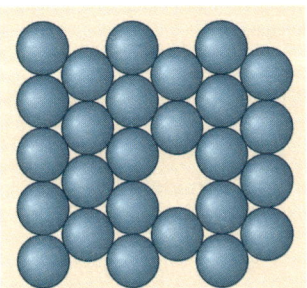

Metals do not usually consist of large perfect crystals. Two imperfections that occur are **missing atoms** (Fig 4) and **dislocations** (Fig 5). Dislocations occur when different crystals meet.

Fig 4 A missing atom in a metal structure

Fig 5 Where two metal crystals have met there is a dislocation

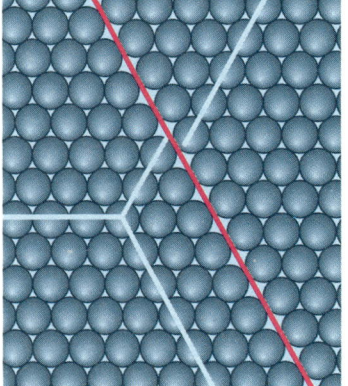

Q2 Why do metals have high melting points?

Q3 Pure metals are usually soft and can be drawn into fine wires. Explain how the structure of a pure metal makes this possible.

Crystallisation in a metal

The crystallisation of a molten metal begins with the formation of small **nuclei** scattered randomly throughout the liquid. At each nucleus, a few atoms may come together in an ordered pattern, and the nucleus grows outwards by the addition of further atoms of metal to its surface. The growth is not necessarily the same in all directions, causing long, needle-shaped crystals to form. Along the line of the crystal, secondary growths may occur to give a crystal skeleton called a **dendrite**. Fig 6 summarises the processes taking place during metal crystallisation.

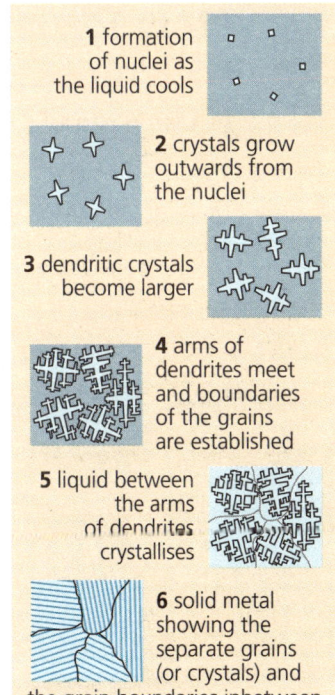

1 formation of nuclei as the liquid cools

2 crystals grow outwards from the nuclei

3 dendritic crystals become larger

4 arms of dendrites meet and boundaries of the grains are established

5 liquid between the arms of dendrites crystallises

6 solid metal showing the separate grains (or crystals) and the grain boundaries inbetween

Fig 6 The process of crystallisation in a metal

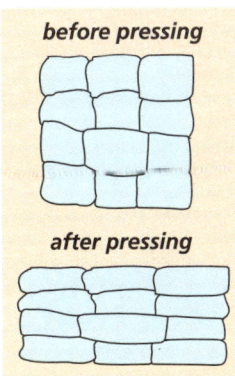

before pressing

after pressing

The physical properties of a metal are greatly affected by the size of the crystal grains. When a molten metal is cooled slowly fewer nuclei are formed and larger crystals are produced.

The effect of cold-working metals, e.g. rolling, extruding and pressing, is to break down the crystal structure and elongate the grains in the direction of working. The metal becomes harder and less ductile. This is shown in Fig 7.

Fig 7 Pressing a metal to alter its properties

A3 Alloys

In this unit you will learn the answers to these questions:
- What is an alloy?
- How are atoms arranged in an alloy?
- What are the common uses of alloys?

Pure metals have relatively few uses. The table summarises some of the uses of pure metals.

Metal	Use	Reason for use
copper	electricity cables	Excellent conductor of electricity. Very ductile
tin	coating cans	Not poisonous
aluminium	kitchen foil	Very malleable. Good heat conductor
iron	wrought-iron gates	Easy to forge. Resists corrosion
lead	flashing on roofs	Soft. Easy to shape. Does not corrode

Pure metals are often too soft and too weak for many uses. Most metals are sold in the form of **alloys** which are intimate mixtures of two or more metals, or of metals and non-metals. Brass is an example of an alloy made by mixing copper and zinc. Steel is an important alloy of iron and between 0.15% and 1.5% carbon.

Alloys are prepared by mixing the constituents in the molten state and allowing them to solidify. Most metals are completely soluble in each other in the liquid state, but in the solid state a range of possibilities exists. The various constituents may be completely miscible, completely immiscible, partially miscible, or they may react with each other to form new compounds.

How forming an alloy affects the structure of a metal

In Unit 6 part of a close-packed layer of atoms in a metal is shown in Fig 3. When an alloy is formed the structure of the metal can be changed in two ways.

1 *Brass*. Brass is an alloy of copper and zinc. Zinc atoms are larger than copper atoms. The different sizes of the atoms in the structure distort the structure (Fig 1) and layers cannot slide as easily over one another.

2 *Steel*. Steel is an alloy of iron and small amounts of carbon. Carbon atoms are very small and fit into the gaps between the iron atoms (Fig 2). The layers of atoms again do not slide as easily over each other.

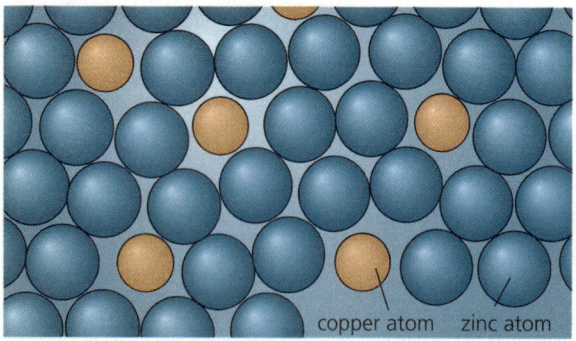

Fig 1 The arrangement of zinc atoms and copper atoms in brass

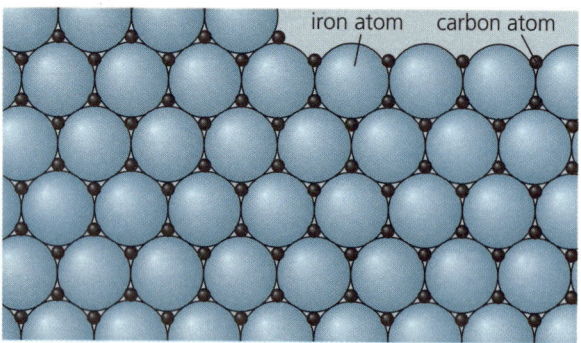

Fig 2 The arrangement of iron atoms and carbon atoms in steel

A Classifying materials

Uses of alloys

The table summarises some of the uses of common alloys, and Fig 3 shows some of their everyday uses.

Alloy	Made from	Special properties	Uses
stainless steel	70% iron, 20% chromium, 10% nickel and small amount of carbon	does not rust	cutlery, sinks, car components
brass	70% copper, 30% zinc	hard, does not corrode	ornaments, screws, hinges
duralumin	aluminium, magnesium, copper and manganese	lightweight and strong	aircraft components, bicycle frames
solder	70% tin, 30% lead	low melting point	joining metals
bronze	95% copper, 5% tin	harder than brass, makes a sound when struck	church bells, statues
coinage bronze	copper, zinc and tin	hard, corrosion resistant	'copper' coins

Q1 Why is pure aluminium used for overhead power cables rather than aluminium alloy?

Q2 Nichrome is an alloy with good electrical properties. Which two metals are mixed together to make it?

Fig 3 Some uses of common alloys

The composition of steel can affect its uses. The table gives some examples of the uses of steel with different compositions.

Type of steel	Percentage of carbon	Examples of uses
low-carbon steel	0.03–0.25	sheet metal for car bodies
medium-carbon steel	0.25–0.50	machine parts, springs
high-carbon steel	0.85–1.20	cutting tools, drills

Q3 How does increasing the percentage of carbon in steel affect its hardness?

12 Solubility

In this unit you will learn the answers to these questions:
- What is solubility?
- How can you find the solubility of a solute at a particular temperature?
- How does the solubility of a solute vary with temperature?
- What is a solubility curve?

We have seen that water is a good **solvent** because it dissolves a wide range of substances (called **solutes**). Some solutes dissolve more than others.

> The solubility of a solute is the mass of the solute that dissolves in 100 g of solvent at a particular temperature.

The solubility of sodium chloride

Fig 1 summarises the steps that should be taken to find the solubility of sodium chloride (salt) in water *at room temperature*.

A beaker is half filled with water at room temperature. Sodium chloride is added to the water in small portions. After each addition, the solution is stirred. Sodium chloride is added until no more sodium chloride will dissolve and some remains undissolved. This is called a **saturated solution**. A dry evaporating basin is weighed and some of the saturated solution, without sodium chloride crystals, is poured into the evaporating basin, which is then weighed again. The solution is carefully evaporated to dryness. After cooling the evaporating basin is weighed again.

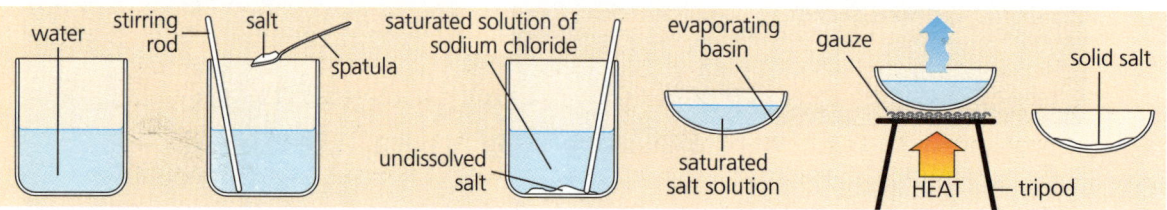

Sample results:

1. Mass of evaporating basin = 50.25 g
2. Mass of evaporating basin + sodium chloride solution = 118.25 g
3. Mass of evaporating basin + solid sodium chloride = 68.25 g

Fig 1 Finding the solubility of sodium chloride in water

From these results:

Mass of sodium chloride solution = **2** − **1** = 118.25 g − 50.25 g = 68.00 g
Mass of solid sodium chloride = **3** − **1** = 68.25 g − 50.25 g = 18.00 g
Mass of water in solution = **3** − **2** = 118.25 g − 68.25 g = 50.00 g

18.00 g of sodium chloride dissolved in 50.00 g of water at room temperature. Therefore, $\frac{18}{50} \times 100$ g of sodium chloride dissolved in 100 g of water at room temperature. The solubility of sodium chloride at room temperature is 36.0 g of sodium chloride per 100 g of water.

B Changing materials

The solubility of potassium chlorate at different temperatures

A weighed mass of potassium chlorate is put into a dry test tube. A measured volume of water is added to the test tube and the test tube is heated until all the solid potassium chlorate has dissolved. The test tube is then allowed to cool and the solution is constantly stirred with a thermometer (Fig 2). The temperature when crystals first start to appear is noted. A known volume of water is added to the test tube and the test tube is reheated and cooled as before. A new temperature is recorded. If this is repeated, a series of volumes of water and temperatures are recorded. Sample results are shown in the table for an experiment using 2.0 g of potassium chlorate.

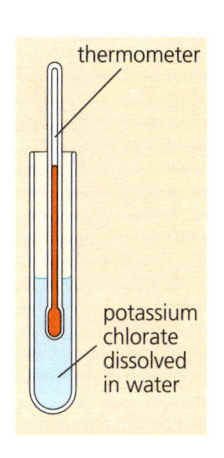

Fig 2

Total volume of water/cm³	Total mass of water/g	Temperature at which crystals are first seen/°C	Solubility (calculated) in g per 100 g of water $\frac{\text{mass of potassium chlorate}}{\text{mass of water}} \times 100$
4	4	90	2/4 × 100 = 50.0
6	6	74	2/6 × 100 = 33.3
8	8	62	2/8 × 100 = 25.0
12	12	48	2/12 × 100 = 16.7
16	16	36	2/16 × 100 = 12.5
20	20	27	2/20 × 100 = 10.0

Note that the mass of 1 cm³ of water is 1 g.

Solubility curves

The experiment with sodium chloride at room temperature could be repeated using saturated solutions prepared at different temperatures. You would then be able to see how the solubility of a solute changes with temperature. This is best shown in a graph, called a **solubility curve**. This is a graph of solubility of a solute (on the vertical, or y, axis) against temperature (on the horizontal, or x, axis).

Fig 3 shows a solubility curve for potassium chlorate in water. You will notice that the solubility of potassium chlorate increases with increasing temperature. This is true with most solutes in water. Use the solubility curve for potassium chlorate to answer the following questions.

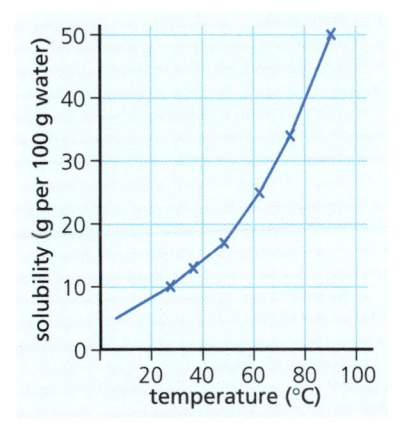

Q1 What is the solubility of potassium chlorate in water at 20°C?

Q2 What is the solubility of potassium chlorate in water at 80°C?

Q3 What mass of potassium chlorate would dissolve in 50 g of water at 40°C?

Q4 If a saturated solution of potassium chlorate containing 100 g of water at 80°C was cooled to 20°C, what mass of potassium chlorate would crystallise out?

Fig 3 Solubility curve of potassium chlorate in water

13 Change

In this unit you will learn the answers to these questions:
- What are temporary (physical) and permanent (chemical) changes?
- How does the mass change during a chemical reaction?
- What are the three types of decomposition?
- What are oxidation and reduction?

Physical and chemical change

Fig 1 shows two changes taking place. In **a)** a block of ice is melting to form a pool of water. This is a temporary or physical change. No chemical reaction has taken place. It is easy to reverse by putting the water back in the freezer. In **b)** wood is burning. This is a permanent or chemical change. It is accompanied by an energy change with energy being lost to the surroundings. It is impossible to reverse the change, i.e. get the wood back from the ashes.

a) Block of ice melting   b) Wood burning

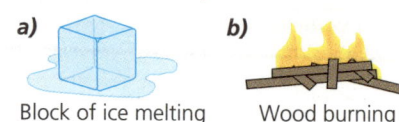

Fig 1 Physical and chemical changes

Are each of the following changes physical (no chemical reaction taking place) or chemical (chemical reaction taking place)?

Q1 A mixture of hydrogen and oxygen explodes.

Q2 Sugar is added to water and the mixture is stirred.

Q3 Water in a kettle is boiled and turned to steam.

Q4 A sparkler firework is lit.

Q5 A piece of iron rusts.

Q6 A sample of flour is sieved to remove lumps.

Q7 A cake mixture is cooked to produce a sponge cake.

Burning magnesium in oxygen is another permanent change. There is an apparent increase in mass when magnesium burns.

0.24 g magnesium before burning   0.40 g residue after burning

However, this is not the whole story. The apparent increase in mass is due to the oxygen which has combined with the magnesium. The sum of the mass of magnesium and the mass of oxygen is equal to the mass of magnesium oxide formed. This is true in all chemical reactions.

> The sum of the masses of the reacting substances = the sum of the masses of the substances produced.

Q8 Copy and complete the following: A physical or _____ change is one where _____ chemical _____ has taken place. A _____ change is one that cannot easily be _____.

Decomposition

Decomposition is a chemical reaction that results in the breaking down of a substance into simpler substances. There are three types of decomposition.

1 Thermal decomposition. A substance is split up by heating, e.g. copper carbonate is split up on heating into copper oxide and carbon dioxide.

2 **Catalytic decomposition.** A substance is split up with the help of a catalyst, e.g. hydrogen peroxide is split into water and oxygen by manganese(IV) oxide.

3 **Electrolytic decomposition.** A substance, which is molten or dissolved in water, is split up by an electric current, e.g. molten lead bromide is split into lead and bromine.

> **Q9** Copy and complete the following: The splitting of a substance into simpler products is called _____ . This can be carried out by heating, using a _____ or by electrolysis.

Oxidation and reduction

A substance which combines with oxygen is said to be **oxidised**. The process is called **oxidation**. Any burning or combustion process is oxidation.

When a piece of magnesium is burned in oxygen, white magnesium oxide is formed.

    magnesium + oxygen ➡ magnesium oxide

Magnesium has gained oxygen and is said to have been oxidised.

Oxidation can also be regarded as a reaction where hydrogen is lost.

Reduction is the opposite of oxidation. A substance is reduced (or reduction has taken place) when it loses oxygen or gains hydrogen.

For example, Joseph Priestley discovered oxygen by heating mercury oxide.

    mercury oxide ➡ mercury + oxygen

The mercury oxide is reduced because it has lost oxygen.

When chlorine reacts with hydrogen, hydrogen chloride is formed.

    hydrogen + chlorine ➡ hydrogen chloride

The chlorine has gained hydrogen and has been reduced.

Redox reactions

Oxidation and reduction reactions occur together. When one substance loses oxygen, another gains it. A reaction where both reduction and oxidation occur is called a **redox reaction**. For example, when hydrogen is passed over heated yellow lead oxide, lead and water are produced.

    lead oxide + hydrogen ➡ lead + hydrogen oxide (water)

Lead oxide loses oxygen during this reaction and is reduced, while hydrogen gains oxygen and is oxidised.

The reduction of lead oxide to lead does not take place on its own. The presence of hydrogen is necessary if reduction is to take place. Hydrogen is called a **reducing agent**. The change of hydrogen to hydrogen oxide uses oxygen from the lead oxide. Lead oxide is called the **oxidising agent**. The overall reaction between hydrogen and lead oxide is a redox reaction.

14 Crude oil and its refining

In this unit you will learn the answers to these questions:
- What makes up crude oil?
- How was crude oil formed in the Earth?
- How is crude oil trapped in the Earth?
- How is crude oil refined?
- What are alkanes?

What is crude oil?

Crude oil (sometimes called petroleum) is an important source of energy and chemicals. It is a source of **organic compounds**, i.e. compounds containing carbon. It is a complex mixture of hydrocarbons (compounds of carbon and hydrogen only). When it comes out of the ground it is a black, treacle-like liquid with an unpleasant smell. Until it could be refined it was of little economic importance. It was used in ancient Babylon to make mortar to stick bricks together. Sir Walter Raleigh (1552–1618) used it to make his wooden ships watertight. Over 100 years ago farmers in Texas used to burn it off when they found it on the surface of their land.

> **Q1** Which two elements are combined in the compounds which make up crude oil?

How crude oil was formed

Crude oil was formed in the Earth millions of years ago. A larger area of the Earth was covered with sea then and the sea was full of all types of animal life. This included tiny sea creatures called plankton.

When these creatures died they sank to the sea bed and were mixed with mud. Over millions of years this layer was compressed by the rocks above and partial decomposition of the remains produced crude oil and the natural gas associated with it.

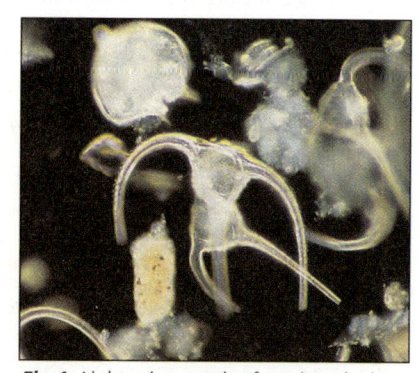

Fig 1 Light micrograph of marine plankton

The layers of sedimentary rocks bent and deposits of crude oil became trapped between layers of impermeable rocks. The crude oil remained trapped until oil explorers drilled down to the deposits. Then the crude oil is forced to the surface under pressure with the natural gas. Fig 2 summarises the processes which produce crude oil.

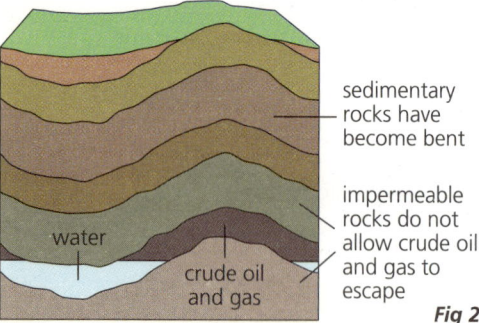

Scientists use a variety of techniques to find underground deposits of crude oil. These include:

1. a geological study of the rocks present;
2. seismic studies – shockwaves are sent through the rock layers and measuring instruments on the surface record the echoes from rock layers;
3. studying fossils from different rocks, which then gives an idea of the age of rocks.

Fig 2 Processes which produce crude oil

B Changing materials

Refining of crude oil

Crude oil is separated into useful saleable fractions by the process of fractional distillation (Unit 10). The fractional distillation separates the crude oil into different fractions. Each fraction has a range of boiling points and contains all of the carbon compounds boiling within the temperature range.

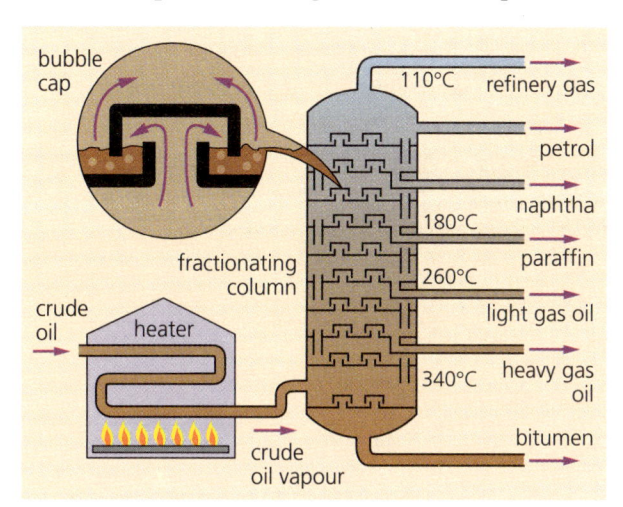

The crude oil is heated in a furnace and the vapour is passed into the bottom of the fractionating column (Fig 3). The hot vapours pass up the column. When each fraction reaches the tray where the temperature is just below its own boiling point it condenses and changes back into a liquid. In this way the different fractions are separated and drawn off separately.

Q2 How do we know that crude oil is a mixture of substances rather than one pure substance?

Fig 3 Fractional distillation of crude oil

The fractions which come off from the top of the column are called **light fractions**. They have low boiling points and are clear, light-coloured, runny liquids which burn readily. Those that condense near the bottom of the column are **heavy fractions**. They are darker in colour, viscous (thick and difficult to pour) and catch alight less easily.

The table contains the properties and uses of the fractions produced by the fractional distillation of crude oil.

Fraction	Boiling point range/°C	Number of carbon atoms in molecules	Uses
refinery gas	up to 40	1 – 4	gases for gas cookers, liquified petroleum gas (LPG)
petrol	40 – 140	5 – 10	fuel for vehicles, chemicals
naphtha	140 – 180	8 – 12	raw material for chemicals and plastics
paraffin	180 – 250	10 – 16	aircraft fuel, heating and raw material for chemicals
light gas oil	250 – 300	14 – 20	fuel for trains and lorries, raw materials for chemicals, plastics
heavy gas oil	300 – 340	20 – 30	fuel for ships, factories, central heating
bitumen	above 340	more than 25	for roads and roofing

Q3 Which fraction boils off first?

Q4 Write down four properties of the petrol fraction.

Q5 Why does the boiling point increase as the number of carbon atoms per molecule increases?

The fractions produced contain hydrocarbons called **alkanes**. Alkanes all fit a general formula C_nH_{2n+2}, e.g hexane is C_6H_{14}. The light fractions contain small alkane molecules and heavy fractions contain large alkane molecules.

15 Uses of alkanes

In this unit you will learn the answers to these questions:
- Why do alkanes make such good fuels?
- What are the products of combustion of alkanes?
- How can methane be made?

Alkanes

The table shows some information about the first six members of the alkane family. Alkanes are **saturated hydrocarbons**, i.e. all of the bonds between the carbon atoms are single covalent bonds.

Alkane	Formula	Structure	Melting point/°C	Boiling point/°C	Mass of 1 mole/g	State at room temperature and pressure
methane	CH_4		−182	−161	16	gas
ethane	C_2H_6		−183	−89	30	gas
propane	C_3H_8		−188	−42	44	gas
butane	C_4H_{10}		−138	0	58	gas
pentane	C_5H_{12}		−130	36	72	liquid
hexane	C_6H_{14}		−95	68	86	liquid

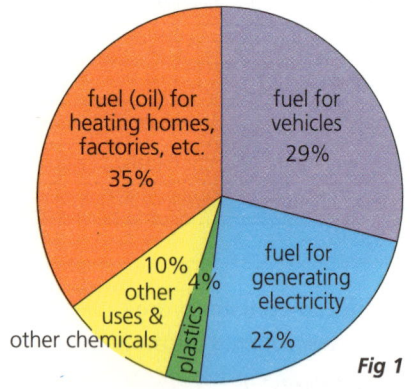

Reactions of hydrocarbons

The hydrocarbons called alkanes are fairly unreactive. Petrol, for example, does not react with sulphuric acid (an acid), sodium hydroxide (an alkali), sodium (metal and strong reducing agent) or potassium manganate(VII) (strong oxidising agent). However, alkanes do burn well to produce energy. Most of the uses of alkanes rely on exothermic reactions when they burn. Fig 1 shows a pie diagram which shows that most crude oil (86%) is used for fuel purposes.

Pie chart:
- fuel (oil) for heating homes, factories, etc. 35%
- fuel for vehicles 29%
- fuel for generating electricity 22%
- plastics 4%
- other uses & other chemicals 10%

Fig 1 *Uses of crude oil*

Burning or **combustion** of hydrocarbons, including alkanes, requires oxygen from the air. Providing there is a *plentiful* supply of oxygen, the products are water vapour and carbon dioxide. The apparatus in Fig 2 can be used to show that carbon dioxide and water are produced when methane burns.

B Changing materials

The table summarises the results of the experiment.

Test with	Before experiment	After experiment	Conclusion
cobalt chloride paper	blue	pink	water produced
limewater	solution clear	solution white and cloudy	carbon dioxide produced

If hydrocarbons, including alkanes, burn in a *limited* supply of oxygen, water vapour is still produced but the poisonous gas carbon monoxide, CO, can be produced.

Fig 2 *Carbon dioxide and water are produced when methane burns*

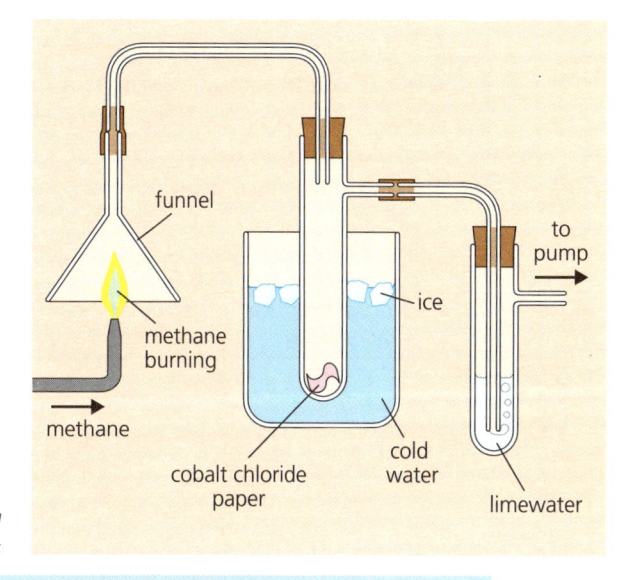

> **Q1** Complete these word equations for the burning of methane:
> plentiful supply of air   methane + oxygen ➡ _____ + _____
> limited supply of air   methane + oxygen ➡ _____ + _____
>
> **Q2** Write balanced symbolic equations for the combustion of methane.

Methane from refuse and animal dung

When rubbish is tipped in landfill sites and covered with soil, bacteria break down the rubbish to form methane gas. In Birkenhead, near Liverpool, gas produced in a landfill site is being used to provide energy for a local factory where sweets and biscuits are made.

> **Q3** Before biodigesters were developed, cow dung and straw were mixed together and dried. These were then used as fuel. What are the advantages of methane produced from biodigesters?
>
> **Q4** What is the waste remaining from the biodigester used for?

In countries such as India where fossil fuels such as coal are very expensive, methane made from animal dung can be used to provide energy. In a biodigester animal dung is broken down by bacteria to produce a gas containing 60% methane.

Making hydrogen from methane

Hydrogen is produced from methane (natural gas) by **steam reforming**. Methane is mixed with steam and passed over a nickel catalyst at a high temperature and pressure.

methane + steam ➡ hydrogen + carbon monoxide
$CH_4(g)$ + $H_2O(g)$ ➡ $3H_2(g)$ + $CO(g)$

The gases are then mixed with more steam and passed over an iron(III) oxide catalyst.

carbon monoxide + steam ➡ carbon dioxide + hydrogen
$CO(g)$ + $H_2O(g)$ ➡ $CO_2(g)$ + $H_2(g)$

The carbon dioxide is removed by dissolving it under pressure in water.

16 Cracking hydrocarbons

In this unit you will learn the answers to these questions:
- What is cracking and why is it important economically?
- What products are formed by cracking alkanes?
- How do you test for unsaturated compounds?
- What are alkenes?

The products of fractional distillation

Fraction	Percentage produced by refining	Percentage demand for finished products
refinery gas	2	4
petrol	8	22
naphtha	10	5
paraffin	14	8
light gas oil	21	23
heavy gas oil	45	38

The table shows the percentage of each fraction produced by the refining of crude oil and the demand for the finished products.

The lighter fractions (e.g. petrol and gas) are in greater demand than the heavier ones (naphtha and paraffin). These large molecules can be broken down into smaller ones. This is called **cracking**.

Cracking alkanes

Alkanes are **saturated** hydrocarbons. They contain only single carbon–carbon and carbon–hydrogen bonds.

E.g. propane

Cracking is a process which breaks down long-chain alkanes into smaller molecules. For example, the breakdown of a decane molecule produces smaller molecules, including some that are **unsaturated**, i.e. they contain one or more carbon–carbon double bonds.

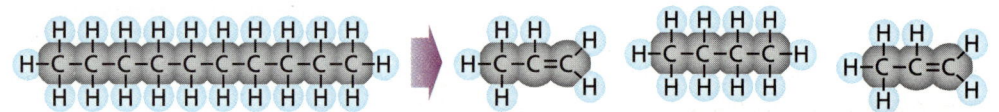

Cracking takes place when alkane vapour is passed over a catalyst at high temperature and pressure. Fig 1 shows how cracking is carried out in industry. The catalyst which is used becomes spent and has to be regenerated for reuse.

It is also possible to change the shape of hydrocarbon molecules by processes of **reforming**.

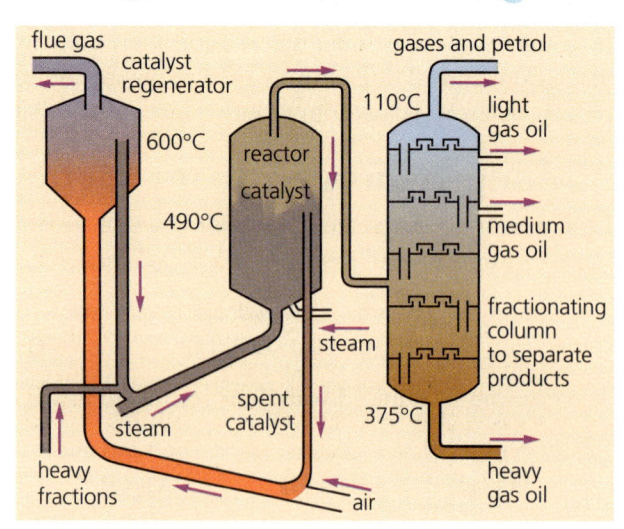

Fig 1 Industrial cracking process

B Changing materials

Cracking liquid paraffin in the laboratory

Liquid paraffin is a mixture of alkanes with about 12 carbon atoms. If liquid paraffin vapour is passed over strongly heated broken china, the vapour is cracked to produce a colourless gas which is insoluble in water and can be collected over water. The apparatus in Fig 2 can be used for cracking liquid paraffin vapour.

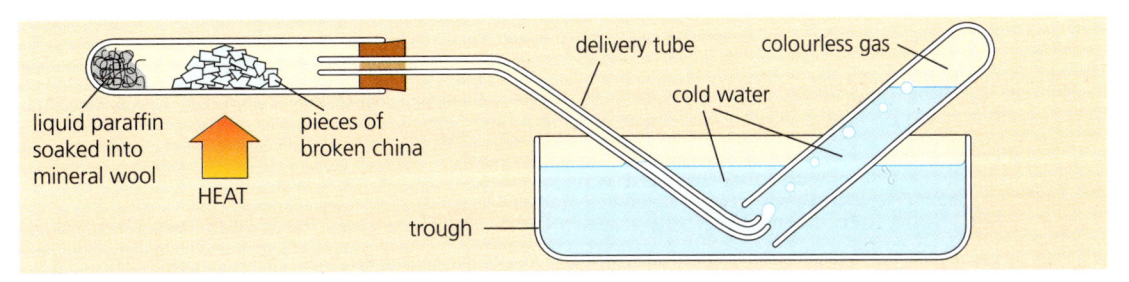

Fig 2 Cracking liquid paraffin vapour

The table summarises the properties of liquid paraffin and the gas which is produced by cracking liquid paraffin.

Property	Liquid paraffin	Gas produced by cracking liquid paraffin
colour	colourless	colourless
state	liquid	gas
smell	no smell	sweet smell
flammable	burns well after heating	burns well with a yellow flame
test with bromine	red colour remains	turns colourless

The colourless gas collected is an alkene called ethene.
The structure of ethene is

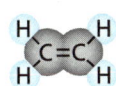

Alkenes can be distinguished from alkanes by the **addition** reaction with bromine. Bromine is red in colour. When it reacts with ethene it produces a colourless product called 1,2-dibromoethane. The solution is therefore decolorised.

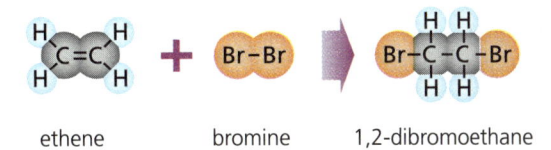

ethene   bromine   1,2-dibromoethane

This test with bromine is used to show if a hydrocarbon is unsaturated. Alkanes contain only single bonds and do not decolorise bromine.

> **Q1** An oily liquid collects on the surface of the water in the trough. What is this liquid and how is it formed?
>
> **Q2** During the experiment water from the trough sometimes enters the delivery tube. Why does this happen?

B1 Fuels

In this unit you will learn the answers to these questions:
- What is a fuel?
- How can we classify fuels?
- What are the advantages and disadvantages of different types of fuel?
- How can methane be produced from refuse and animal waste?
- How can the products of the combustion of methane be identified?
- How can the energy content of a fuel be found?

A fuel is a substance which burns to release energy. There are some fuels that release energy but do not burn, for example uranium in a nuclear reactor.

Fuels can be classified in different ways.

1 Solid fuels, liquid fuels and gaseous fuels. **2** Fossil fuels and renewable fuels.

Solid fuels include coal, coke, peat and wood. They have to be stored and are usually difficult to set alight. They often do not burn cleanly, producing smoke and other impurities. Liquid fuels include petrol, diesel oil and central-heating oil. They are easier to light and cleaner to burn than solid fuels. They require some kind of tank to store them. Gaseous fuels include methane (natural gas) and hydrogen. They burn easily and cleanly. However, mixtures of gaseous fuel and air can be explosive and care must be taken with storage.

Fossil fuels include coal, petrol and natural gas. They have been produced in the Earth over millions of years. When they are used up they cannot be replaced. They are a **finite resource**. Fuels such as wood, sugar cane and ethanol are **renewable**. New supplies can be grown every year to replace the supply used.

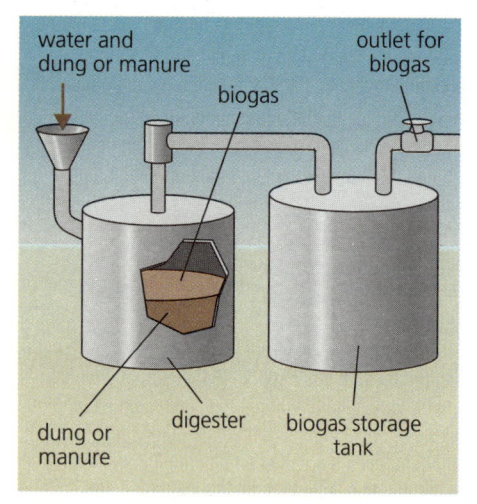

Fig 1 Biodigester

Producing methane in landfill sites and biodigesters

When refuse is tipped in landfill sites and covered with soil, bacteria decompose the refuse and produce methane gas. The production of this gas has to be carefully monitored to prevent explosions. One explosion in Loscoe in Derbyshire demolished a bungalow and threatened other properties.

Methane is often piped off old refuse sites. In Birkenhead, near Liverpool a factory making sweets and biscuits is powered by gas from a local refuse site.

In countries such as India people cannot afford to buy fossil fuels. Traditionally they have burned dung from their animals to provide energy for cooking. This dung is, however, a good fertiliser and if it is burnt the soil does not benefit. One solution is to use a biodigester (Fig 1). Dung and water are put into the digester and bacteria break down the dung producing methane gas which can be used as a fuel. The waste from the digester is then used as a fertiliser.

B Changing materials

Products of burning methane

Fig 2 shows how the products of the burning of methane can be investigated. The pump sucks the products of combustion through the apparatus. In test tube A a colourless liquid collects. The table shows the results of tests on this liquid.

Fig 2 Investigating the products when methane is burnt

Test	Result
add cobalt(II) chloride paper	paper turns from blue to pink
add anhydrous copper(II) sulphate	turns from white to blue
boiling point	100°C

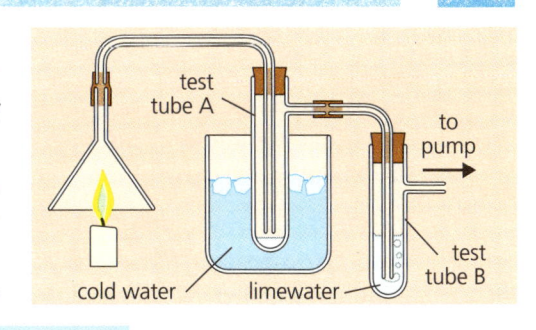

Q1 What can be concluded from the results of the tests in the table?

In tube B the limewater turns milky.

Q2 What can be concluded from the result of this test?

Q3 What are the products of combustion of methane?

Q4 Methane has the formula CH_4. Write a balanced symbol equation for the reaction of methane with oxygen.

Q5 How would the results be different if a jet of hydrogen gas was used in place of methane?

Energy content of a fuel

Fig 3 shows apparatus which can be used to find the energy of the liquid fuel in a spirit lamp. The lamp is weighed before and after the experiment to find the mass of fuel used. The mass of the calorimeter and the mass of the water in the calorimeter are found. The temperature of the water in the calorimeter is taken at the start and finish of the experiment.

Fig 3 Finding the energy of liquid fuel

Sample results:

1. Mass of spirit lamp before experiment = 86.7 g
2. Mass of spirit lamp after experiment = 86.2 g
3. Mass of liquid fuel burned = 0.5 g
4. Mass of metal calorimeter = 65.0 g
5. Mass of water in the calorimeter = 100 g
6. Temperature of water at the beginning of the experiment = 20°C
7. Temperature of water at the end of the experiment = 30°C

Q6 Often it is better to compare the energy content of fuels per mole rather than per gram. Why do you think this is so?

From these results:

Temperature rise = 10°C

Energy required to raise the temperature of 100 g of water by 10°C
= mass of water × specific heat capacity of water × temperature rise (specific heat capacity of water is 4200 J/kgK)
= 0.1 × 4200 × 10 = 4.2 kJ

Energy required to raise the temperature of 65 g of metal (the calorimeter) by 10°C
= mass of metal × specific heat capacity of metal × temperature rise (specific heat capacity of metal is 420 J/kgK)
= 0.065 × 420 × 10 = 0.27 kJ

The total energy required = 4.47 kJ
0.5 g of liquid fuel produces 4.47 kJ.
The energy content of the fuel is 4.47 × 2 = 8.94 kJ/g.

17 Addition polymerisation

In this unit you will learn the answers to these questions:
- What are addition polymers and how are they made?
- What are addition polymers used for?
- What is a copolymer?

Materials we commonly call plastics are more correctly called **polymers**. They are made by a process of **polymerisation** by joining together small molecules called **monomers**. The process is summarised by:

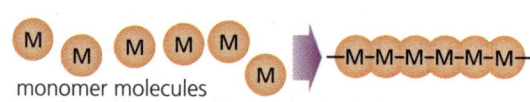

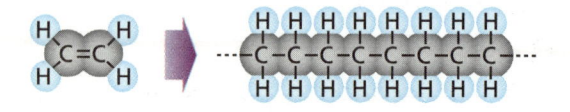

monomer molecules

The most common polymer is poly(ethene), which is made from joining together many ethene molecules to form long poly(ethene) chains.

The polymer is formed by a series of **addition** reactions and is therefore called an **addition polymer**. You will notice that the monomer molecules contain a carbon–carbon double bond but the polymer does **not** contain double bonds.

The conditions used to produce poly(ethene) can vary and the properties of the final polymer will depend upon the reaction conditions.

1 If ethene is heated at high temperatures and high pressures in the presence of a catalyst, **low density poly(ethene)** is produced.

2 If ethene is bubbled through an organic solvent containing complex catalysts, **high density poly(ethene)** is formed.

Both contain poly(ethene) chains.

Q1 In which form of poly(ethene) are the chains more closely packed together?

Q2 The average relative molecular mass of a poly(ethene) chain is 140 000. The relative molecular mass of an ethene molecule is 28. How many ethene molecules are there in an average poly(ethene) chain?

Polymers made from crude oil

The process of cracking (Unit 16) produces unsaturated alkenes from long-chain alkanes. These alkenes can be used to make a wide range of polymers. The table gives information about some common addition polymers.

Polymer	Structure of polymer	Monomer	Uses of polymer
poly(styrene) or poly(phenylethene)	$[-C(C_6H_5)(H)-C(H)(H)-]_n$	styrene or phenylethene $C_6H_5(H)C=C(H)(H)$	flowerpots, yoghurt cartons, plastic model kits, ceiling tiles
poly(vinyl chloride) or PVC or poly(chloroethene)	$[-C(Cl)(H)-C(H)(H)-]_n$	vinyl chloride or chloroethene $Cl(H)C=C(H)(H)$	artificial leather for furniture, luggage cases, clothes
poly(tetrafluoro-ethene) or PTFE	$[-C(F)(F)-C(F)(F)-]_n$	tetrafluoroethene $F(F)C=C(F)(F)$	non-stick coatings in saucepans

B Changing materials

Q3 Propene, C_3H_6, has a structure of

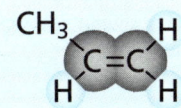

CH_3 \ / H
   $C=C$
 H / \ H

Draw the structure of part of a poly(propene) chain.

Uses of polymers

Polymers have become increasingly useful in recent years for several reasons.

1 There is a wider range of different polymers around now and each polymer has its own properties.

2 Traditional materials such as wood and metals have become less available and more expensive.

3 The density of polymers is much less than metals.

4 The reactivity of polymers is very low and so, unlike metals, there are no corrosion problems.

Factors which may affect the properties of a polymer

The properties of a polymer can be altered by changing its structure either during its making or by treatment afterwards.

1 Chain length

The average chain length of a polymer can be altered by the conditions used when polymerisation takes place.

The longer the chain length the higher will be the melting point of the polymer. Many polymers melt over a range of temperature and soften first before melting.

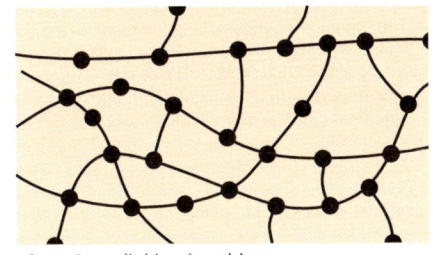

Fig 1 Cross-linking in rubber

2 Cross-linking

Natural rubber is an addition polymer formed from the latex of the rubber tree.

Before natural rubber can be used for car tyres it has to be hardened by a process called vulcanisation. The rubber is mixed with sulphur and cross-linking takes place between the polymer chains (Fig 1).

3 Degree of crystallisation

Fig 2 shows the chains in two polymers. In **a)** the chains are more regularly arranged than in **b)**. The polymer in **a)** is more crystalline.

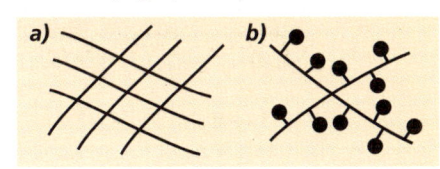

Fig 2 Degree of crystallisation

Copolymers

A polymer such as poly(ethene) contains one unit repeated over and over again. In practice, a more suitable polymer is often produced using two monomers polymerised together. For example, there is a copolymer of chloroethene and dichloroethene which has a trade name of Saran. It is used for making food wrappings.

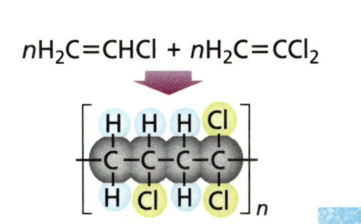

$nH_2C=CHCl + nH_2C=CCl_2$

$$\left[\begin{array}{cccc} H & H & H & Cl \\ | & | & | & | \\ -C-C-C-C- \\ | & | & | & | \\ H & Cl & H & Cl \end{array} \right]_n$$

B2 Condensation polymerisation

In this unit you will learn the answers to these questions:
- What is a condensation reaction?
- What is a condensation polymer?
- What are examples of condensation polymers?
- What are thermoplastic and thermosetting polymers?
- Why are plastics replacing metals for many uses?

Condensation reactions

A condensation reaction is a reaction between two molecules to form a larger molecule and to leave a small molecule, such as water (H_2O), or hydrogen chloride (HCl). For example the reaction between ethanoic acid and ethanol produces an ester and water (see Unit 18 on ethanol).

$$CH_3-C\binom{O}{O-H} + CH_3CH_2OH \rightleftharpoons CH_3-C\binom{O}{O-CH_2CH_3} + H_2O$$

ethanoic acid + ethanol ⇌ ethyl ethanoate + water

This could be represented in a simplified form by:

$$\bullet-C\binom{O}{O-H} + \blacksquare-O-H \rightleftharpoons \bullet-C\binom{O}{O-\blacksquare} + H_2O$$

The symbols ● and ■ are used to represent the hydrocarbon parts of the molecules. These are not involved in the changes. The reaction is between the –OH group in the alcohol and the –COOH group in the acid.

Another example of a condensation reaction is:

$$\bullet-C\binom{O}{Cl} + \blacksquare-N\binom{H}{H} \rightarrow \bullet-C\binom{O}{N\binom{H}{\blacksquare}} + HCl$$

acid chloride + amine ➡ amide + hydrogen chloride

Condensation polymers

Condensation polymers are formed when a series of condensation reactions takes place. The **monomer** molecules, which make up the polymer, must contain at least two reactive groups. Part of the polymer chain produced is shown here. Each time a link between two monomer molecules is made, a water molecule is lost.

$$\cdots\bullet-C\binom{O}{O-\blacksquare-O}C\binom{O}{}-\bullet-C\binom{O}{O-\blacksquare-O}C\cdots + H_2O$$

The resulting polymer is a **polyester**, made from a series of esterification reactions. It is an example of a **condensation polymer**.

A different condensation polymer is produced when acid chlorides and amines react. Again the monomer molecules must contain two reactive groups:

$$\binom{O}{Cl}C-\bullet-C\binom{O}{Cl} \quad H\!\!>\!\!N-\blacksquare-N\!\!<\!\!H$$

Part of the chain produced is shown here.

This is a **polyamide**, formed by a series of amide-forming reactions. It is called nylon.

$$\cdots C\binom{O}{}-\bullet-C\binom{O}{N\binom{}{H}}-\blacksquare-N\binom{}{H}C-\bullet-C\binom{O}{}\cdots + HCl$$

B Changing materials

There are many naturally occurring condensation polymers including cellulose, starch and proteins (see Unit B3 on the chemistry of food).

Thermoplastic and thermosetting polymers

Polymers can be classified according to how they change on heating. They can be classified as **thermoplastic** or **thermosetting** polymers.

A thermoplastic polymer becomes soft and mouldable on heating, without undergoing any significant chemical change. On cooling it hardens again. This softening and hardening can be repeated over and over again.

Thermosetting polymers (or thermosets) are plastics that are resistant to high temperatures and cannot be melted. They decompose before they melt and therefore cannot be softened and re-moulded. They are insoluble and swell only slightly in most organic solvents. At room temperature they are usually hard and brittle.

> **Q1** Can you think of examples, around the home, of thermoplastic and thermosetting polymers?
>
> **Q2** Which would be easier to recycle, thermoplastic or thermosetting polymers?

The differences between thermoplastic and thermosetting polymers can be understood by comparing the arrangement of chains in them. Fig 1 shows the arrangement in **a)** a thermoplastic polymer and **b)** a thermosetting polymer.

In a thermoplastic polymer there are only weak intermolecular attractions between the chains. On melting, the chains become free to move, and on cooling, no new bonds are formed.

In a thermosetting polymer, strong covalent bonds form cross-links between the chains. It is not possible for the chains to become free without breaking down the whole structure. The thermosetting polymer does not melt.

Fig 1 *The arrangement of chains in* **a)** *thermoplastic polymer and* **b)** *thermosetting polymer*

Over the past thirty or so years many objects traditionally made from wood, metal, or leather have been replaced by objects made from polymers. Fig 2 shows a graph of the mass of polymer per car over the years 1960–1994.

In a certain make of new car there are nearly 3000 different parts and over one-third of them is made from polymers.

Fig 2 *Graph showing the mass of polymer per car in car manufacture*

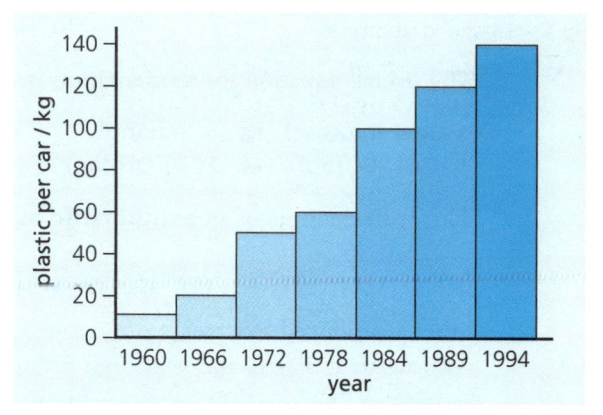

> **Q3** Why do you think so many car components are made from polymers?
>
> **Q4** Select parts of a car and suggest what they would have been made from before polymers were used. For example, car bumpers were made of steel, which was then electroplated.

18 Ethanol

In this unit you will learn the answers to these questions:
- How can ethanol be prepared from sugar and from ethene?
- What is produced when ethanol burns?
- What are the uses of ethanol?
- What effects can ethanol have on the human body?

Ethanol is a compound with the formula C_2H_5OH, commonly called alcohol. Its structural formula is:

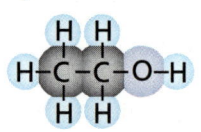

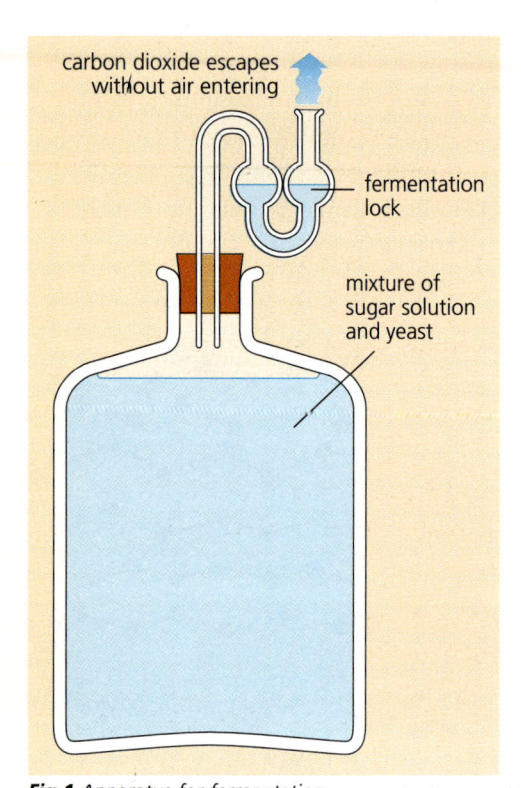

Fig 1 Apparatus for fermentation

It can be prepared by the process of **fermentation**. This involves the action of enzymes in yeast on sugar or carbohydrate solution. The apparatus in Fig 1 can be used to produce a solution of ethanol in water by fermentation. The valve in the neck of the jar allows the escape of carbon dioxide gas, produced during the fermentation, without allowing air into the jar.

Q1 What may happen if air is allowed to enter during the fermentation?

Q2 What precaution is taken with the fermenting equipment before using it to produce wine?

Fermentation is an example of **anaerobic respiration** (respiration without oxygen). Fermentation stops when the ethanol content reaches about 14% as the enzymes cannot survive in high ethanol concentrations. More concentrated ethanol solutions can be produced by fractional distillation (see whisky production, Unit 10).

The overall equation for fermentation is:

sugar (glucose) ➡ ethanol + carbon dioxide + energy
$C_6H_{12}O_6$ (aq) ➡ $2C_2H_5OH$ (aq) + $2CO_2$ (g) + 84 kJ

This is an example of an **exothermic** reaction.

Q3 How does the equation tell you that the reaction is exothermic?

Manufacture of ethanol from ethene

Ethene, produced by cracking fractions from crude oil, undergoes an addition reaction with steam at 300°C and very high pressure to produce ethanol.

$C_2H_4(g) + H_2O(g)$ ➡ $C_2H_5OH(g)$

B Changing materials

Uses of ethanol

Ethanol has four important uses.

1 **As a solvent**. Ethanol is a very good solvent, dissolving a wide range of different substances. It is very volatile, i.e. it evaporates easily. It is used as a solvent in paints, varnishes and perfumes. Ethanol evaporates quickly, causing the product to dry rapidly.

2 **As a fuel**. Ethanol burns with a clean, non-smoky flame. It is used for spirit burners. It is sold in the form of methylated spirits (meths) for this purpose with substances added to make it unsuitable for drinking.

Ethanol burns in a plentiful supply of air to produce carbon dioxide and water.

$$\text{ethanol} + \text{oxygen} \rightarrow \text{carbon dioxide} + \text{water}$$
$$C_2H_5OH(l) + 3O_2(g) \rightarrow 2CO_2(g) + 3H_2O(l)$$

In Brazil motorists use a mixture of ethanol and petrol as the fuel in motor cars. Ethanol is made from fermentation of sugar for this purpose.

Fig 2 *An ethanol and petrol pump in Brazil*

Q4 Why has ethanol been developed as a fuel in Brazil but not in Western Europe?

3 **In alcoholic drinks**.

4 **A useful reactant in the chemical industry**. Ethanol is used widely to make other chemicals. Ethanol reacts with ethanoic acid to form an **ester**, called ethyl ethanoate.

$$\text{ethanoic acid} + \text{ethanol} \rightleftharpoons \text{ethyl ethanoate} + \text{water}$$
$$CH_3COOH(l) + C_2H_5OH(l) \rightleftharpoons CH_3COOC_2H_5(l) + H_2O(l)$$

Ethyl ethanoate is used to make nail-varnish remover. Esters are important compounds which are responsible for the fragrant odours of fruits and flowers. Synthetic esters are used in the food industry as flavouring agents.

Q5 Methyl butanoate is present in pineapples and gives the smell and flavour to the fruit. The structure of methyl butanoate is: $CH_3CH_2CH_2\overset{\overset{O}{\|}}{C}OCH_3$
Write down the acid and the alcohol which can be used to make methyl butanoate.

Esters occur naturally in fats and oils. They are split up by hydrolysis into acid and alcohol. This process, using sodium hydroxide solution, is called **saponification**. The word saponification comes from the Latin word *sapo*, which means soap. Soap is produced when animal fat is hydrolysed by an alkali.

$$\text{animal fat} + \text{sodium hydroxide (alkali)} \rightarrow \text{soap} + \text{alcohol (glycerol)}$$

$$\begin{array}{l} CH_2OOCR \\ CHOOCR \\ CH_2OOCR \end{array} + 3NaOH \rightarrow 3RCOONa + \begin{array}{l} CH_2OH \\ CHOH \\ CH_2OH \end{array}$$

R represents carbon chains of between 12 and 18 carbon atoms, e.g. $C_{12}H_{25}-$.

B3 The chemistry of food

In this unit you will learn the answers to these questions:
- What types of chemicals are present in foods?
- What are carbohydrates?
- What are proteins?
- What is the job of vitamins and minerals in the diet?
- What are food additives and why are they used?
- How is margarine manufactured?

Chemicals in foods

There are many different chemicals present in our foods. These include **carbohydrates**, **fats**, **proteins**, **vitamins** and **minerals**. Vitamins and minerals are chemicals which are present in our bodies in very small amounts and control important processes in the body.

Carbohydrates are compounds containing carbon, hydrogen and oxygen. All carbohydrates have a general formula $C_x(H_2O)_y$.

Carbohydrates are grouped into **monosaccharides** (e.g. glucose and fructose, both with the formula $C_6H_{12}O_6$), **disaccharides** (e.g. sucrose and maltose, both $C_{12}H_{22}O_{11}$) and **polysaccharides** (e.g. starch, pectin and cellulose). Polysaccharides are condensation polymers (see Unit B2 on condensation reactions) made from chains of monosaccharide molecules. Polysaccharides in vegetables are more soluble in hot water than in cold. When vegetables are cooked these compounds are released into the water.

Starch is a condensation polymer, with glucose as the monomer. It is stored in plants as a reserve of energy. It can be broken down into simpler carbohydrates by **hydrolysis** in aqueous solution. The breakdown involves the reaction of the starch with water and unless a catalyst is present the reaction is extremely slow. The reaction can be catalysed in two ways.

1 **Acid-catalysed hydrolysis.** This is carried out by heating starch solution with dilute acid. The product is glucose.

2 **Enzyme-catalysed hydrolysis.** The hydrolysis reaction may also be catalysed by the enzyme α-amylase which is present in saliva. This reaction takes place at room temperature and produces maltose.

Fats are esters of acids and the alcohol, glycerol (see Unit 18). Fig 1 shows how a fat molecule can be made from acid and alcohol.

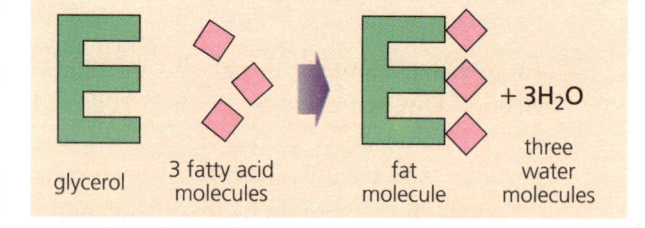

Fig 1 A fat molecule is made from three fatty acid molecules and one glycerol molecule

Proteins differ from carbohydrates and fats because they contain other elements in addition to carbon, hydrogen and oxygen. They contain nitrogen, and often sulphur and phosphorus. They are very complicated condensation polymers (see Unit B2) formed from large numbers of simple monomers called **amino acids**.

B Changing materials

The diagram represents a simple amino acid, where R can be a hydrogen atom, or some other group. The simplest amino acid is **glycine**.

$$H-\underset{NH_2}{\overset{R}{C}}-COOH \quad \text{simple amino acid}$$

$$H-\underset{NH_2}{\overset{H}{C}}-COOH \quad \text{glycine, where R is a hydrogen atom}$$

A single protein can contain as many as 500 amino acid units combined together. When each link, called a **peptide link**, is formed an $-NH_2$ group and a $-COOH$ group react and a molecule of water is eliminated.

A protein can be represented as a coil, with each loop held in position by weak cross-links (Fig 2).

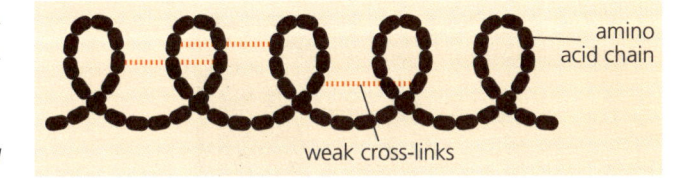

Fig 2 Part of a protein coil

Egg white contains a protein called ovalbumin. When it is heated the weak links which hold the protein in place break and the coiled chains unfold. This is what happens when egg white turns to a white solid. The change is called **coagulation**.

Many proteins are affected by acids and alkalis and also by beating them. When an egg white is beaten, it becomes foamy due to partial coagulation.

Food additives

Food additives are substances added to food that are not naturally present in the food. They include artificial colourings, preservatives, artificial sweeteners, solvents, emulsifiers etc. There are only a limited number of approved additives.

Q1 Look at a selection of food labels. What food additives have been added? Say why you think they have been added.

Q2 The use of food additives often causes controversy. Can you think of examples of food additives being harmful?

Manufacture of margarine

Margarine is widely used as an alternative to butter. Both butter and margarine are **water-in-oil emulsions**. This means that fine droplets of water are suspended in oil. Fig 3 shows what can be seen under a microscope.

Margarine is produced when fats and oils are hardened using hydrogen. Natural fats and oils are unsaturated (see Units 15 and 16). Hydrogen gas is bubbled through the liquid oil, in the presence of a nickel catalyst, at a temperature of 140°C. The hydrogen molecules add on to the fat and oil molecules to form a saturated product. Finally, vitamins and preservatives are added, and the margarine is coloured with an appropriate yellow dye.

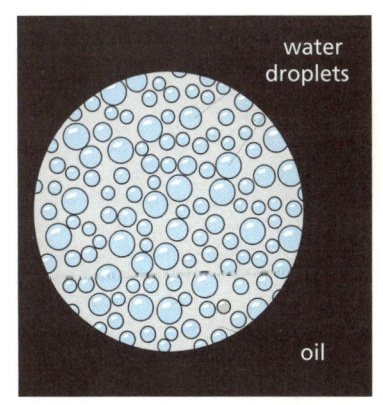

Fig 3 Margarine is a fine suspension of water droplets in oil, as seen under a microscope

51

B4 The carbon cycle

In this unit you will learn the answers to these questions:
- What is the carbon cycle and how does it maintain the balance of gases in the atmosphere?
- What is the greenhouse effect?
- What are the possible consequences of global warming?

Fig 1 shows sugar cane growing in a field. As the cane grows photosynthesis takes place. Carbon dioxide is taken in by the plant and oxygen is given out.

Fig 1 Sugar cane crop

Fig 2 shows a sugar refinery where sugar is extracted from harvested cane using hot water. The remains of the cane are burned. This burning uses up oxygen in the atmosphere and releases carbon dioxide back into the atmosphere.

Fig 2 Sugar cane at a sugar refinery. Smoke is a by-product

Q1 Burning the remains of sugar cane releases energy. Suggest **two** uses for the energy released.

Q2 Finish the word equation for photosynthesis and the word equation for combustion using words from this list:

    carbon dioxide   oxygen   water

_____ + _____ →(energy / chlorophyll) sugars + _____

sugars + _____ → _____ + _____

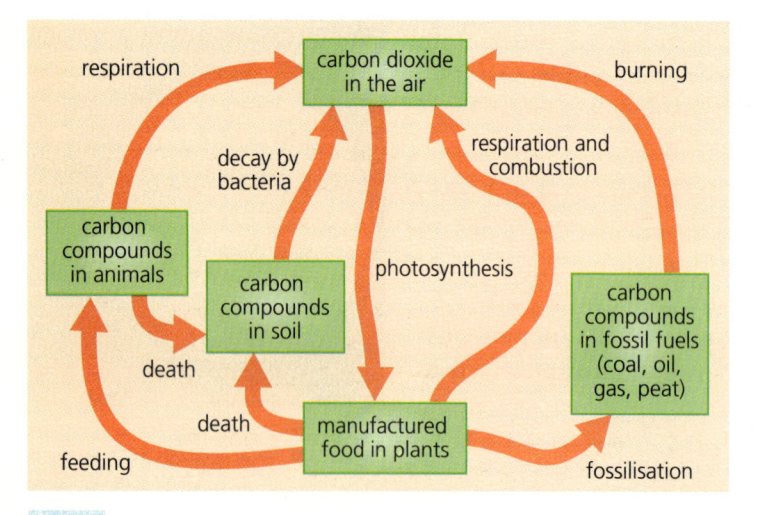

Photosynthesis and combustion are just two processes which help to maintain a balance between oxygen and carbon dioxide in the atmosphere. Fig 3 summarises processes which maintain this balance.

Fig 3 The carbon cycle

B Changing materials

The oceans have a vital role in maintaining the balance of carbon dioxide in the atmosphere. Green algae in the sea absorb vast amounts of carbon dioxide by photosynthesis. Also carbon dioxide is absorbed by the oceans in processes resulting in the formation of carbonates.

There is some evidence that concentrations of carbon dioxide in the atmosphere have increased in the past two hundred years. In 1880 there were 280 ppm (parts per million) of carbon dioxide in the atmosphere, and by 1990 this had risen to 350 ppm. It is predicted that by 2030 the level of carbon dioxide will have risen to 560 ppm.

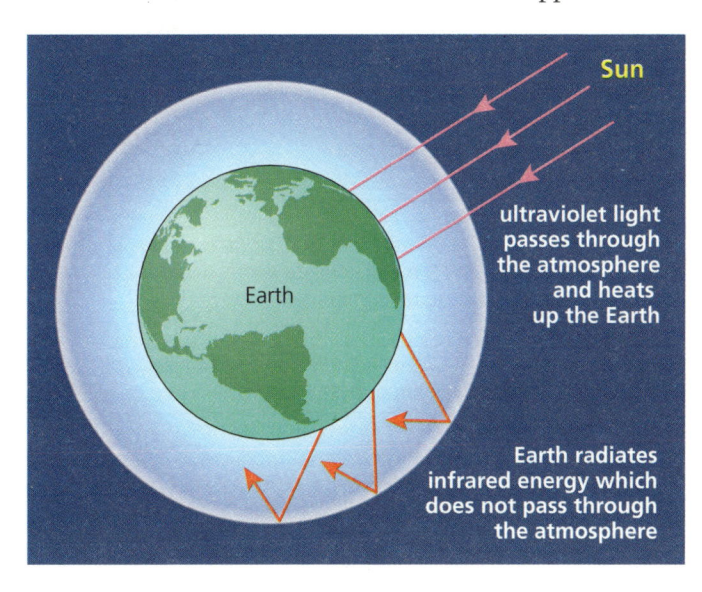

Q3 How can the pollution of the seas with toxic chemicals increase the concentrations of carbon dioxide in the atmosphere?

Q4 Suggest changes which have caused carbon dioxide concentrations in the air to rise.

Q5 Suggest action that could be taken to prevent further increases in the levels of carbon dioxide.

The increase in carbon dioxide concentrations in the atmosphere reduces the loss of energy reflected back into space. This is summarised in Fig 4. More energy is trapped than was normal in the past. This is called the **greenhouse effect** and the problem which follows is called **global warming**. It is estimated that the temperature of the Earth could rise by 4°C in the next fifty years.

Fig 4 *The greenhouse effect*

Possible consequences of global warming

No scientist is absolutely sure what changes might occur if concentrations of carbon dioxide increase and the temperature of the Earth's surface rises.

A temperature rise could melt more of the icecaps putting more water into the oceans. Also, rising temperatures would cause water to expand. The result could be flooding of low-lying land. Two-thirds of the cities with populations above 2.5 million people are on the coast.

There could be possible climatic changes with more extremes of weather – colder winters and hotter summers. Changed rainfall patterns could mean new deserts in Africa and dustbowls in Mid-Western states of America and the Soviet Union.

Q6 Can you suggest any other possible consequences of a rise in the temperature of the Earth?

19 Reactivity series

In this unit you will learn the answers to these questions:
- How do different metals react with air, water and dilute hydrochloric acid?
- How can metals be arranged in order of reactivity using reactions with air, water and dilute acid?
- What are displacement reactions and when will they take place?

Reactions of metals

There is a wide variety in the way metals react with air, water and dilute hydrochloric acid. The table compares the reactivity of some metals.

Metal	Reaction with air	Reaction with water	Reaction with dilute hydrochloric acid
potassium	burn in air or oxygen to form an oxide	reacts violently with cold water to produce hydrogen; hydrogen burns with a lilac flame	violent reaction to produce hydrogen (dangerous)
sodium		reacts quickly with cold water to produce hydrogen; hydrogen does not ignite	
calcium		reacts slowly with cold water to produce hydrogen	
magnesium		reacts very slowly with cold water; violent reaction with steam	react with acid to produce a metal chloride and hydrogen; react more slowly down list
zinc		fairly fast with steam	
iron		reacts only reversibly with steam	
lead	converted to the oxide by heating in air or oxygen but do not burn	no reaction with water	exceedingly slow reaction to produce hydrogen
copper			hydrogen not produced; no reaction with dilute hydrochloric acid
silver	not affected by oxygen or air		

In the table the metals have been arranged in order of reactivity. The most reactive metals are at the top of the list and the least reactive metals at the bottom. This order of metals is called the **reactivity series**. Other metals can be included in the series, as shown here. This reactivity series can be used to explain many reactions which take place.

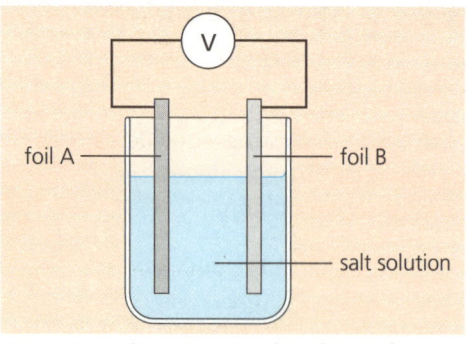

The same order of metals can be obtained by measuring the voltages of simple cells. Two pieces of metal rod or foil are dipped into a beaker containing salt solution (Fig 1). The voltage produced is measured on a voltmeter.

most reactive
potassium
sodium
calcium
magnesium
aluminium
zinc
iron
lead
copper
silver
gold
least reactive

Fig 1 Measuring the voltages of simple cells

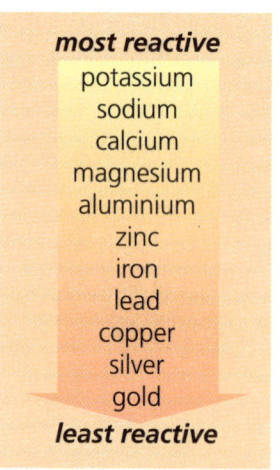

B Changing materials

The results of a series of experiments are shown in the table.

When the voltages are arranged in descending order, the metals are in the same order as the reactivity series.

Foil A	Foil B	Voltage measured /V
magnesium	copper	1.0
zinc	copper	0.6
iron	copper	0.3
lead	copper	0.02
copper	copper	0.0
silver	copper	−0.05

Displacement reactions of metals

A displacement reaction is a reaction where one metal replaces another during a chemical reaction. For example, if an iron nail is put into blue copper(II) sulphate solution, a displacement reaction takes place.

iron + copper(II) sulphate ➡ iron(II) sulphate + copper
$Fe (s) + CuSO_4 (aq)$ ➡ $FeSO_4 (aq) + Cu (s)$

The blue colour of copper(II) sulphate solution fades and a brown deposit of copper forms on the nail. The reaction takes place because iron is more reactive than copper. Iron is higher in the reactivity series than copper.

No reaction takes place when zinc is added to magnesium sulphate. Zinc is less reactive than magnesium (zinc is below magnesium in the reactivity series).

Q1 Write a word equation for the reaction which takes place when zinc is added to silver nitrate solution.

Displacement reactions can take place when a metal is added to an aqueous solution of a metal compound. They can also take place when a mixture of a powdered metal and a powdered metal oxide is heated.

One industrial application of a displacement reaction is the Thermit reaction used to weld lengths of railway track together (Fig 2). If a mixture of aluminium powder and iron(III) oxide is heated, a very violent reaction takes place. Aluminium, being more reactive than iron, replaces iron in iron(III) oxide.

Fig 2 A Thermit reaction used to weld rail tracks

aluminium + iron(III) oxide ➡ aluminium oxide + iron
$2Al (s) + Fe_2O_3 (s)$ ➡ $Al_2O_3 (s) + 2Fe (l)$

Q2 Suggest a metal which could be used instead of aluminium for this reaction.

20 Stability of compounds

In this unit you will learn the answers to these questions:
- How is the stability of metal compounds related to the position of the metal in the reactivity series?
- How does the method used for extracting metals from their ores depend on the position of the metal in the reactivity series?

In Unit 19 we arranged metals in order of reactivity according to reactions with air, water and dilute hydrochloric acid. We called the list of metals the reactivity series. We used the reactivity series to predict displacement reactions.

We can also use the reactivity series to predict the stability of compounds. That is, we can predict how easily compounds will be split up on heating.

The reactivity series and the stability of compounds

Consider the analogy of hitting nails into a piece of wood. In Fig 1 there are two identical nails.

Nail A is hit gently with a hammer but nail B is hit with a hard blow by the hammer. You will see that nail A does not go as far into the wood as nail B. When it comes to removing the nails, the reverse process to hammering them in, nail A is easier to pull out than nail B.

If we react magnesium with oxygen, a very exothermic reaction takes place and a large quantity of energy is lost to the surroundings. If copper is reacted with oxygen, copper oxide is formed but there is no significant energy loss to the surroundings.

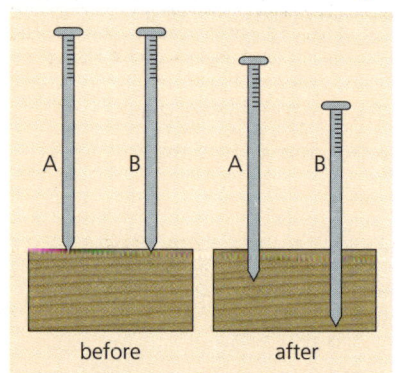

Fig 1 Hitting nails into a piece of wood. Nail B is hit harder than nail A and so goes further into the wood

When it comes to splitting up magnesium oxide and copper oxide, much more energy is required to produce magnesium and oxygen from magnesium oxide than to produce copper and oxygen from copper oxide.

Metals high in the reactivity series are most reactive. This means that when they react to form compounds, they produce the largest energy losses (Fig 2).

Compounds of metals high in the reactivity series are difficult to split up. The energy lost on compound formation must be returned if the compound is to be split up.

Q1 Which one of the following oxides decomposes on heating: sodium oxide, silver oxide, calcium oxide, iron(III) oxide?

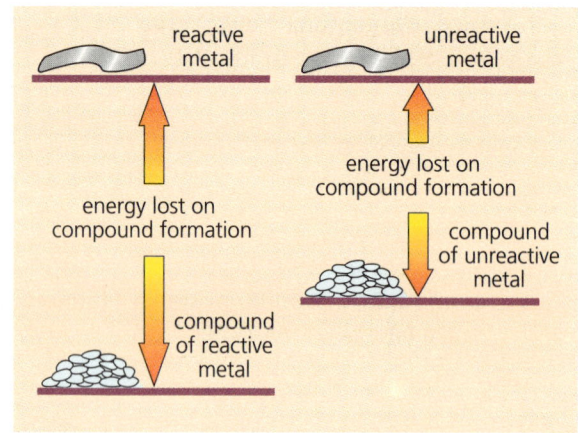

Fig 2 Metals higher in the reactivity series lose more energy when forming compounds

B Changing materials

Stability of metal carbonates

The table shows what is observed when metal carbonates are heated. The stability decreases as you move down the reactivity series.

Q2 Which gas is produced when all carbonates (except sodium and potassium) are heated?

Metal carbonate	Action of heat
potassium carbonate	not decomposed even at very high temperatures
sodium carbonate	
calcium carbonate	decomposed on heating into the oxide and carbon dioxide; ease of decomposition increases as you move down the list
magnesium carbonate	
zinc carbonate	
iron carbonate	
lead carbonate	
copper carbonate	
silver carbonate	unstable – does not exist at room temperature

Stability of metal nitrates

This table shows what is observed when metal nitrates are heated. Again the stability decreases as you move down the reactivity series. The same sort of pattern is seen if other metal compounds are considered.

Q3 Which gas is produced when *all* nitrates are decomposed by heating?

Q4 Why is potassium nitrate used in gunpowder?

The stability of compounds is important when considering the methods used to extract metals from their ores.

Metal nitrate	Action of heat
potassium nitrate	on heating, oxygen is lost at high temperatures; a nitrite remains; no nitrogen dioxide is produced
sodium nitrate	
calcium nitrate	decomposed on heating producing the oxide of the metal, nitrogen dioxide and oxygen gas
magnesium nitrate	
zinc nitrate	
iron nitrate	
lead nitrate	
copper nitrate	
silver nitrate	decomposed producing the metal, oxygen and nitrogen dioxide

Metal extracted	Method of extraction
potassium	electrolysis of fused chloride
sodium	
calcium	
magnesium	
aluminium	electrolysis of oxide dissolved in molten electrolyte
zinc	reduction with carbon or other reducing agent
iron	
lead	
copper	
silver	heating
mercury	

Extracting metals from their ores

The table summarises the methods used to extract metals from their ores.

The table shows that if there is a metal high in the reactivity series present in a compound which is difficult to split up, it can be extracted by electrolysis. This method requires a large amount of energy.

Metals in the middle of the reactivity series are extracted by reduction – usually with carbon.

Metals low in the reactivity series are present in compounds which are unstable. The metal can be extracted just by heating.

B5 Corrosion of metals – 1

In this unit you will learn the answers to these questions:
- What is corrosion?
- Why are reactive metals stored under oil?
- What causes iron and steel to rust?
- How can rusting be prevented?

Corrosion

Corrosion is the reaction of a metal with air or oxygen to form an oxide. Corrosion is an oxidation process.

In general, metals high in the reactivity series will corrode quickly and metals low in the reactivity series (see Unit 19) are most resistant to corrosion.

Potassium and sodium are very reactive metals at the top of the reactivity series. They are stored under oil.

Q1 Why are potassium and sodium stored under oil?

Rusting of iron and steel

The corrosion of iron and steel is commonly called **rusting**. It has been estimated that rusting costs the World at least £2 500 000 000 each year. Because rusting is such an economic problem, a great deal of money has been spent trying to reduce its effects.

The chemical composition of rust is complicated. It is probably best thought of as hydrated iron(III) oxide, $Fe_2O_3.xH_2O$. The process of rusting is best summarised by the ionic equation:

$$Fe \rightarrow Fe^{3+} + 3e^-$$

The experiment in Fig 1 shows what causes rusting. Four test tubes are set up containing identical iron nails. In test tube **1** the nail is in contact with air and water. In test tube **2**, air is present but no water, as anhydrous calcium chloride absorbs water. In test tube **3**, there is water but no air, as air is expelled by boiling. Finally, in test tube **4**, the oil excludes air and water.

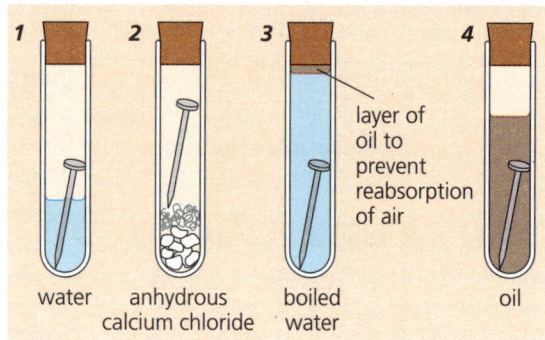

Fig 1 Testing for conditions of rusting

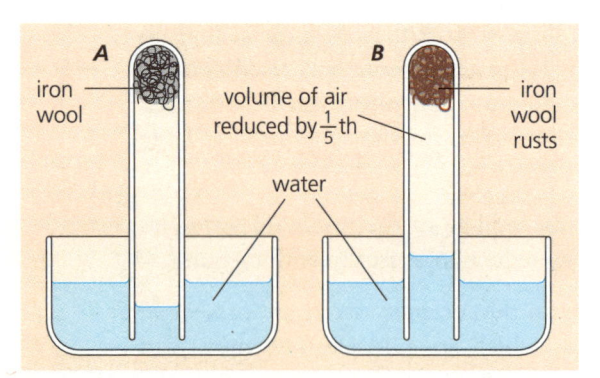

After one week there is rusting in test tube **1** but no rusting in the other three tubes. The conclusion from this is that air and water are necessary for rusting to take place.

The experiment in Fig 2 shows that it is the oxygen in the air which causes rusting. Only one-fifth of the air is used up in rusting.

Q2 Why is iron wool used in the experiment in Fig 2, not an iron nail?

Fig 2 Experiment to show that oxygen is used up during rusting

B Changing materials

Rusting is speeded up by dissolved carbon dioxide or salt. This explains why cars rust more quickly near the sea.

Ways of preventing rusting

Rusting can be prevented by excluding air and/or water. The following methods are used.

1 **Iron can be painted by spraying, dipping or brushing**. Provided the paint surface is not broken, rusting will not take place. The paint coating prevents oxygen and water coming into contact with the iron. When the paint coating is broken, rusting will take place. This type of protection is used to protect cars from rusting and for protecting large bridges (e.g. Forth Bridge in Scotland) and iron railings.

2 **Iron can be coated with oil or grease**. Again, air and water cannot come into contact with the iron and rusting does not take place. A smearing of oil on a saw blade will prevent it from rusting. It is a good method for treating moving parts.

3 **Iron can be coated with a layer of zinc**. This process is called **galvanising**. The zinc coating can be put on by dipping or spraying. If the zinc coating is deeply scratched to expose bare iron, rusting will not take place (see Unit B6) as the zinc corrodes in preference to the iron.

4 **Iron can be protected by sacrificial protection**. This is useful for protecting ships and piers where the steel is constantly in contact with sea water and air. If blocks of magnesium metal are attached to the steel, the magnesium will corrode away but the steel will remain intact. When the magnesium has completely corroded away, new blocks of magnesium can be attached.

An alternative way of protecting pier legs or a ship involves using steel anodes (Fig 4) by connecting them to a d.c. generator. The pier legs are made the cathode (negative) and a piece of steel is made the anode (positive). The pier will not rust away but the steel anodes will. They can easily be replaced.

Fig 3 *Magnesium blocks on the ship's sides prevent rusting of its hull*

5 **Rusting can be prevented by electroplating** (see Unit 22).

> **Q3** Car manufacturers have spent a great deal of money preventing rusting in cars. What is done to reduce the rusting of a car?

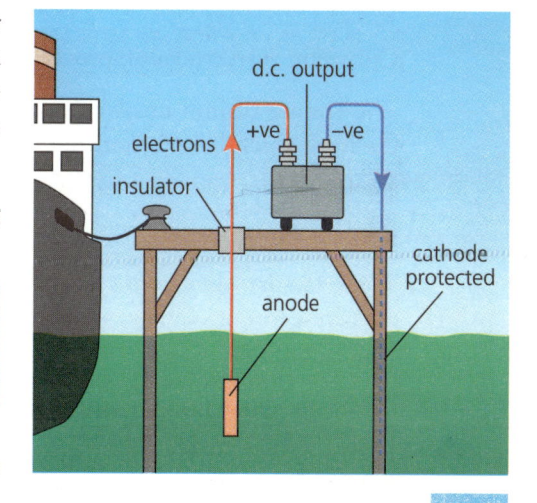

Fig 4 *Protecting pier legs from rusting*

B6 Corrosion of metals – 2

In this unit you will learn the answers to these questions:
- Why does aluminium resist corrosion?
- How can oxide coatings on aluminium be thickened by electrolysis?
- How can corrosion be explained in terms of electron transfer?
- Do unreactive metals corrode?

Corrosion of aluminium

Aluminium is above iron in the reactivity series (see Unit 19). It would be reasonable to expect aluminium to corrode more rapidly than iron. This is not the case.

On the surface of aluminium there is a thin coating of aluminium oxide which stops air and water coming into contact with the metal underneath. Because of its lack of corrosion, aluminium has a wide range of uses.

Q1 Give examples of the uses of aluminium.

If a piece of aluminium foil is dipped into mercury, the oxide coating is removed. If this foil is left at room temperature in contact with the air, the aluminium rapidly oxidises and forms aluminium oxide.

Anodising

Anodising is a process for finishing aluminium and aluminium products. Anodising involves thickening the oxide layer by electrolysis and dyeing it.

Fig 1 shows how a piece of aluminium can be anodised. The object to be anodised is made the anode and aluminium is used as the cathode. Oxygen is produced at the anode and this thickens the oxide layer. If a dye is put into the acid, the dye will colour the oxide layer.

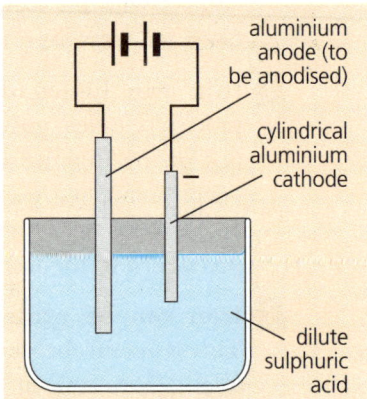

Fig 1 Apparatus used to anodise aluminium

Q2 Write ionic equations for the reactions at the anode and cathode during anodising.

Corrosion in terms of electron transfer

Corrosion is an oxidation process which can be explained in terms of electron transfer.

The rusting of iron involves various stages. There are two factors about the surface of the iron which help to start the process.

1. Impurities and mechanical strains cause imperfections in the iron.
2. Differences in amounts of dissolved oxygen in contact with the surface.

These factors cause some areas of the iron to become **anodic**. Here there is a lower oxygen content. Other areas become **cathodic** where there is a higher oxygen concentration.

In the anodic area, iron atoms are oxidised by losing electrons to the cathodic areas. Iron(II) irons are formed and go into solution:

$$Fe(s) \rightarrow Fe^{2+}(aq) + 2e^-$$

These ions are further oxidised by dissolved oxygen to form iron(III) ions.

$$Fe^{2+}(aq) \rightarrow Fe^{3+}(aq) + e^-$$

In the cathodic areas, oxygen takes up the electrons coming from the anodic areas. The oxygen is reduced in the presence of water to form hydroxide ions.

$$\tfrac{1}{2}O_2(aq) + H_2O(l) + 2e^- \rightarrow 2OH^-(aq)$$

The iron(III) ions combine with the hydroxide ions to form iron(III) hydroxide which then loses some of its water to the atmosphere.

$$2Fe(OH)_3(s) \rightarrow Fe_2O_3 \cdot xH_2O(s) + (3-x)H_2O(l) \qquad \text{where } x = 1 \text{ or } 2$$

This mechanism shows that both oxygen and water are needed for rusting.

Ferroxyl indicator is useful when studying rusting. The indicator consists of a mixture of phenolphthalein solution and potassium hexacyanoferrate(III) solution. Hydroxyl ions produced during rusting turn phenolphthalein pink. Iron(II) ions, also formed, turn hexacyanoferrate(III) blue. The blue colour shows where the iron is unprotected and pink where it is protected.

Galvanising

A piece of galvanised iron has a coating of zinc. If the zinc layer is broken, the two metals come into contact. In the presence of an electrolyte such as rain water, a simple cell is set up.

Zinc is the negative pole and iron is the positive pole. The likely reactions at the zinc and iron are:

negative $Zn(s) \rightarrow Zn^{2+}(aq) + 2e^-$
positive $2H^+(aq) + 2e^- \rightarrow H_2(g)$

Electrons are transferred from the zinc to the iron. These are taken up by the hydrogen ions. The zinc is oxidised in preference to the iron. The iron surface becomes coated with a protective layer of basic zinc(II) carbonate.

Tin-plating

Iron can also be protected by tin. If a tin can is scratched exposing the two surfaces to an electrolyte solution, the iron becomes the negative pole and the tin becomes the positive pole. The iron therefore rusts more quickly than it would otherwise do.

negative $Fe(s) \rightarrow Fe^{2+}(aq) + 2e^-$
positive $2H^+(aq) + 2e^- \rightarrow H_2(g)$

Corrosion of copper

Copper is low in the reactivity series. It is very slow to corrode. In fact, copper is often used for decorative purposes because it forms a decorative coating of basic copper(II) carbonate. Fig 2 shows the roofscape of part of the city of Salzburg, Austria.

Fig 2 *Copper is often used for a decorative effect*

21 Extraction of metals – 1

In this unit you will learn the answers to these questions:
- How do metals exist in the earth?
- How can sodium and aluminium be extracted from their ores?

In Unit 20 it was shown that the method of extraction of a metal depends on the position of the metal in the reactivity series. Metals at the top of the reactivity series form stable compounds and require electrolysis to extract them. Metals in the middle of the reactivity series are extracted by reduction, often with carbon. Metals at the bottom of the reactivity series are usually extracted by heating alone.

Metal	Common ore	Chief chemical constituent of ore	Formula of chief constituent
sodium	rock salt	sodium chloride	NaCl
mercury	cinnabar	mercury sulphide	HgS
copper	copper pyrites	copper sulphide and iron sulphide	$CuFeS_2$
aluminium	bauxite	aluminium oxide	Al_2O_3
zinc	zinc blende	zinc sulphide	ZnS
iron	haematite	iron(III) oxide	Fe_2O_3
calcium	limestone	calcium carbonate	$CaCO_3$
lead	galena	lead sulphide	PbS
potassium	carnallite	potassium magnesium chloride	$KMgCl_3.6H_2O$
magnesium	carnallite	potassium magnesium chloride	$KMgCl_3.6H_2O$
	dolomite	magnesium calcium carbonate	$MgCO_3.CaCO_3$

Metal ores

Few metals are found uncombined in the Earth. Most metals are usually present in the Earth as **ores**. An ore is a rock containing a mixture of substances including a compound of the metal that is to be extracted. The aluminium ore bauxite, for example, consists of about 40% aluminium oxide (a compound of aluminium and oxygen) with iron oxide, sand and titanium dioxide.

The table gives the names and chemical constituents of common ores.

Q1 Is there any link between the position of a metal in the reactivity series and the type of compound present in the ore – chloride, carbonate, sulphide?

Q2 It has been estimated that one cubic mile of sea water contains £100 000 000 worth of gold. Why can't gold be extracted economically from sea water?

Extraction of sodium

Sodium is extracted from molten sodium chloride by electrolysis in the Downs cell (Fig 1). Calcium chloride is added to the sodium chloride to lower the melting point of the electrolyte from about 800°C to 600°C. At the cathode (negative electrode), sodium is formed and, because of its low density, it floats upward and is collected in an 'upside down' trough. It can be tapped off from here. A little calcium is also produced at

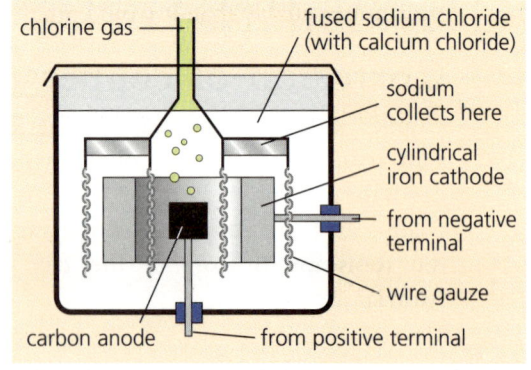

Fig 1 Extraction of sodium

B Changing materials

the cathode but this crystallises and can be removed. Chlorine is produced at the anode (positive electrode) and then escapes through the hood. The chlorine produced is a useful by-product.

Q3 What is the economic advantage of adding calcium chloride to the sodium chloride in the cell?

Q4 Why is it important to keep the sodium and chlorine apart?

The cell reactions are :

cathode sodium ions + electrons ➡ sodium atoms
Na^+ + e^- ➡ Na

anode chloride ions ➡ chlorine molecules + electrons
$2Cl^-$ ➡ Cl_2 + $2e^-$

Extraction of aluminium

Although aluminium is present in small quantities in almost every handful of soil, it is extracted from bauxite.

Q5 Why is it not economic to use soil which would not have to be transported?

Bauxite is found mainly in tropical and subtropical parts of the world – Australia, Guinea, Jamaica, Indonesia, India and Brazil.

Fig 2 Open cast mining of bauxite in Australia

Q6 How is the bauxite obtained from the ground?

Removing the ore in this way leaves ugly scars on the landscape (Fig 2).

Purification of the bauxite takes place at the mining site. During the purification, the ore is treated with strong alkali. The main impurity is red iron oxide which forms a red mud which is pumped into huge ponds and left. These also spoil the landscape.

Q7 What are the advantages of purifying the bauxite and producing pure aluminium oxide at the mining site?

The extraction of aluminium is carried out by electrolysis of molten aluminium oxide dissolved in molten cryolite (sodium aluminium fluoride). Electrolysis takes place in carbon-lined steel tanks called pots. The carbon lining acts as a cathode and carbon anodes are used (Fig 3).

The products of electrolysis are aluminium (produced at the cathode) and oxygen (produced at the anode).

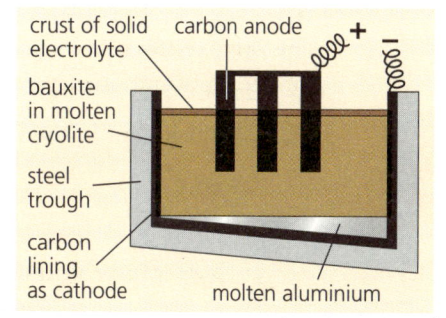

Fig 3 Extraction of aluminium

cathode aluminium ions + electrons ➡ aluminium atoms
Al^{3+} + $3e^-$ ➡ Al

anode oxide ions ➡ oxygen molecules + electrons
$2O^{2-}$ ➡ O_2 + $4e^-$

The aluminium collects at the bottom of the pot and can be removed. The carbon anodes burn in the oxygen produced and have to be replaced from time to time. The exhaust gases from the pots are bubbled through water to remove soluble gases.

22 Extraction of metals – 2

In this unit you will learn the answers to these questions:
- How is iron extracted from iron ore?
- How is steel produced from iron?
- How is copper purified by electrolysis?
- What affects the price of a metal?

Extraction of iron

Ores containing large amounts of iron (called 'rich' ores) include haematite and magnetite (both oxides of iron). These are often mixed with 'poorer' ores for extraction.

Iron is produced in a blast furnace (Fig 1). A furnace is about 70 metres high, made of steel and lined with fireproof bricks. The raw materials are iron ore, coke (carbon) and limestone. They are loaded from time to time through the top of the furnace.

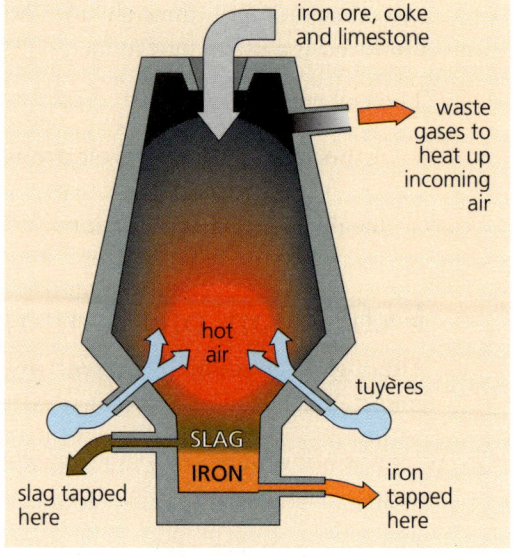

Fig 1 Extraction of iron in a blast furnace

Hot air is blown into the base of the furnace through a series of pipes called **tuyères**. Burning the coke produces sufficient heat to raise the temperature inside the furnace to 1900°C, sufficient to melt the contents of the furnace. Carbon monoxide is produced in the furnace. This acts as the reducing agent which reduces the iron oxide to iron.

The limestone (calcium carbonate) added to the furnace removes the impurities, especially the sand, forming slag – calcium silicate.

The hot waste gases escaping from the blast furnace contain carbon monoxide.

Q1 What are the three solid materials added to the blast furnace?

Q2 What is the reducing agent in the furnace?

Q3 What can the waste gases be used for?

Q4 What are the two liquids tapped off the furnace?

The main reactions in the blast furnace are:

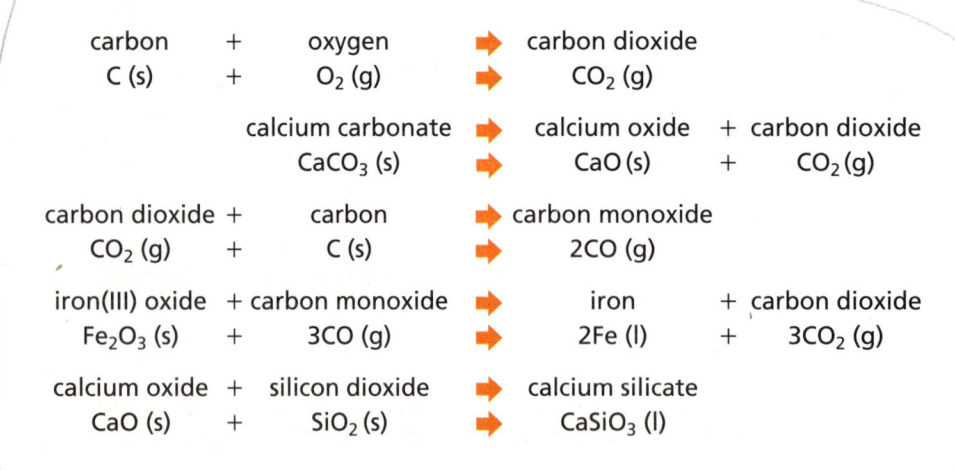

carbon + oxygen ➡ carbon dioxide
$C (s)$ + $O_2 (g)$ ➡ $CO_2 (g)$

calcium carbonate ➡ calcium oxide + carbon dioxide
$CaCO_3 (s)$ ➡ $CaO (s)$ + $CO_2 (g)$

carbon dioxide + carbon ➡ carbon monoxide
$CO_2 (g)$ + $C (s)$ ➡ $2CO (g)$

iron(III) oxide + carbon monoxide ➡ iron + carbon dioxide
$Fe_2O_3 (s)$ + $3CO (g)$ ➡ $2Fe (l)$ + $3CO_2 (g)$

calcium oxide + silicon dioxide ➡ calcium silicate
$CaO (s)$ + $SiO_2 (s)$ ➡ $CaSiO_3 (l)$

B Changing materials

> **Q5** Give two reasons why limestone is added to the blast furnace.

The iron obtained is impure, containing carbon, phosphorus and silicon. Most of the iron produced is immediately turned into steel. The steel-making furnace (Fig 2) is tilted and loaded with 30% scrap iron and 70% molten iron from the blast furnace. A water-cooled lance is lowered into the upright furnace and pure oxygen is blown, under high pressure, onto the surface of the molten iron. The oxides of carbon and phosphorus escape as gases. Limestone is added to remove other impurities as slag. Finally, any additional substances are added for the grade of steel being produced.

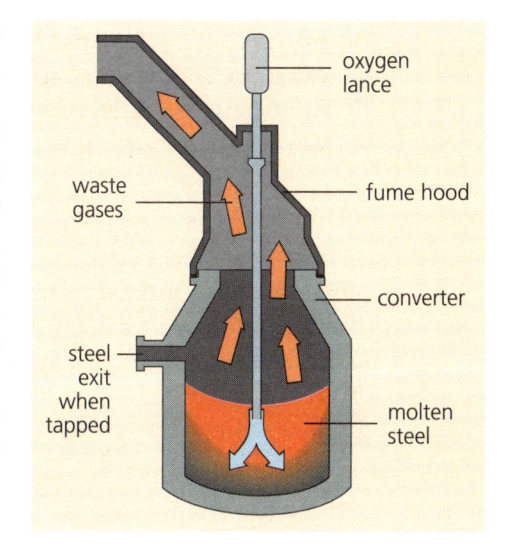

Fig 2 Steel-making furnace

Purification of copper by electrolysis

Copper is extracted by reduction but for many purposes, e.g. electrical wiring, is required in a high state of purity. Copper is purified by electrolysis (Fig 3) with the anode made of an impure copper plate and the cathode a pure copper plate. The electrolyte is copper(II) sulphate solution.

During the electrolysis the anode dissolves and pure copper is deposited on the cathode.

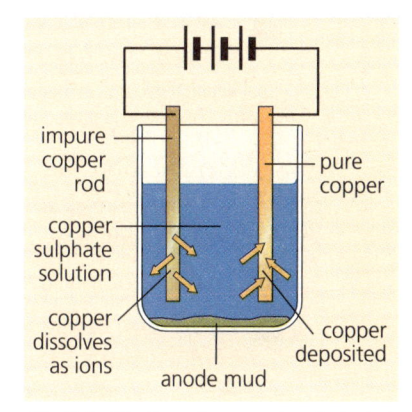

Anode copper atoms → copper ions + electrons
$$Cu \rightarrow Cu^{2+} + 2e^-$$

Cathode copper ions + electrons → copper atoms
$$Cu^{2+} + 2e^- \rightarrow Cu$$

Fig 3 Purification of copper by electrolysis

The impurities that were in the impure plate collect at the bottom of the cell as 'anode mud'. This can be refined to produce precious metals such as silver, gold and platinum.

Factors affecting the price of a metal

The price of a metal depends upon a number of factors. These include:

1. the amount of the metal available in ores in the Earth;
2. where the ores are;
3. the ease of extraction;
4. the quantity of metal re-cycled;
5. the demand for the metal by industry.

Fig 4 Steel production: a worker taking the slag from a blast furnace

23 Types of rock

In this unit you will learn the answers to these questions:
- What are sedimentary, igneous and metamorphic rocks?
- How are these different rock types formed?
- What tests do geologists use to identify minerals in rocks?

What is a rock?

A rock is a solid part of the Earth's crust. Although some rocks are almost pure substances, most rocks are usually made up of a mixture of chemicals called **minerals**. The properties of a rock will depend upon:

1 the type of minerals; **2** the concentration of the minerals in the rock;

3 how the minerals are held together.

Identifying the minerals in rocks

A **geologist** identifies the particular minerals in a rock by carrying out a series of tests. These include:

1 Colour There can be considerable variations in the colours of minerals. Many minerals can have a variety of colours, so using colour as the only way of identifying a mineral can lead to wrong conclusions.

2 Streak test The colour of the mineral in a powdered form is helpful in identification. The simplest way of doing this is a streak test where the mineral is scratched across an unglazed ceramic tile called a **streak plate**. Different materials produce different colours.

3 Lustre Look at the mineral – is it shiny, glassy, dull, etc.?

4 Hardness Hardness is measured on Moh's scale. This is a scale of hardness from 1 to 10 using certain standard materials. If a mineral can be scratched with a fingernail it has a hardness of about 2. A 2p coin has a hardness of about 3.5 and a steel penknife about 6. These tests give a geologist a guide to the hardness of a mineral.

5 Density The density can give a guide to identifying the minerals present. For example, galena (lead sulphide) has a very high density.

6 Testing with acid When dilute acid is added to a carbonate mineral such as calcite (a form of calcium carbonate), fizzing will be seen as carbon dioxide is produced.

7 Crystal shape This can also be useful in identifying minerals present in a rock (see Unit 4).

Moh's scale	Mineral
1	talc
2	gypsum
3	calcite
4	fluorite
5	apatite
6	feldspar
7	quartz
8	topaz
9	corundum
10	diamond

Rocks can be divided into three groups according to the way they are formed. These three groups are **sedimentary rocks**, **igneous rocks** and **metamorphic rocks**.

Sedimentary rocks

A sedimentary rock is formed when a layer of mud, sand or other natural debris is compressed. This process is called **consolidation**. The sedimentary rocks are laid

B Changing materials

down in layers, called **beds**, and the joins between layers are called **bedding planes** (Fig 1). New rocks are deposited on existing rocks and so the older the rocks are, the lower they are in the Earth's crust. After being deposited, these layers can tilt and twist. Examples of sedimentary rocks are shown in Fig 2.

Fig 1 A cliff of sedimentary rocks, showing the layered structure

Fig 2 Examples of sedimentary rocks

limestone   sandstone   conglomerate

Igneous rocks

Igneous rocks are hard rocks formed when the molten magma inside the Earth's crust crystallises. These rocks are composed of crystals of different minerals. The crystals are not packed together in any pattern. The sizes of the crystals are determined by the rate of cooling of the magma. If the crystallisation is slow, large crystals are formed, while rapid cooling produces small crystals. There are two types of igneous rock – **intrusive** and **extrusive**. Intrusive rocks solidify within the Earth's crust and are found at the Earth's surface only when overlying rocks are worn away. Because they are formed on slow cooling, they usually contain larger crystals. Granite is an example of an intrusive igneous rock. Extrusive rocks solidify on the surface of the Earth when liquid magma reaches the Earth's surface. Basalt is an example of an extrusive rock. Some igneous rocks contain tiny bubbles formed because molten magma contains gases. Examples of igneous rocks are shown in Fig 3.

granite

basalt

Fig 3 Examples of igneous rocks

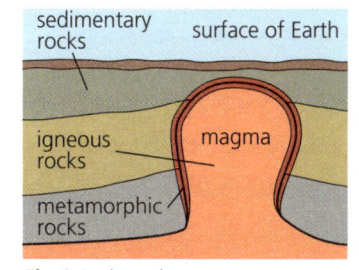

Fig 4 An intrusion

Magma from deep inside the Earth can push its way close to the surface. These 'upwellings' of magma are called **intrusions** (Fig 4). They cool to form igneous rocks.

Q1 Why are the crystals of extrusive rocks generally smaller than the crystals of intrusive rocks?

Metamorphic rocks

Metamorphic rocks are also hard rocks formed when high temperatures and high pressures act on other rocks. For example, the action of high temperatures and high pressures on the sedimentary rock limestone produces marble. Around a magma intrusion, the high temperatures and high pressures cause rocks to change to metamorphic rocks.

Fossils, the remains of plants and animals from millions of years ago, are commonly found in sedimentary rocks and less commonly in metamorphic rocks. An example of a metamorphic rock is shown in Fig 5.

marble

Fig 5 Example of a metamorphic rock

Q2 Why are fossils not found in igneous rocks?

24 Uses of rocks

In this unit you will learn the answers to these questions:
- What are natural rocks used for?
- What factory-made materials can be used as substitutes for rocks?

Stone for buildings

Fig 1 shows the two houses we used in Unit 1.

The old cottage is made of limestone blocks and has a roof made of slate. Limestone is a sedimentary rock and slate is a metamorphic rock produced by the action of high temperatures and high pressures on mud. These traditional materials have properties which make them suitable for use in house-building.

Fig 1 An old stone cottage and a modern brick house

> **Q1** Write down the properties of
> a) limestone
> b) slate
> which make them suitable for house-building.

Fig 2 A slate mine in North Wales showing the slates in sheets

However, with the growth in the number of houses built in this century, these materials have become expensive and alternatives have been developed. The walls of a modern house are often made of bricks and the roof made of ceramic tiles. Both of these are made from clay and the clay is baked in an oven. The formation of bricks and tiles resembles the formation of metamorphic rock. The change taking place is permanent and the resulting products are hard and brittle.

> **Q2** In areas of natural beauty, there are often restrictions on the types of building materials which can be used. Fig 3 shows a village in the Peak District in Derbyshire. What sort of building materials would you recommend and what sort of building materials would you not recommend?

Fig 3 A village in the Peak District

B Changing materials

Using stone for statues

Igneous and metamorphic rocks are frequently used for statues. They are generally harder than sedimentary rocks.

Action of acid rain on rocks

Rainwater has a pH of about 5.5, but often the pH is much lower due to dissolved chemicals such as sulphur dioxide and oxides of nitrogen. Fig 4 shows a limestone carving on a cathedral. The detail of the carving has been eaten away by the acid rain.

Fig 4 *A limestone carving badly eroded by acid rain*

Cement and concrete

Cement is a very useful material produced by heating limestone powder with clay. When water is added to cement, a chemical reaction takes place which causes the cement to harden.

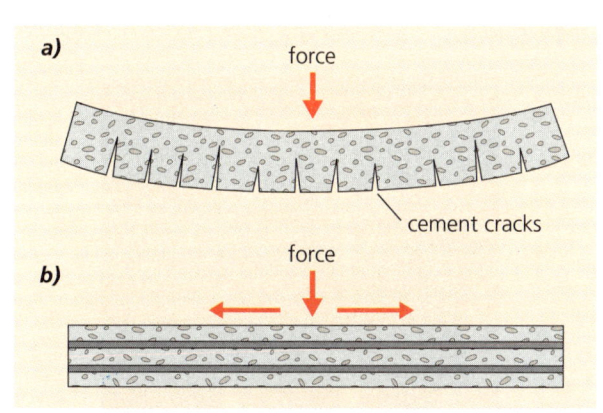

Fig 5 **a)** *The vertical force causes the concrete to break*
b) *The reinforcing steel rods transfer the force sideways*

Usually cement is mixed with water, sand and gravel to produce concrete. Concrete is a very useful building material. It is poured into moulds to produce concrete railway sleepers, beams, lamp-posts, etc. However, concrete is not a strong material unless it is reinforced. In Fig 5 it can be seen that a vertical force will cause the beam to bend and break. Reinforcing the concrete with steel rods transfers the forces sideways and makes the beam stronger.

Fig 6 shows the reconstructed Library of Celsus in Ephesus, Turkey. In the reconstruction, missing parts of the structure were made using reinforced concrete mixed with chippings of marble. This gives it an appearance similar to the original marble.

Fig 6 *The Library of Celsus in Ephesus, Turkey*

25 The rock cycle

In this unit you will learn the answers to these questions:
- What is weathering or erosion of rocks?
- What is the rock cycle?

Breaking down of rocks

The rocks in the Earth's crust are constantly being broken down by **weathering** or **erosion**. These processes are caused by the action of wind and rain, water and ice.

Water attacks certain minerals as it passes through rocks. In granite areas, minerals called feldspars in granite are attacked and turned into soft clay minerals. This causes the granite to crumble and the other minerals present – quartz and mica – then fall loose and are carried away as sand.

Rainwater is naturally acidic due to dissolved carbon dioxide. It can be called carbonic acid and has a pH of about 5.5. Rainwater attacks limestone, which is almost entirely made up of the mineral calcite. Calcite reacts with dilute acids.

$$CaCO_3\ (s)\ +\ H_2O\ (l)\ +\ CO_2\ (g)\ \rightleftharpoons\ Ca(HCO_3)_2\ (aq)$$
limestone · calcium hydrogencarbonate

The action of rainwater on limestone produces large underground caverns (Fig 1). The stalactites and stalagmites are formed when the calcium hydrogencarbonate decomposes and re-forms calcite.

> **Q1** Stalactites and stalagmites are made of solid calcium carbonate in the form of calcite. In Fig 1, which ones are stalactites and which ones are stalagmites?
>
> **Q2** How is the calcium carbonate formed in stalactites and stalagmites?
>
> **Q3** Some stalactites and stalagmites are stained brown. What causes the brown stain?

Fig 1 A limestone cavern

Rocks can be broken down by repeated freezing and thawing (Fig 2). When water freezes it expands considerably, forcing rocks apart. This process occurs over and over again, eventually breaking down the rock.

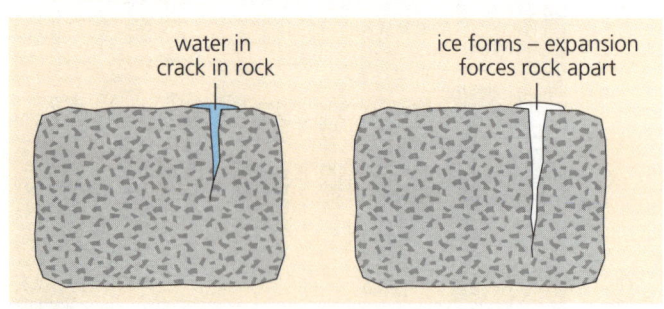

water in crack in rock

ice forms – expansion forces rock apart

Fig 2 Repeated freezing and thawing breaks down rocks

Rocks break down even in the absence of water. Rocks in a dry desert area can be broken down by the wind. The wind picks up sand particles and hurls them at exposed rocks. This natural 'sandblasting' produces more sand, which

B Changing materials

continues the process. The erosion of the Sphinx in Egypt by sand is a good example of this type of weathering (Fig 3).

The rock fragments produced by these forms of weathering often get washed into rivers. As the fragments get carried along in rivers they become more rounded, losing sharp edges. As the speed of the river slows, the fragments drop and are deposited on the river bed. Heavy fragments drop first and fine fragments are carried further.

Conglomerate is a rock containing large fragments (see Unit 23). This will be deposited close to where the river enters the sea (Fig 4). Shale is made of very fine particles and is formed away from the entry of the river into the sea.

Fig 3 *The Sphinx, Egypt, eroded by 'sandblasting'*

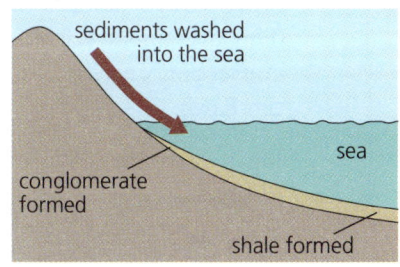

Fig 4 *Formation of conglomerate and shale*

The rock cycle

Rocks are being constantly broken down and new rocks are being formed. Molten rocks in the magma are crystallised to form igneous rocks. Weathering and erosion of rocks produces sediments which are deposited to produce sedimentary rocks. Metamorphic rocks can be produced from sedimentary rocks. Rocks returning to the magma complete the cycle. The rock cycle is summarised in Fig 5.

The rock cycle is driven by two energy processes. On the surface, processes are powered by the Sun's energy. Within the Earth, energy is provided by radioactive decay.

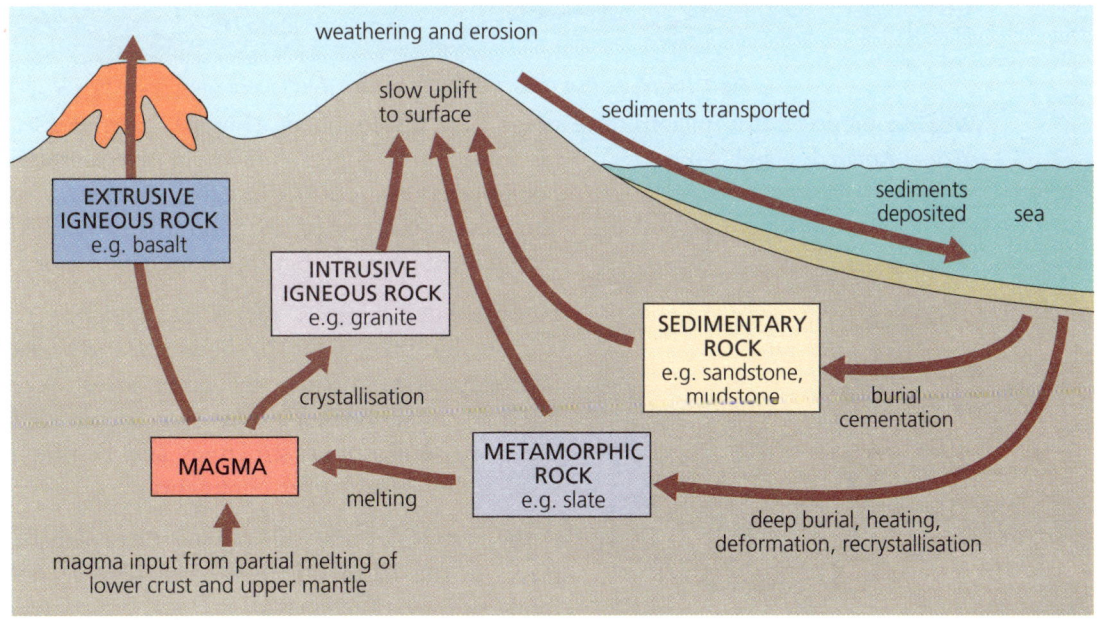

Fig 5 *The rock cycle*

26 Plate tectonics

In this unit you will learn the answers to these questions:
- What is the theory of plate tectonics?
- What are constructive and destructive plate margins?
- How are rocks recycled?

Until the beginning of the twentieth century it was believed that the Earth's crust had remained unchanged over millions of years. In 1912, a German scientist, Alfred Wegener, proposed his theory of plate tectonics. This theory proposed that the Earth's crust had cracked into huge sections called **plates**. These plates were then able to move slowly (about 1–2 cm each year) floating on the liquid mantle below the crust. This movement was due to convection currents. The energy required to set up these convection currents comes from the energy given out by radioactive decay within the Earth.

Fig 1 shows the plates which cover the surface of the Earth.

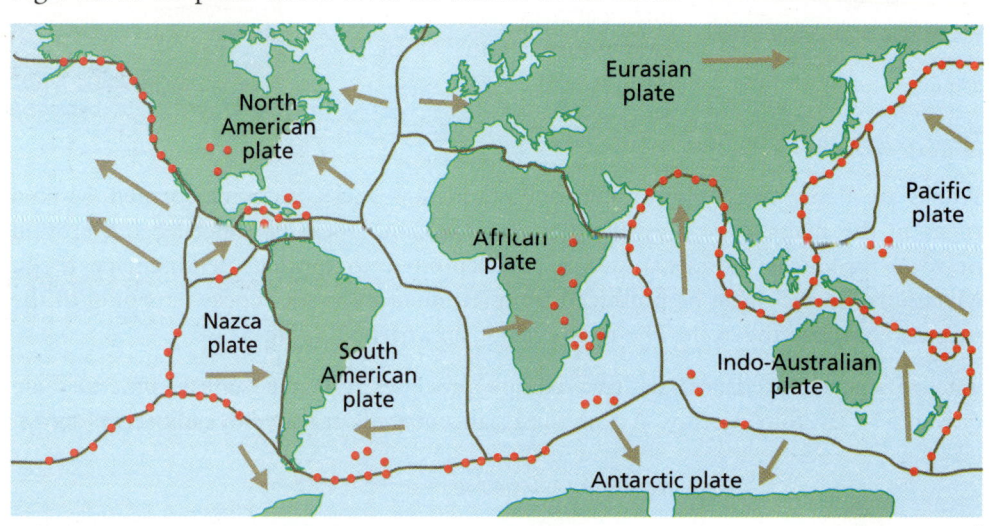

Fig 1 The plates that cover the Earth's surface (earthquake sites shown by ● ● ● ●)

Wegener proposed that millions of years ago all of the continents (Europe, America, Asia, Africa, Antarctica and Australasia) were joined in a supercontinent in the southern hemisphere. He called this the **Pangaea**. The continents then moved apart until they reached their present positions, but they continue to move.

He presented various pieces of evidence to support his theory. Fig 2 shows the way that South America, Africa and other areas once fitted together. Investigations have shown that there are similar rock structures and common fossils found between the continents.

If the vast plates are still moving there will be places in the Earth where we will observe the results of these movements.

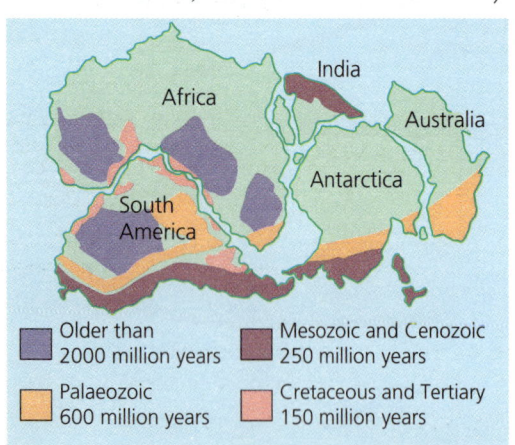

Fig 2 The continents fitting together. Note the continuity of rocks across continents

- Older than 2000 million years
- Palaeozoic 600 million years
- Mesozoic and Cenozoic 250 million years
- Cretaceous and Tertiary 150 million years

B Changing materials

Earthquakes

If you look back to Fig 1 you will notice that most earthquake sites exist on or near to the boundaries of plates. When plates slide past each other, stresses and strains build up in the Earth's crust. If these stresses and strains are released suddenly the effect is called an earthquake. The ground breaks as the Earth moves. These breaks in the ground are called **faults**. One famous fault is the San Andreas Fault in California.

> **Q1** How is the strength of an earthquake measured?
>
> **Q2** Engineers sometimes try to prevent an earthquake by pumping large amounts of water into the Earth. Why do they do this?

Constructive plate margins

When two plates are moving apart, hot molten rock from the magma comes to the surface of the earth and forms new rocks. This is called a **constructive plate margin**. An important example of this is the submerged ocean ridge along the boundary of plates down the centre of the Atlantic Ocean. Fig 3 shows this constructive plate margin and the changes in magnetic field which accompany it.

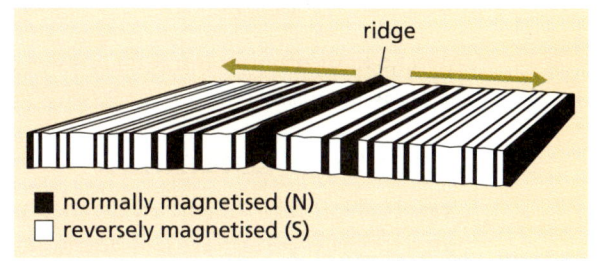

Fig 3 *A constructive plate margin*

The magnetic field of the Earth is constantly changing. In the past 3.6 million years it has changed at least nine times. Magnetic detectors dragged through the sea behind ships have shown alternating bands of normal and reversed magnetism in the ocean floor. The pattern of magnetism is the same on both sides of the plate margin. When molten rock escapes from the magma and solidifies as rock, the internal magnetism of the rock lines up with the Earth's magnetic field and is fixed.

Destructive plate margins

When two plates collide the rocks are squeezed together. The Andes mountains in South America were formed by the collision of the Nazca plate and the South American plate.

> **Q3** These plates are still moving together. Why do the Andes Mountains not get higher each year?

Fig 4 shows two plates moving together. One plate is a continental crust plate with an average density of 2.7 g per cm³, the other plate is a thinner ocean floor plate which has a density of about 3.3 g per cm³. The ocean floor plate is forced under the continental plate and melts back into the magma.

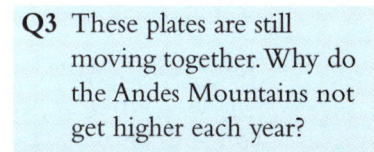

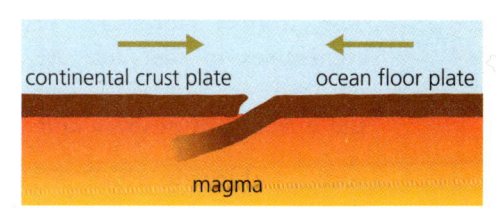

Fig 4 *A destructive plate margin*

Recycling of rocks

The theory of plate tectonics explains the recycling of rocks. New igneous rocks are produced at plate boundaries. These igneous rocks are then weathered to produce sediments which, in turn, produce sedimentary rocks. Rocks return to the magma at destructive plate boundaries.

27 Chemical equations

In this unit you will learn the answers to these questions:
- How do you write chemical formulae?
- What are chemical equations and how do you write them?
- What are ionic equations?

In a chemical reaction new substances are formed. The substances that react are called **reactants** and the new substances made are called **products**.

A chemical reaction can be represented by a **chemical equation** which summarises, in words or symbols, the change taking place. Substances which remain unchanged during the reaction are not shown in the equation. For example, the burning of magnesium in oxygen has the equation:

magnesium + oxygen ➡ magnesium oxide
2Mg + O_2 ➡ 2MgO
reactants   *product*

In a chemical reaction the reactants are on the left-hand side and the products are on the right-hand side.

Chemical formulae

Correct chemical formulae are needed in order to write correct symbol equations. Chemical formulae can be obtained by carrying out experiments (Unit 29). They are determined by finding the masses of the different elements which combine in the compound. Magnesium oxide is written as MgO rather than MgO_2 or Mg_2O because one atom of magnesium combines with one atom of oxygen.

> **Q1** Write the correct chemical formulae of iron oxides using the information given. The symbols of iron and oxygen are Fe and O.
> a) 1 atom of iron combines with 1 atom of oxygen.
> b) 2 atoms of iron combine with 3 atoms of oxygen.
> c) 3 atoms of iron combine with 4 atoms of oxygen.

You can write correct chemical formulae using the ions with the correct charges.

The correct formulae of compounds in the table are obtained by ensuring that **the number of positive and negative charges are the same**.

	Cl^-	O^{2-}	OH^-	NO_3^-	SO_4^{2-}	CO_3^{2-}
Na^+	NaCl					Na_2CO_3
Mg^{2+}						
Al^{3+}		Al_2O_3				

> **Q2** Now copy out the table and complete it.

sodium chloride Na^+ Cl^-
   number of positive charges = number of negative charges
so write **NaCl** (ignoring charges).

sodium carbonate Na^+ CO_3^{2-}
   number of positive charges = half the number of negative charges
To get equal numbers of positive and negative charges you need to have two Na^+, so write Na_2CO_3.

aluminium oxide Al^{3+} O^{2-}

To get equal numbers of positive and negative charges you need two Al^{3+} and three O^{2-}, so write Al_2O_3.

Diatomic gases

Common gases such as oxygen, nitrogen and chlorine are composed of molecules each containing two atoms. These are called diatomic gases. In equations, therefore, we write O_2, H_2, N_2 and Cl_2.

Writing symbol equations

1 Calcium carbonate decomposes on heating to produce calcium oxide and carbon dioxide. We can write a word equation.

calcium carbonate ➡ calcium oxide + carbon dioxide

Then we can write the symbol equation.

$CaCO_3$ ➡ CaO + CO_2

This equation is already **balanced**. There is the same number of each type of atom on both the right-hand side and left-hand side of the equation.

$Ca = 1, C = 1, O = 3$

Finally, state symbols can be added.

$CaCO_3$ (s) ➡ CaO (s) + CO_2 (g)

2 Calcium burns in oxygen to form calcium oxide.

calcium + oxygen ➡ calcium oxide

Now, writing in the correct symbols and formulae:

Ca + O_2 ➡ CaO

This equation then has to be balanced and state symbols added.

LHS: $Ca = 1, O = 2$; RHS: $Ca = 1, O = 1$

$2Ca$ (s) + O_2 (g) ➡ $2CaO$ (s)

(s) = solid
(g) = gas
(l) = liquid
(aq) = aqueous (in solution)

Ionic equations

Ionic equations are useful because they emphasise the important changes taking place in a chemical reaction. For example, the equation for the neutralisation reaction between sodium hydroxide and hydrochloric acid is:

sodium hydroxide + hydrochloric acid ➡ sodium chloride + water

$NaOH$ (aq) + HCl (aq) ➡ $NaCl$ (aq) + H_2O (l)

Since all of the reactants and products (except water) are composed of ions, this equation could be written:

Na^+ (aq) OH^- (aq) + H^+ (aq) Cl^- (aq) ➡ Na^+ (aq) Cl^- (aq) + H_2O (l)

An equation should show change and therefore anything present before and after the reaction can be deleted. The simplest ionic equation, deleting Na^+ (aq) and Cl^- (aq), is therefore:

OH^- (aq) + H^+ (aq) ➡ H_2O (l)

28 The mole

In this unit you will learn the answers to these questions:
- What is a mole?
- How can we use relative atomic masses, obtained from the Periodic Table, to calculate the mass of 1 mole of different substances?

Atoms are very small and it is impossible to weigh and measure individual atoms in the school laboratory. It is helpful to consider atoms in larger numbers.

- A magnesium atom weighs 24 times as much as a hydrogen atom.
- Ten magnesium atoms weigh 24 times as much as ten hydrogen atoms.
- x magnesium atoms weigh 24 times as much as x hydrogen atoms.

Chemists usually use a very large number called Avogadro's number (L). Avogadro's number is approximately 6×10^{23} or 600 000 000 000 000 000 000 000. To give you some idea of the size of this number, if the whole population of the world wished to count up to this number between them and they worked without any breaks, twenty-four hours each day, it would take six million years to finish. Alternatively, a line 6×10^{23} mm long would stretch from the Earth to the Sun and back two million times.

- 1 mole of hydrogen atoms weighs 1 g.
- 1 mole of magnesium atoms weighs 24 g.
- 1 mole of sulphur atoms weighs 32 g.
- A mole of magnesium atoms weighs 24 times as much as a mole of hydrogen atoms.

> The amount of a substance which contains Avogadro's number of particles is called 1 mole.

Look at the Periodic Table on page 91.

Q1 What is the significance of the **mass** of 1 mole of hydrogen atoms, 1 mole of magnesium atoms and 1 mole of sulphur atoms?

Q2 A sample of magnesium weighs 6 g. What mass of sulphur contains the same number of atoms as 6 g of magnesium?

Q3 Use the Periodic Table to help you work out the mass of:
  a) 1 mole of sodium atoms, Na;
  b) 1 mole of oxygen atoms, O;
  c) 1 mole of oxygen molecules, O_2
    (each oxygen molecule contains two oxygen atoms);
  d) 0.5 moles of bromine atoms, Br;
  e) 0.1 moles of chlorine molecules, Cl_2;
  f) 2 moles of calcium atoms, Ca;
  g) 3 moles of helium atoms, He;
  h) 0.25 moles of carbon atoms, C;
  i) 0.5 moles of nitrogen atoms, N;
  j) 0.5 moles of nitrogen molecules, N_2.

B Changing materials

Because the mass of electrons is negligible compared to other particles in an atom, the mass of 1 mole of magnesium atoms, for example, is the same as the mass of 1 mole of magnesium ions.

> **Q4** Work out the mass of:
> **a)** 1 mole of chloride ions, Cl^-;
> **b)** 1 mole of aluminium ions, Al^{3+};
> **c)** 0.1 moles of calcium ions, Ca^{2+};
> **d)** 0.25 moles of sulphide ions, S^{2-};
> **e)** 1 mole of hydroxide ions, OH^-;
> **f)** 1 mole of oxide ions, O^{2-};
> **g)** 0.25 moles of magnesium ions, Mg^{2+};
> **h)** 0.25 moles of copper ions, Cu^{2+}.

The mass of one mole of compounds can be calculated using the correct formula.

1 calcium carbonate $CaCO_3$

The masses of 1 mole of calcium, carbon and oxygen are 40, 12 and 16, respectively.

The mass of 1 mole of calcium carbonate
$= 40 + 12 + (3 \times 16)$
$= 100\,g$

2 calcium hydroxide $Ca(OH)_2$

The mass of 1 mole of calcium hydroxide
$= 40 + 2(16 + 1)$
$= 74\,g$

3 calcium nitrate $Ca(NO_3)_2$

The mass of 1 mole of calcium nitrate
$= 40 + 2[14 + (3 \times 16)]$
$= 164\,g$

4 hydrated copper(II) sulphate $CuSO_4.5H_2O$

The mass of 1 mole of hydrated copper(II) sulphate
$= 64 + 32 + (4 \times 16) + 5[(2 \times 1) + 16]$
$= 250\,g$

> **Q5** Work out the mass of 1 mole of:
> **a)** calcium oxide, CaO;
> **b)** magnesium chloride, $MgCl_2$;
> **c)** barium hydroxide, $Ba(OH)_2$;
> **d)** chromium(III) sulphate, $Cr_2(SO_4)_3$;
> **e)** magnesium sulphate, $MgSO_4.7H_2O$;
> **f)** calcium hydrogencarbonate, $Ca(HCO_3)_2$;
> **g)** iron(III) sulphate, $Fe_2(SO_4)_3$;
> **h)** iron(II) sulphate, $FeSO_4$;
> **i)** aluminium sulphate, $Al_2(SO_4)_3$;
> **j)** sodium carbonate, $Na_2CO_3.10H_2O$.
>
> **Q6** Work out the mass of:
> **a)** 0.5 moles of calcium hydroxide, $Ca(OH)_2$;
> **b)** 0.1 moles of sodium hydroxide, $NaOH$;
> **c)** 0.1 moles of sulphuric acid, H_2SO_4;
> **d)** 0.5 moles of nitric acid, HNO_3;
> **e)** 2 moles of hydrochloric acid, HCl.

$$\text{number of moles} = \frac{\text{mass in g}}{\text{mass of 1 mole in g}}$$

29 Chemical formulae by experiment

In this unit you will learn the answer to this question:
■ How can the formula of a compound be found by experiment?

Every chemical formula can theoretically be found as a result of a chemical experiment.

Formula of magnesium oxide

A weighed mass of magnesium is burned in air and the mass of magnesium oxide formed is found.

a Mass of crucible and lid	=	25.15 g
b Mass of crucible, lid and magnesium	=	25.27 g
Mass of magnesium **b** − **a**	=	0.12 g
c Mass of crucible, lid and magnesium oxide	=	25.35 g
Mass of magnesium oxide **c** − **a**	=	0.20 g

From these results:

■ 0.12 g of magnesium combines with (0.20 − 0.12) g of oxygen to form 0.20 g of magnesium oxide.

■ 0.12 g of magnesium combines with 0.08 g of oxygen.

■ In Unit 28 it was shown that

$$\text{number of moles} = \frac{\text{mass in g}}{\text{mass of 1 mole in g}}$$

Therefore $\frac{0.12}{24}$ moles of magnesium combines with $\frac{0.08}{16}$ moles of oxygen atoms.

■ 0.005 moles of magnesium combines with 0.005 moles of oxygen atoms.

The simplest formula of magnesium oxide is, therefore, MgO.

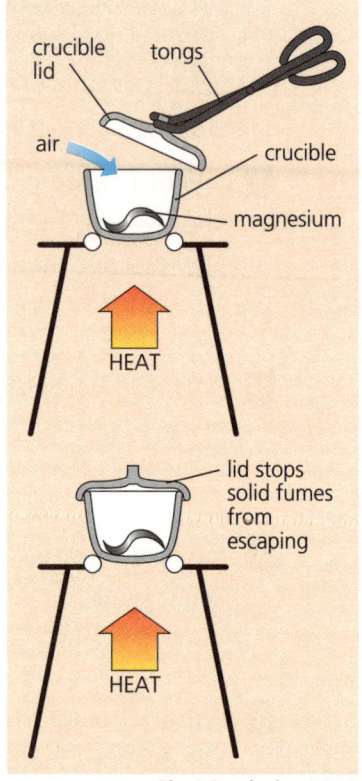

Fig 1 Producing MgO

Formula of silicon chloride

Silicon chloride is a liquid produced when dry chlorine is passed over a heated sample of silicon.

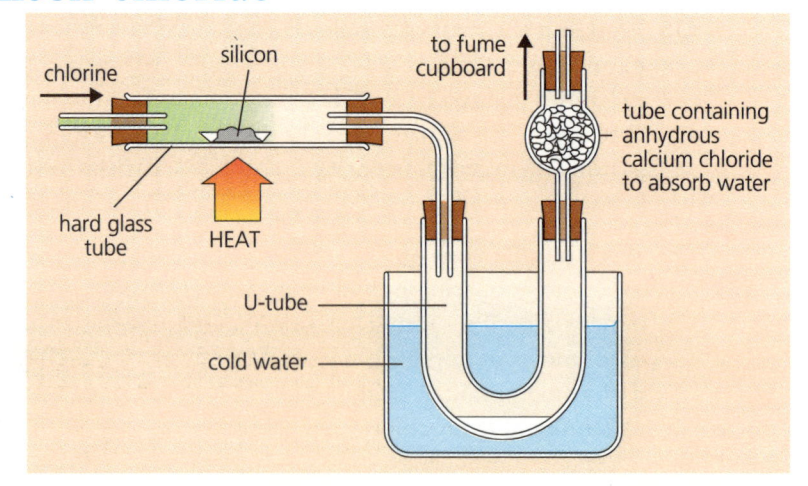

Fig 2 Producing silicon chloride

B Changing materials

The silicon and the hard glass tube are weighed before and after heating to find the mass of silicon used. The mass of silicon chloride is found by weighing the U-tube before and after the experiment.

a Mass of hard glass tube and silicon before heating = 38.86 g
b Mass of hard glass tube and silicon after heating = 38.30 g
Mass of silicon used **a** − **b** = 0.56 g
c Mass of U-tube before experiment = 145.40 g
d Mass of U-tube after experiment = 148.80 g
Mass of silicon chloride formed **d** − **c** = 3.40 g

From these results:

- 0.56 g of silicon combines with 2.84 g of chlorine to produce 3.40 g of silicon chloride.

- $\frac{0.56}{28}$ moles of silicon atoms combines with $\frac{2.84}{35.5}$ moles of chlorine atoms.

- 0.02 moles of silicon atoms combines with 0.08 moles of chlorine atoms.

There are four times as many chlorine atoms as silicon atoms. The formula is, therefore, $SiCl_4$.

Formulae of copper oxides

There are two copper oxides – black copper oxide and red copper oxide. The formulae of the two oxides can be found by reducing the metal oxides to copper using hydrogen as the reducing agent.

copper oxide + hydrogen ➡ copper + water

The apparatus shown could be used.

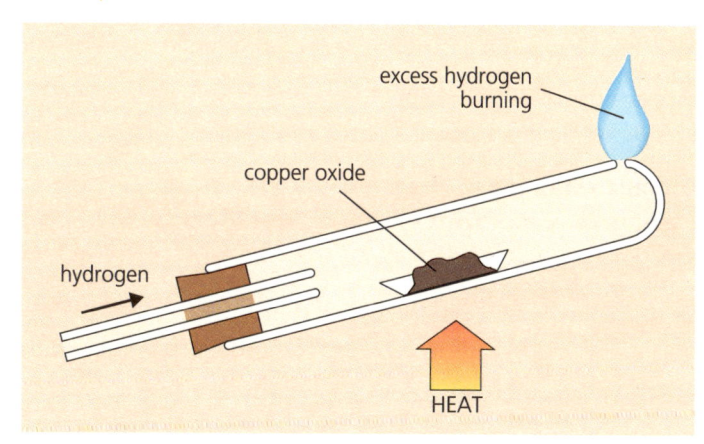

Fig 3 Reducing copper oxide

Q1 The following results were obtained. Work out the formulae of the two oxides.

	Black copper oxide	Red copper oxide
mass of copper oxide	0.80 g	0.72 g
mass of copper	0.64 g	0.64 g

30 Calculations from equations

In this unit you will learn the answer to this question:
■ How can calculations of masses of reactants and products be carried out using a balanced chemical equation?

Balanced symbol equations summarise the reactants and products in a chemical reaction. They also enable us to work out the masses of substances that react and the masses of the products formed. This is vital, for example, for a chemical manufacturer who is then able to work out the costs of making a given mass of a chemical and so calculate the price that must be charged to make a profit.

Working out masses from a chemical equation

The equation for the reaction between calcium carbonate and dilute hydrochloric acid is

calcium carbonate + hydrochloric acid → calcium chloride + water + carbon dioxide

$$CaCO_3\,(s) + 2HCl\,(aq) \rightarrow CaCl_2\,(aq) + H_2O\,(l) + CO_2\,(g)$$

Mass of 1 mole of calcium carbonate = $40 + 12 + (3 \times 16)$ = 100 g
Mass of 2 moles of hydrochloric acid = $2\,(1 + 35.5)$ = 73 g
Mass of 1 mole of calcium chloride = $40 + (35.5 \times 2)$ = 111 g
Mass of 1 mole of water = $(2 \times 1) + 16$ = 18 g
Mass of 1 mole of carbon dioxide = $12 + (2 \times 16)$ = 44 g

If you add up the sum of the masses of the reactants it should always equal the sum of the masses of the products. Checking at this point will prevent arithmetical errors.

Calculate the mass of calcium chloride produced when 50 g of calcium carbonate reacts with excess hydrochloric acid

From the equation:
■ 100 g of calcium carbonate reacts to produce 111 g of calcium chloride.
■ 1 g of calcium carbonate reacts to produce $\frac{111}{100}$ g of calcium chloride.
■ 50 g of calcium carbonate reacts to produce $50 \times \frac{111}{100}$ g = 55.5 g of calcium chloride.

Calculate the mass of carbon dioxide produced when 4 g of calcium carbonate reacts with excess hydrochloric acid

From the equation:
■ 100 g of calcium carbonate reacts to produce 44 g of carbon dioxide.
■ 1 g of calcium carbonate reacts to produce $\frac{44}{100}$ g of carbon dioxide.
■ 4 g of calcium carbonate reacts to produce $4 \times \frac{44}{100}$ g = 1.76 g of carbon dioxide.

Volumes of gases used up or produced

When dealing with reactants or products that are gases it is often better to use volumes rather than masses. For example:

hydrogen + chlorine → hydrogen chloride
$$H_2\,(g) + Cl_2\,(g) \rightarrow 2HCl\,(g)$$

B Changing materials

1 mole of hydrogen molecules reacts with 1 mole of chlorine molecules to form 2 moles of hydrogen chloride molecules.

2 g of hydrogen reacts with 71 g of chlorine to produce 73 g of hydrogen chloride.

The volume of a fixed mass of gas changes with changes in pressure and temperature. At room temperature and atmospheric pressure, one mole of any gas has a volume of $24\,dm^3$. So, in this example, $24\,dm^3$ of hydrogen reacts with $24\,dm^3$ of chlorine to produce $48\,dm^3$ of hydrogen chloride.

Calculate the volume of hydrogen chloride produced when $10\,dm^3$ of hydrogen reacts with $10\,dm^3$ of chlorine

From the equation:

- 1 mole of hydrogen reacts with 1 mole of chlorine to produce 2 moles of hydrogen chloride.
- Volume of hydrogen chloride produced, at room temperature and atmospheric pressure = $20\,dm^3$.

Calculate the volume of carbon dioxide, at room temperature and atmospheric pressure, produced when 4 g of calcium carbonate reacts with excess hydrochloric acid

$$CaCO_3\,(s) + 2HCl\,(aq) \rightarrow CaCl_2\,(aq) + H_2O\,(l) + CO_2\,(g)$$

- 100 g of calcium carbonate reacts to produce $24\,dm^3$ of carbon dioxide.
- 1 g of calcium carbonate reacts to produce $\frac{24}{100}\,dm^3$ of carbon dioxide.
- 4 g of calcium carbonate reacts to produce $4 \times \frac{24}{100}\,dm^3 = 0.96\,dm^3$ of carbon dioxide.

Unlike the masses, the volume of the reactants and products are not always the same. For example:

$$2NH_3\,(g) \rightarrow N_2\,(g) + 3H_2\,(g)$$

Volume of reactants at room temperature and atmospheric pressure = $48\,dm^3$.

Volume of products at room temperature and atmospheric pressure:
$$24 + (3 \times 24)\,dm^3 = 96\,dm^3.$$

Percentage yield

So far in these calculations we have assumed that all of the reactants are turned into products, i.e. the yield is said to be 100% and there is no waste. This is usually not the case, especially in some reactions involving organic chemicals when the percentage yield is often between 50% and 80%.

Q1 The equation of methane burning in excess oxygen is
$$CH_4\,(g) + 2O_2\,(g) \rightarrow CO_2\,(g) + 2H_2O\,(l)$$
a) What volume of carbon dioxide is formed when $1\,dm^3$ of methane is burned in excess oxygen?
b) What volume of water is formed when $1\,dm^3$ of methane is burned in excess oxygen?

Q2 The equation for the decomposition of calcium carbonate is
$$CaCO_3 \rightarrow CaO + CO_2$$
When 1 tonne of calcium carbonate was heated 0.5 tonnes of calcium oxide were produced. What was the percentage yield?

If the equation indicates that 10 g of product can be produced and 6 g is actually obtained, the percentage yield is $\frac{6}{10} \times 100 = 60\%$.

31 Concentration calculations

In this unit you will learn the answers to these questions:
- How do we work out the concentration of a solution?
- What is the advantage of using molar concentrations?

Molar concentrations

Concentrations of solutions can be expressed in different ways. One way is mass of solute per unit volume of liquid, for example g per dm^3 or g/dm^3.

For example, if 4g of sodium hydroxide is dissolved in 100g of water, the concentration of the solution is 40g per dm^3.

Q1 Calculate the concentration, in g per dm^3, of a solution containing 2g of sodium chloride in 25g of water.

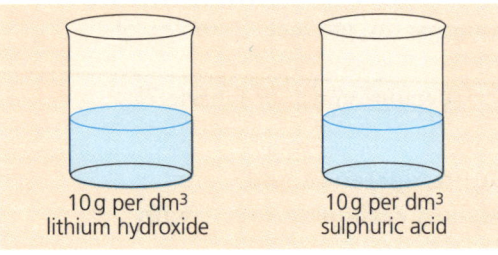

Fig 1 Two solutions with the same concentration, but different numbers of particles

10g per dm^3 lithium hydroxide

10g per dm^3 sulphuric acid

Fig 1 shows two solutions with the same concentration. However, there is no easy comparison of the number of particles. As the particles have different masses, the number of particles in each solution will be different.

If **concentrations in moles per dm^3** are used, we can make a direct comparison of the number of particles present.

> The concentration in moles per dm^3 can be calculated by dividing the mass in 1 dm^3 by the mass of 1 mole of the solute:
>
> $$\text{concentration in moles per } dm^3 = \frac{\text{mass in 1 } dm^3 \text{ of solution}}{\text{mass of 1 mole}}$$

Compare the number of particles present in 10g per dm^3 lithium hydroxide and 10g per dm^3 nitric acid

10g per dm^3 lithium hydroxide, LiOH
The mass of 1 mole of lithium hydroxide = 7 + 16 + 1 = 24g
Molar concentration = $\frac{10}{24}$ = 0.42 moles per dm^3

10 g per dm^3 nitric acid, HNO_3
The mass of 1 mole of nitric acid = 1 + 14 + (3 × 16) = 63g
Molar concentration = $\frac{10}{63}$ = 0.16 moles per dm^3

Because the mass of 1 mole of nitric acid is approximately $2\frac{1}{2}$ times the mass of 1 mole of lithium hydroxide, this disguises the difference in the number of particles present. There are approximately $2\frac{1}{2}$ times as many particles of lithium hydroxide as particles of nitric acid.

Sometimes a solution with a molar concentration of 2 moles per dm^3 is written as 2M.

Q2 Calculate the molar concentrations of the following solutions. (Refer to the Periodic Table on page 91 for the relative atomic masses you will need.)
  a) 10.6g of sodium carbonate, Na_2CO_3, dissolved to make 1 dm^3 of solution.
  b) 73g of hydrogen chloride, HCl, dissolved to make 500 cm^3 of solution.
  c) 117g of sodium chloride, NaCl, dissolved to make 2 dm^3 of solution.

B Changing materials

Q3 What do these three solutions have in common?

100 cm³
1 mole per dm³

10 cm³
10 moles per dm³

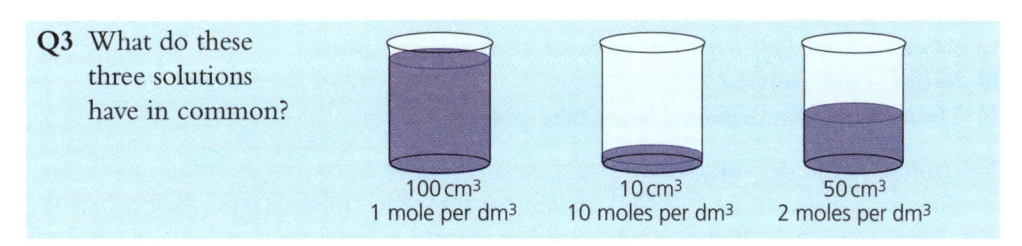

50 cm³
2 moles per dm³

Reacting volumes of solutions

In Unit 30 we saw that calculations can be made using masses of reacting substances and masses of products. We can extend this to include reactions between solutions of known concentrations. For example, the reaction of sodium hydroxide and sulphuric acid:

$$2NaOH\ (aq) + H_2SO_4\ (aq) \rightarrow Na_2SO_4\ (aq) + 2H_2O\ (l)$$

From the equation, 2 moles of sodium hydroxide react with 1 mole of sulphuric acid to form 1 mole of sodium sulphate and 2 moles of water.

How many moles of sodium hydroxide, NaOH, are present in 50 cm³ of solution of molar concentration 2 mole per dm³?

1 dm³ of solution (2 mole per dm³) contains 2 moles of NaOH.
50 cm³ is $\frac{50}{1000}$ of 1 dm³ (i.e. $\frac{1}{20}$).
Number of moles of NaOH = $2 \times \frac{1}{20}$ = 0.1 moles.

How many moles of sulphuric acid would react with 50 cm³ of solution of NaOH of molar concentration 2 mole per dm³?

Because 2 moles of sodium hydroxide react with 1 mole of sulphuric acid, the number of moles of sulphuric acid reacting with 0.1 moles of NaOH = 0.05.

What volume of sulphuric acid (2 mole per dm³) reacts completely with 50 cm³ of solution of NaOH of molar concentration 2 mole per dm³?

A solution of sulphuric acid with a molar concentration of 1 mole per dm³ contains 1 mole of H_2SO_4 in each dm³ (1000 cm³). The volume of this solution containing 0.05 moles of H_2SO_4 is:

$0.05 \times \frac{1000}{2}$ = 25 cm³.

Titrations

The reaction between sodium hydroxide and sulphuric acid is an example of a reaction producing a soluble salt (Unit 48). Fig 2 shows how this experiment could be carried out to find the volume of 2M sulphuric acid (2 mole per dm³) which reacts with 50 cm³ of sodium hydroxide solution (2 mole per dm³) can be carried out.

This is called a **titration**.

Fig 2 Apparatus to find the volume of sulphuric acid which reacts with sodium hydroxide solution

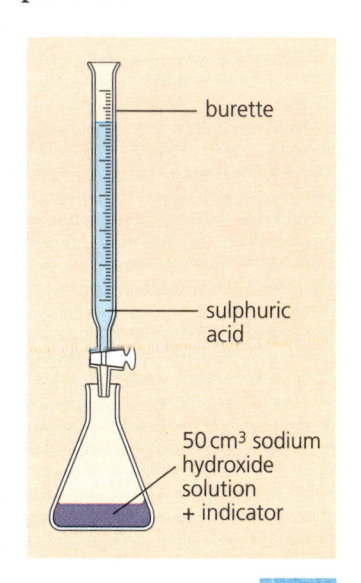

— burette
— sulphuric acid
— 50 cm³ sodium hydroxide solution + indicator

B7 Electrochemistry – 1

In this unit you will learn the answers to these questions:
- What is electrolysis?
- Under what conditions does it take place?

Electrolysis is the **decomposition** of a compound by electricity. A compound which is split up by electrolysis is called an **electrolyte**. Electrolysis takes place when the electrolyte is molten (liquid) or dissolved in water (an aqueous solution). Electrolytes are made up of ions (see Unit 6). In the solid state, the ions can vibrate but are not free to move. When the electrolyte is melted or dissolved in water the regular arrangement of ions (or **lattice**) breaks down and the ions are free to move. Electrolytes can be acids, alkalis, bases or salts.

Electrolysis of molten lead(II) bromide

Lead(II) bromide is made up of Pb^{2+} and Br^- ions. Fig 1 shows the diagram for the electrolysis of lead(II) bromide.

Q1 Why are there twice as many bromide ions as lead(II) ions in the lead(II) bromide lattice?

Q2 What material is used for the electrodes? What properties make this a suitable material for this purpose?

Q3 What name is given to the electrode connected to:
  a) the positive terminal of the battery?
  b) the negative terminal of the battery?

Q4 How will the bulb in the circuit change as the lead(II) bromide is heated until it melts?

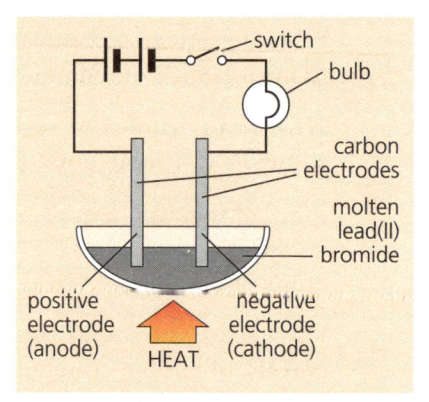

Fig 1 Apparatus used to electrolyse lead(II) bromide

The products of this electrolysis are lead (formed at the cathode) and bromine (formed at the anode).

Fig 2 shows what happens during this electrolysis. The process is in two stages – migration and discharge.

1 Migration. When lead(II) bromide is melted, positively charged lead(II) ions move towards the cathode and negatively charged bromide ions move towards the anode.

2 Discharge. The cathode has a surplus of electrons and the anode has a shortage. Electron transfers take place and the ions are said to be discharged.

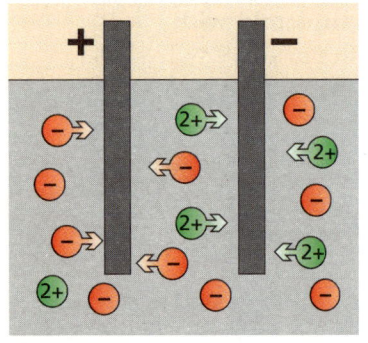

Fig 2 Ion movement during electrolysis of lead(II) bromide

At the cathode, each lead ion gains two electrons to form a lead atom.

$$Pb^{2+} + 2e^- \rightarrow Pb$$

At the anode, each bromide ion loses an electron and forms a bromine atom.

$$Br^- \rightarrow Br + e^-$$

Two bromine atoms join together to form a bromine molecule.

$$Br + Br \rightarrow Br_2$$

B Changing materials

Oxidation and reduction

Oxidation is a process where electrons are *lost* and reduction is a process in which electrons are *gained*.

Q5 Which ions, lead(II) or bromide, are oxidised and which are reduced?

Q6 At which electrode does:
a) oxidation occur? b) reduction occur?

Electrolysis of aqueous solutions

In pure water some of the molecules are split into H^+ and OH^- ions. This very slight ionisation explains the very slight electrical conductivity of pure water. An aqueous solution of copper(II) sulphate will therefore contain Cu^{2+} and SO_4^{2-} ions (from the copper(II) sulphate) and H^+ and OH^- ions (from the water). Both positive ions (Cu^{2+} and H^+) migrate to the negative electrode and both negative ions (SO_4^{2-} and OH^-) migrate to the positive electrode. At each electrode, one or both of the ions may be discharged. The table summarises some electrolysis experiments.

Electrolyte solution	Electrodes	Ion discharged at +ve electrode	Ion discharged at –ve electrode	Product at +ve electrode	Product at –ve electrode
dilute sulphuric acid	carbon	OH^-(aq)	H^+(aq)	oxygen	hydrogen
dilute sodium hydroxide	carbon	OH^-(aq)	H^+(aq)	oxygen	hydrogen
copper(II) sulphate	carbon	OH^-(aq)	Cu^{2+}(aq)	oxygen	copper
copper(II) sulphate	copper	none	Cu^{2+}(aq)	none	copper
very dilute sodium chloride	carbon	OH^-(aq)	H^+(aq)	oxygen	hydrogen
concentrated sodium chloride	carbon	Cl^-(aq)	H^+(aq)	chlorine	hydrogen

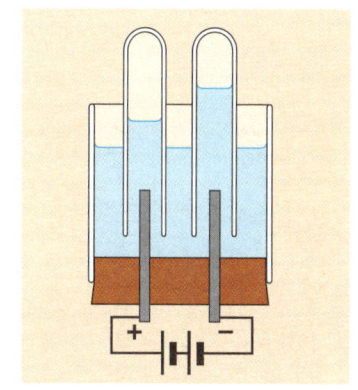

The apparatus in Fig 3 can be used for the electrolysis of aqueous solutions and to collect gaseous products.

Q7 Which of the following would increase the electrolysis speed?
a) Using larger electrodes. b) Lifting the test tubes.
c) Increasing the current flowing.
d) Diluting the electrolyte with water.

The following points about the electrolysis of aqueous solutions should be remembered.

1 Metals, if produced, are discharged at the negative electrode.

2 Hydrogen is produced at the negative electrode only.

3 Non-metals, apart from hydrogen, are produced at the positive electrode.

4 Reactive metals, such as sodium, are not produced during the electrolysis of aqueous solutions.

5 The products obtained can depend upon the concentration of the electrolyte and the nature of the electrolyte.

6 Providing the concentrations of the negative ions in solution are approximately the same, the order of discharge is:

Fig 3 Apparatus used for the electrolysis of aqueous solutions and to collect gaseous products

OH^-(aq)
I^-(aq)
Br^-(aq)   decreasing
Cl^-(aq)   ease of
NO_3^-(aq)   discharge
SO_4^{2-}(aq)

B8 Electrochemistry – 2

In this unit you will learn the answers to these questions:
- What are common applications of electrolysis?
- How can the quantity of product obtained by electrolysis be related to the quantity of electricity used?

Applications of electrolysis

1. **Extraction and purification of metals.** Units 21 and 22 give examples of electrolysis used in this way.

2. **Electroplating.** This is the coating of a metal with a thin coating of another metal using electrolysis. Iron or steel can be plated with a thin coating of nickel to prevent rusting. Finally, a thin coating of chromium is deposited on the nickel surface to give a shiny appearance. Fig 1 shows how a piece of steel can be electroplated with nickel. The steel object to be plated is made the cathode in the cell. Nickel is deposited on the cathode during electrolysis.

Q1 What happens at the anode during electroplating of steel?

Q2 Complete the ionic equation for the reaction taking place when nickel is deposited on steel.
Ni^{2+} + _____ ➡ _____

Q3 Is the process taking place in **Q2** oxidation or reduction?

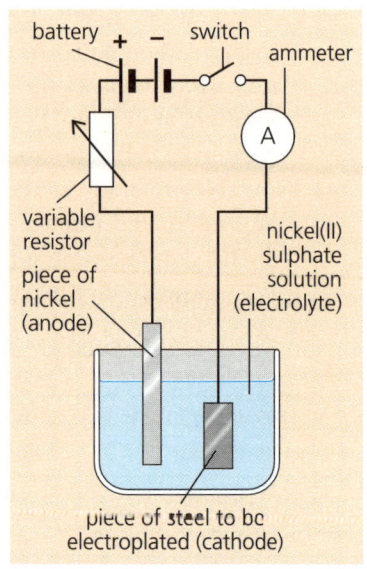

Fig 1 Electroplating a piece of steel with nickel

3. **Electrolysis of brine (sodium chloride solution).** Brine (sodium chloride solution) is an important raw material in the chemical industry. Electrolysis of brine produces sodium hydroxide, chlorine gas and hydrogen gas. Fig 2 shows the diaphragm cell which is used for the electrolysis of brine. In this cell the electrolysis of purified, saturated brine takes place with a titanium anode and a steel cathode. The anode and cathode are in separate compartments separated by a diaphragm that allows brine to pass through but prevents the products, chlorine and sodium hydroxide solution from coming into contact.

The direction of flow of the solution is from the anode compartment to the cathode compartment.

Q4 Look at Fig 2. How does the design of the cell ensure that the flow of the solution is from the anode compartment?

The reactions at the electrodes are:
Anode $2Cl^-(aq)$ ➡ $Cl(g) + 2e^-$
Cathode $2H^+(aq) + 2e^-$ ➡ $H_2(g)$

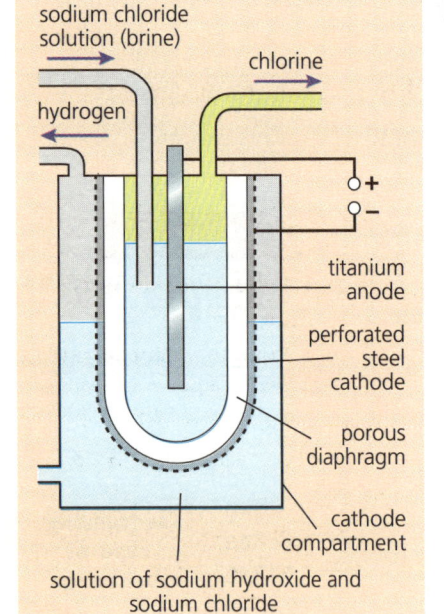

Fig 2 Diaphragm cell used to electrolyse brine (sodium chloride solution)

B Changing materials

The solution leaving the cathode compartment contains approximately 12% by mass of sodium hydroxide and 15% sodium chloride. When this is evaporated to about one-fifth of its volume, the solution contains 50% sodium hydroxide and less than 1% sodium chloride. This is sufficient purity for many applications of sodium hydroxide.

Quantitative electrolysis

Fig 3 shows apparatus for studying the quantity of electricity required to deposit a given mass of product.

> **Q5** What jobs do the ammeter and variable resistor have in this circuit?

Experiments show that the masses of the products is proportional to both current passing and time, i.e. the quantity of electricity.

> quantity of electricity =
>   current (in amperes) × time (in seconds)

If a current of 1 ampere (1 A) is passed for 1 second, the quantity of electricity is 1 coulomb, C.

> **Q6** Calculate the number of coulombs passed when:
> a) a current of 2 A is used for 1 minute;
> b) a current of 5 A is used for 1 hour.

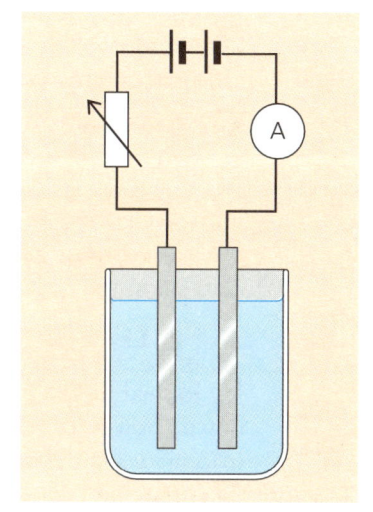

Fig 3 Apparatus used to study the quantity of electricity needed to deposit a given mass of product during an electrolysis

The number of coulombs used in an experiment is often a very large number. The unit called the faraday is a larger unit than the coulomb.

> A faraday is the amount of electricity carried by 1 mole of electrons.
> 1 faraday (F) = 96 500 C

> **Q7** Calculate the number of faradays passed when 1 A is used for 1930 seconds.

The quantity of electricity required to deposit 1 mole of atoms depends upon the charge on the ion being discharged.

If the ion has a single positive charge or single negative charge, e.g. Na^+ or Cl^-, 1 faraday is required to deposit 1 mole of atoms.

If the ion has a double positive charge or a double negative charge, e.g. Cu^{2+} or O^{2-}, 2 faradays are required to deposit 1 mole of atoms.

If the ion has a triple positive charge or triple negative charge, e.g. Al^{3+}, 3 faradays are required to deposit 1 mole of atoms.

> **Q8** Calculate the number of faradays needed to deposit:
> a) 1 mole of nickel atoms from Ni^{2+};
> b) 1 mole of iodine atoms from I^- ions;
> c) 0.5 moles of calcium atoms from Ca^{2+} ions.
>
> **Q9** Calculate the mass of potassium deposited by 0.1 F from K^+ ions. (A_r (K) = 39.)

32 The Periodic Table

In this unit you will learn the answers to these questions:

- **What is the Periodic Table?**
- **How can it help us to organise our knowledge of Chemistry?**
- **How are the properties of elements related to their position in the Periodic Table?**
- **What are periodic graphs?**

In the middle of the nineteenth century chemists were discovering a large number of new elements. They were also able to determine atomic weights of the elements (now called atomic masses) accurately.

Attempts were made by chemists, including Johann Dobereiner, John Newlands and Lothar Meyer, to produce a system to classify the elements.

John Newlands, in 1865, arranged the known elements in order of increasing atomic weight. He realised that every eighth element in the series was similar.

H **Li** Be B C N O F **Na** Mg Al Si P S Cl **K**

He likened this to music and called it the Law of Octaves. It fell down, however, because some of the atomic weights were inaccurate and there were elements that had not been discovered.

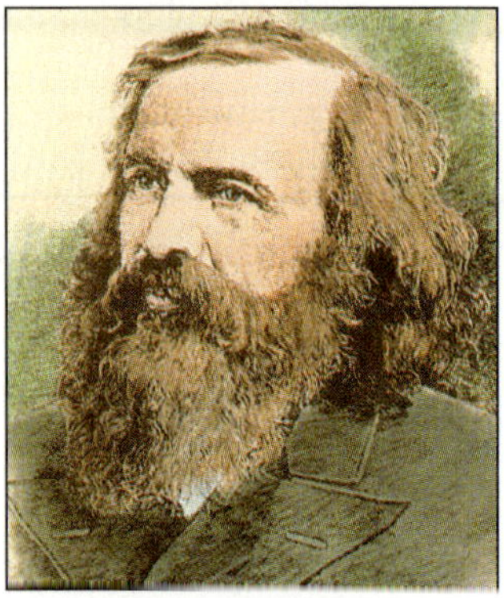

***Fig 1** Mendeleev (1834 1907)*

In 1869, the Russian chemist Dmitri Mendeleev produced a classification of the elements which has survived in the form of the modern Periodic Table (page 91). Mendeleev arranged the known elements in order of increasing atomic weight but in such a way that elements with similar properties were in the same vertical column. He called these vertical columns **groups** and the horizontal rows **periods**. If necessary he left gaps in the table and predicted the discovery of new elements to fill these gaps. He even changed the order slightly in places where elements were obviously misplaced.

Fig 2 shows a copy of Mendeleev's original table. Although the notes are in Russian, it is possible to make out the symbols of the elements. In this table, elements with similar properties are in the same row, e.g. Li, Na, K, Rb, Cs.

но въ ней, мнѣ кажется, уже ясно выражается примѣнимость выставляемаго мною начала ко всей совокупности элементовъ, пай которыхъ извѣстенъ съ достовѣрностію. На этотъ разъ я и желалъ преимущественно найдти общую систему элементовъ. Вотъ этотъ опытъ:

			Ti=50	Zr=90	?=180.
			V=51	Nb=94	Ta=182.
			Cr=52	Mo=96	W=186.
			Mn=55	Rh=104,4	Pt=197,4
			Fe=56	Ru=104,4	Ir=198.
			Ni=Co=59	Pl=106,6,	Os=199.
H=1			Cu=63,4	Ag=108	Hg=200.
	Be=9,4	Mg=24	Zn=65,2	Cd=112	
	B=11	Al=27,4	?=68	Ur=116	Au=197?
	C=12	Si=28	?=70	Sn=118	
	N=14	P=31	As=75	Sb=122	Bi=210
	O=16	S=32	Se=79,4	Te=128?	
	F=19	Cl=35,5	Br=80	I=127	
Li=7	Na=23	K=39	Rb=85,4	Cs=133	Tl=204
		Ca=40	Sr=87,6	Ba=137	Pb=207.
		?=45	Ce=92		
		?Er=56	La=94		
		?Yt=60	Di=95		
		?In=75,6	Th=118?		

***Fig 2** Mendeleev's Periodic Table*

Q1 How many elements did Mendeleev include in his table?

Q2 How did Mendeleev represent elements which had not been discovered?

C Patterns of behaviour

Q3 Look at each of the following sets of elements.
   a) F Cl Br I   **b)** Ca Sr Ba Pb   **c)** N P As Sb Bi   **d)** Be Mg Zn Cd
   In which of these sets are **all** of the elements in the same column in the modern Periodic Table (page 91)?

Relating the electronic arrangement to the position in the Periodic Table

The electron arrangement in a sodium atom is 2, 8, 1. Sodium has three electron shells and is therefore in period 3.

The table shows the number of electrons in the outer shell for the first three elements. Finish this table for the first 20 elements. Use the Periodic Table on page 91 to complete it.

Element	Order of increasing atomic weight (atomic mass)	Number of electrons in outer energy level
hydrogen	1	1
helium	2	2
lithium	3	1

You should notice that the number of electrons in the outer energy level is the same as the group number in the Periodic Table, except for the noble gases in group 0.

Q4 Copy and complete the bar graph of number of electrons in the outer energy level against the order of the elements in the table above.

Q5 Look carefully at the elements potassium and argon in the bar graph. Why would they fit better if they were changed round?

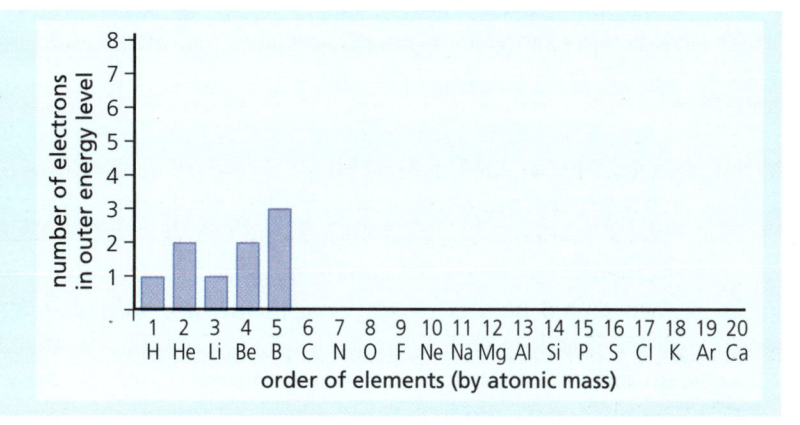

You will notice that the graph consists of a series of peaks and troughs which repeat. This is called a **repeating** or **periodic** pattern.

Lothar Meyer saw similar periodic graphs when he plotted physical properties against atomic weight.

Q6 a) Write down the name of the element which is at the top of each peak in your graph. Use the modern Periodic Table on page 91 to predict which element would be at the top of the next peak.
   b) Write down the name of the element which is at the bottom of each trough in your graph. Use the modern Periodic Table on page 91 to predict which element would be at the bottom of the next trough.

Q7 Use the Periodic Table to identify the elements whose atoms have the following electron arrangements.
   a) 2, 8, 18, 5   **b)** 2, 8, 18, 8, 2   **c)** 2, 8, 18, 7

33 Structure of the Periodic Table

In this unit you will learn the answer to this question:
■ How can the Periodic Table be used in lessons and examinations? (You will have a copy of it with you in the examination.)

The modern Periodic Table is a way of classifying the elements. The elements are arranged in order of increasing **atomic number** to avoid any elements out of order when atomic masses are used. The Periodic Table can help you to make predictions about elements you have not yet met. Fig 1 shows the main parts of the Periodic Table. The **main block** of the Periodic Table consists of eight chemical families (i.e. groups I–VII and group 0). Between groups II and III are three rows of **transition metals**.

Elements are classified as metals and non-metals. The bold red line which goes down through the main block elements in steps separates metals on the left-hand side of it from non-metals on the right-hand side of it.

In Unit 32 we saw that there were repeating patterns in physical properties. There are also repeating patterns in the main block of the Periodic Table in the formulae of compounds formed by these elements. The table shows the chemical formulae of the chlorides of some of the elements in the main block.

Q1 Are there more metals or more non-metals in the Periodic Table?

Q2 What change occurs across period 2 from lithium to neon?

Q3 What change occurs down group IV from carbon to lead?

Group	I	II	III	IV	V	VI	VII	0
period 2	LiCl	$BeCl_2$	BCl_3	CCl_4	NCl_3	OCl_2	FCl	no chlorides
period 3	NaCl	$MgCl_2$	$AlCl_3$	$SiCl_4$	PCl_3	SCl_2	–	no chlorides
period 4	KCl	$CaCl_2$	$GaCl_3$	$GeCl_4$	$AsCl_3$	$SeCl_2$	BrCl	no chlorides

You should be able to see patterns in these formulae. Elements in the same group form chlorides with a similar formula, e.g. LiCl and NaCl. The number of chlorine atoms combined with one of the atoms of the element is the same as the group number or the group number subtracted from eight. For example:

$AlCl_3$ three chlorine atoms combined with one aluminium atom
PCl_3 8 – 5 chlorine atoms combined with one phosphorus atom

Q4 Use the modern Periodic Table to write the formulae of:
a) caesium chloride b) barium chloride c) tellurium chloride d) iodine chloride.

Similar patterns can be seen with oxides.

Group	I	II	III	IV	V	VI	VII	0
period 2	Li_2O	BeO	B_2O_3	CO_2	N_2O_3	–	F_2O	no oxides
period 3	Na_2O	MgO	Al_2O_3	SiO_2	P_2O_3	SO_2	Cl_2O	no oxides
period 4	K_2O	CaO	Ga_2O_3	GeO_2	As_2O_3	SeO_2	Br_2O	no oxides

Q5 Use the modern Periodic Table to write the formulae of:
a) caesium oxide b) barium oxide c) tellurium oxide.

C Patterns of behaviour

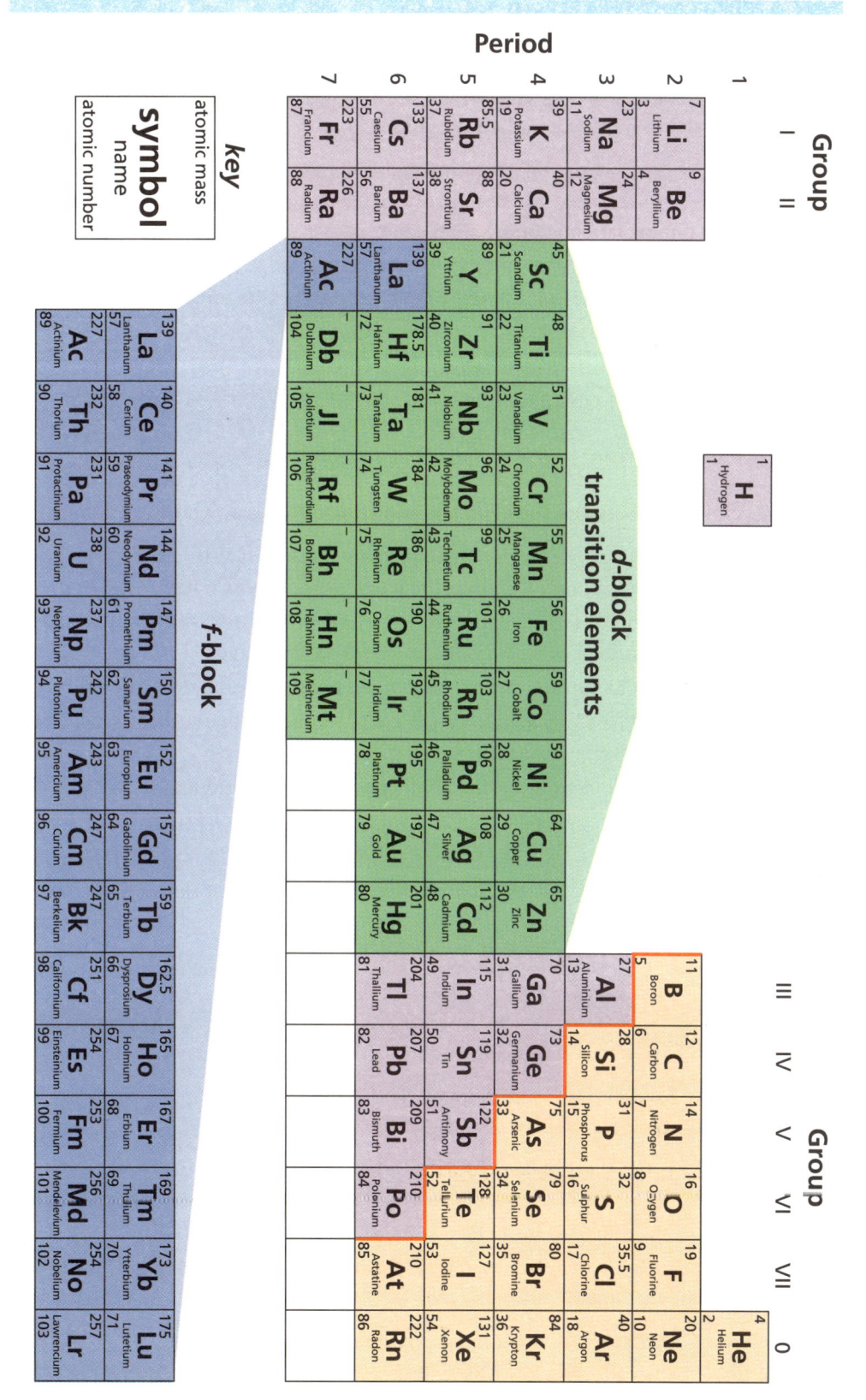

Fig 1 The Periodic Table of elements

34 The alkali metals

In this unit you will learn the answers to these questions:
- What are the alkali metals and where are they placed in the Periodic Table?
- How does the reactivity of alkali metals change down the group?

The elements in group I of the Periodic Table include lithium, sodium, potassium, rubidium and caesium. These form a family of elements called **alkali metals**. The table gives some information about these elements.

Element	Symbol	Atomic number	Melting point (°C)	Boiling point (°C)	Density (g per cm^3)	Date of discovery
lithium	Li	3	181	1331	0.54	1817
sodium	Na	11	98	890	0.97	1807
potassium	K	19	63	766	0.86	1807
rubidium	Rb	37	39	701	1.53	1861
caesium	Cs	55	29	685	1.87	1861

There are similarities between the elements and certain trends down the group.

Fig 1 Sir Humphrey Davy (1778 – 1829): he discovered potassium and sodium by electrolysis

1. All of the elements are reactive metals. They are stored under paraffin oil to prevent reaction with air and water.
2. All of the elements are soft metals that can be easily cut with a knife. The softness increases down the group.
3. The melting points and boiling points decrease down the group.
4. The alkali metals are generally less strong than other metals but have better heat and electrical conductivities.
5. The densities generally increase down the group.

Because of the great stability of the compounds of alkali metals, they were undiscovered at the start of the nineteenth century. They were all discovered by the electrolysis of molten materials.

Q1 When an alkali metal is cut, a shiny surface is produced. This quickly turns dull. Suggest why this is so.

Reactions of alkali metals with oxygen (air)

All alkali metals burn in oxygen to form solid oxides. For example:

sodium + oxygen ➡ sodium oxide
$4Na (s) + O_2 (g)$ ➡ $2Na_2O (s)$

The solid oxides are alkaline, hence the name alkali metals.

Reactions of alkali metals with cold water

All alkali metals react with cold water to form a soluble alkaline hydroxide and hydrogen gas. For example:

sodium + water ➡ sodium hydroxide + hydrogen
$2Na (s) + 2H_2O (l)$ ➡ $2NaOH (aq) + H_2 (g)$

C Patterns of behaviour

All reactions of alkali metals with cold water are exothermic. The table compares the reactivity of some of the alkali metals with cold water.

Alkali metal	Reaction with cold water
lithium	Lithium floats on water, gently fizzing and producing a colourless gas. The gas burns with a squeaky pop (hydrogen). Remaining solution is alkaline.
sodium	Sodium floats on water, fizzing rapidly and producing a colourless gas. The gas burns with a squeaky pop (hydrogen). Remaining solution is alkaline.
potassium	Potassium floats on water, fizzing violently and producing a colourless gas. From time to time hydrogen ignites and burns with a lilac-pink flame. Remaining solution is alkaline.
rubidium	Rubidium sinks (denser than water). Very violent reaction over in a fraction of a second. Remaining solution is alkaline.

It can be seen that the reactivity of alkali metals increases down the group. In all reactions of alkali metals, atoms lose one electron to form a single, positively charged ion. For example:

$$Na \rightarrow Na^+ + e^-$$

The metals become **more reactive** down the group because the outer electron is lost more easily as the group is descended.

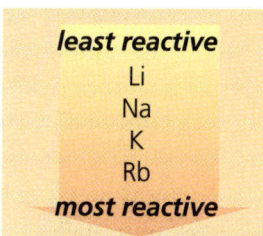

least reactive
Li
Na
K
Rb
most reactive

Reactions of alkali metals with chlorine

All of the alkali metals burn in chlorine gas to form a salt. For example:

lithium + chlorine → lithium chloride
$2Li (s) + Cl_2 (g) \rightarrow 2LiCl (s)$

sodium + chlorine → sodium chloride
$2Na (s) + Cl_2 (g) \rightarrow 2NaCl (s)$

potassium + chlorine → potassium chloride
$2K (s) + Cl_2 (g) \rightarrow 2KCl (s)$

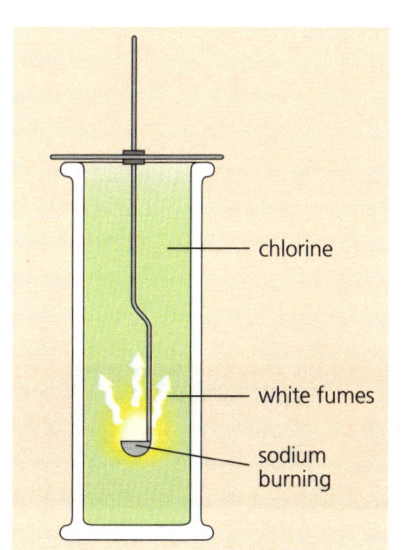

A small piece of alkali metal is heated in the bowl of a combustion spoon until it starts to burn. The spoon is then lowered into a gas jar of chlorine (Fig 2). As the alkali metal continues to burn, it combines with the chlorine gas to produce white fumes of sodium chloride that settle as a solid on the cool sides of the gas jar.

Fig 2 Apparatus to show the reaction of an alkali metal (sodium) with chlorine

Uses of alkali metals

There are few uses of alkali metals because of their great reactivities. There are, however, many uses of alkali metal compounds. A small quantity of metallic sodium is used in sodium street lights, which have a characteristic orange colour. Sodium is used as a coolant in some nuclear power stations. It is a good conductor of heat and removes heat from the reactor.

35 Noble gases

In this unit you will learn the answer to this question:
■ What are noble gases and what are they used for?

The noble gases are a family of unreactive gases placed in group 0 of the Periodic Table.

These gases were not known in 1869 when Mendeleev devised the Periodic Table (Unit 32) and had to be added later. These gases occur in the atmosphere, sometimes, as in the case of argon, in fairly large amounts. The reason they were not discovered earlier was their great unreactivity.

helium	He
neon	Ne
argon	Ar
krypton	Kr
xenon	Xe
radon	Rn

History of the discovery of the noble gases

In 1894, Lord Rayleigh was accurately measuring the densities of common gases. He produced several samples of nitrogen from different chemicals and, within the limits of experimental error, obtained a value for the density of nitrogen of 1.2505 g per dm³ at 0°C and atmospheric pressure.

Fig 1 Lord Rayleigh (1842 – 1919)

However, he also prepared samples of nitrogen from the air by removing oxygen, water vapour and carbon dioxide. The density of nitrogen prepared in this way was always 1.2575 g per dm³ under the same conditions.

Fig 2 William Ramsay (1852 – 1916)

In order to solve this mystery, Lord Rayleigh enlisted the help of William Ramsay. Ramsay was a young Professor of Chemistry at University College London. Ramsay believed that the reason for the difference in density was the presence of a heavier gas in the nitrogen obtained from the air, and within a few months he had proved this to be correct.

Nitrogen is an unreactive gas but it will react with burning magnesium to form solid magnesium nitride:

$$3Mg\,(s) + N_2\,(g) \rightarrow Mg_3N_2\,(s)$$

Magnesium was used to remove the nitrogen from a sample of nitrogen made from the air. The gas that resulted did not react with magnesium and produced an entirely different spectrum from nitrogen. This, together with experiments carried out by Rayleigh, confirmed the presence of a new element called argon in 1894.

Fig 3 The spectrum of the Sun, analysis of which led to the discovery of helium

In another experiment, a gas was obtained from heating certain uranium minerals, and this was also, like argon, very inert. It was found to be identical to the element helium, first discovered in spectroscopic examination of light from the Sun (Fig 3). Later other noble gases were obtained by careful fractional distillation of liquid air by M. W. Travers.

Ramsay's discoveries brought him international fame. In 1904 he was awarded the Nobel prize for Chemistry. In the same year Rayleigh received the Nobel prize for Physics.

C Patterns of behaviour

Reactions of noble gases

Until about forty years ago it was believed that noble gases did not react with other chemicals under any conditions. However, it is now possible to form a number of noble gas compounds. The first one, xenon tetrafluoride, XeF_4, was discovered by accident. A mixture of xenon and fluorine was passed through a heated nickel tube. When the resulting gases were cooled, white crystals of xenon tetrafluoride were formed.

$$Xe\,(g) + 2F_2\,(g) \rightarrow XeF_4\,(s)$$

Q1 Why is a compound between xenon and fluorine more likely than compounds between neon and fluorine or xenon and iodine?

Uses of noble gases

Helium is used for filling weather balloons and airships. It is denser than hydrogen and therefore is not as good as hydrogen for lifting balloons. Its main advantage is that it is not flammable and can be used safely without fire risks.

Nitrogen dissolved in the blood under pressure can cause a severe condition called diver's bends when a diver comes back to the surface. To avoid this, nitrogen is not used in a diver's breathing apparatus. A diver's breathing apparatus contains a mixture of helium and oxygen.

Neon is used to fill light tubes for advertising signs. The tubes are filled with neon at low pressure and an electric spark is passed through the tube.

Argon and argon/nitrogen mixtures are used to fill electric light bulbs. The tungsten filament is heated by an electric current until it glows. Oxygen must not be inside the bulb or the filament will burn out.

Krypton and xenon are used in special bulbs for lighthouses and projectors.

Radon is a radioactive gas and is used in the treatment of cancers.

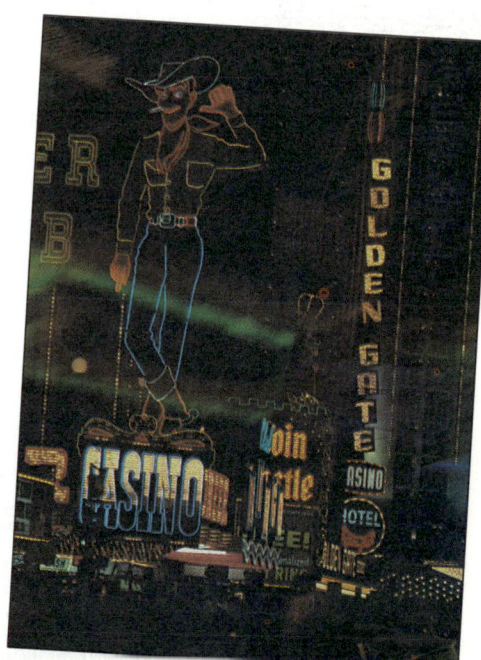

Fig 4 *Neon is used to fill the light tubes for advertising signs*

Fig 5 *Lighthouses use special bulbs which contain krypton and xenon*

36 The halogens – 1

In this unit you will learn the answers to these questions:
- What are the halogen elements and where can they be found in the Periodic Table?
- How do the physical properties such as melting and boiling point change down group VII?
- How does the reactivity of halogens decrease down group VII?

The halogens are a family of reactive non-metallic elements placed in group VII of the Periodic Table.

fluorine	F
chlorine	Cl
bromine	Br
iodine	I
astatine	At

The table contains information about the halogens.

Element	Atomic number	Melting point (°C)	Boiling point (°C)	Density at room temperature and atmospheric pressure/g per dm³	Appearance at room temperature and atmospheric pressure
fluorine F	9	−220	−188	1.58	colourless gas
chlorine Cl	17	−101	−34	2.99	greenish-yellow gas
bromine Br	35	−7	58	3.12	dark red liquid
iodine I	53	114	183	4.94	black shiny solid
astatine At	85				

Although the halogens show similarities to one another in physical and chemical properties, there is a gradual change down the group. All of the halogens have simple molecular structures with diatomic molecules, i.e. Cl_2, Br_2, I_2. The covalent bonds are strong but the bonds between separate molecules are weak. The molecules are therefore easily separated and so their boiling points are relatively low.

Q1 Use the table to predict the physical properties of astatine.

As we move down the group, the halogen molecules get heavier and larger. Therefore, from fluorine to iodine, they are gradually more difficult to melt and vaporise. This is shown by their increasing melting and boiling points.

Reactions of halogens with water

The table summarises the reactions of halogens with cold water.

Halogen	Reaction with cold water
fluorine	Violent reaction with cold water forming oxygen and hydrogen fluoride gases. $2F_2 + 2H_2O \rightarrow 4HF + O_2$
chlorine	Forms a mixture of hydrochloric acid and hypochlorous acid. The solution is strongly acidic and a strong bleach. $Cl_2 + H_2O \rightarrow HCl + HOCl$
bromine	Forms a solution of hydrobromic acid and hypobromous acid. The solution is acidic and a bleach.
iodine	Only reacts slightly with water. Very slightly acidic and a mild bleach.

These reactions clearly show a decrease in reactivity down the group.

Q2 Suggest how astatine would react with cold water.

C Patterns of behaviour

Reactions of halogens with metals

The word 'halogen' means salt-producer. All halogens react with metals to produce salts. For example, sodium burns in chlorine to form sodium chloride (see Unit 34):

sodium + chlorine ➡ sodium chloride
2Na (s) + Cl_2 (g) ➡ 2NaCl (s)

In similar reactions, fluorine forms fluorides, bromine forms bromides and iodine forms iodides. The table shows the reactivity of halogens with hot iron.

Halogen	Reaction with hot iron
chlorine	reacts rapidly to form iron(III) chloride iron + chlorine ➡ iron(III) chloride 2Fe (s) + $3Cl_2$ (g) ➡ $2FeCl_3$ (s)
bromine	reacts slowly iron + bromine ➡ iron(III) bromide 2Fe (s) + $3Br_2$ (g) ➡ $2FeBr_3$ (s)
iodine	reacts very slowly iron + iodine ➡ iron(III) iodide 2Fe (s) + $3I_2$ (g) ➡ $2FeI_3$ (s)

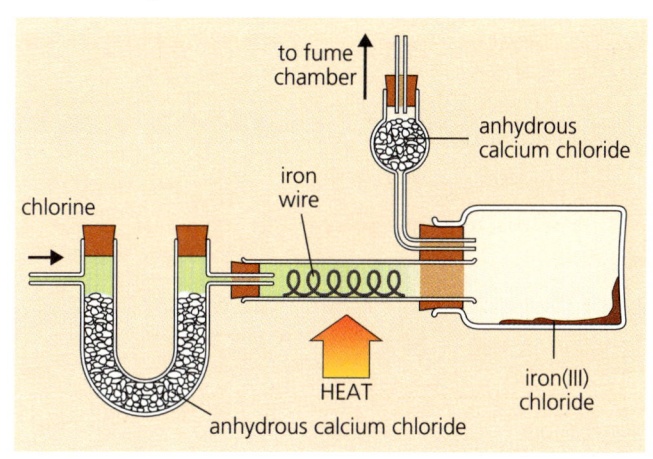

Fig 1 shows apparatus which can be used to produce iron(III) chloride from iron and dry chlorine.

Fig 1 Preparation of iron(III) chloride

Q3 Write a word and symbol equation for the reaction of aluminium and chlorine to produce aluminium chloride, $AlCl_3$.

Reactions of halogens with hydrogen

The reactions of halogens with hydrogen clearly show the differences in reactivity of the halogens.

Mixtures of fluorine and hydrogen react explosively to produce hydrogen fluoride.

hydrogen + fluorine ➡ hydrogen fluoride
H_2 (g) + F_2 (g) ➡ 2HF (g)

Chlorine and hydrogen can be mixed together without reaction providing they are kept in the dark. In sunlight they react together explosively.

hydrogen + chlorine ➡ hydrogen chloride
H_2 (g) + Cl_2 (g) ➡ 2HCl (g)

Mixtures of bromine and hydrogen react together on heating to produce hydrogen bromide.

hydrogen + bromine ➡ hydrogen bromide
H_2 (g) + Br_2 (g) ➡ 2HBr (g)

Iodine and hydrogen only react partially when they are heated.

hydrogen + iodine ⇌ hydrogen iodide
H_2 (g) + I_2 (g) ⇌ 2HI (g)

From these reactions the order of reactivity can be established.

most reactive
fluorine
chlorine
bromine
iodine
least reactive

37 The halogens – 2

In this unit you will learn the answers to these questions:
- What are displacement reactions?
- How can hydrochloric acid be produced from sodium chloride?
- What are the uses of fluorine, chlorine, bromine and iodine?

In Unit 36 we saw that the order of reactivity of the halogens is:

This was established by the reactivity of halogens with hydrogen, water and metals. The order can be confirmed by looking at displacement reactions of halogens.

most reactive
fluorine
chlorine
bromine
iodine
least reactive

Displacement reactions of halogens

If chlorine gas is passed through colourless potassium iodide solution, the solution turns brown as free iodine forms.

potassium iodide + chlorine → potassium chloride + iodine
$2KI\ (aq)\ +\ Cl_2\ (g)\ →\ 2KCl\ (aq)\ +\ I_2\ (aq)$

This reaction occurs because chlorine is more reactive than iodine and replaces it in the potassium iodide. Iodine is displaced.

A similar reaction takes place when chlorine is bubbled through potassium bromide solution. A red solution containing bromine is produced.

Q1 What are the products of the reaction between bromine and potassium iodide solution?

$2KBr\ (aq)\ +\ Cl_2\ (g)\ →\ 2KCl\ (aq)\ +\ Br_2\ (aq)$

No reaction occurs when chlorine is bubbled through potassium fluoride solution as chlorine is less reactive than fluorine.

A displacement reaction is important in the extraction of bromine from sea water. Chlorine is bubbled through a concentrated sea water solution, rich in bromide. A displacement reaction takes place to produce bromine.

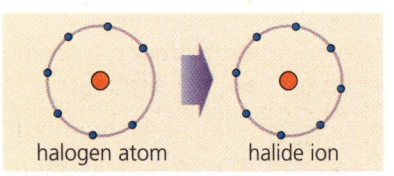

halogen atom → halide ion

The high reactivity of halogens compared to many other elements can be related to electronic structure. All halogens, in group VII of the Periodic Table, have seven electrons in their outer shell. This is one electron less than the stable electron arrangements of noble gases. Therefore all halogens gain one electron to form an ion with a single negative charge (e.g. F^-, Cl^-, Br^-).

As we go down the group the atoms become larger and less able to attract electrons. The reactivity therefore decreases.

Halogen	Electron arrangement in Atom	Ion		
fluorine	2, 7	2, 8	$F + e^- →$	F^-
chlorine	2, 8, 7	2, 8, 8	$Cl + e^- →$	Cl^-
bromine	2, 8, 18, 7	2, 8, 18, 8	$Br + e^- →$	Br^-

Hydrogen halides

When concentrated sulphuric acid is added to sodium chloride a colourless, steamy gas is produced, as shown on the next page.

C Patterns of behaviour

sodium chloride + conc. sulphuric acid → sodium hydrogensulphate + hydrogen chloride

$NaCl(s) + H_2SO_4(l) \rightarrow NaHSO_4(s) + HCl(g)$

This gas turns damp blue litmus paper red. The gas dissolves well in water to form a colourless solution.

This apparatus can be used to produce a solution of the gas in water.

The table shows the properties of the aqueous solution.

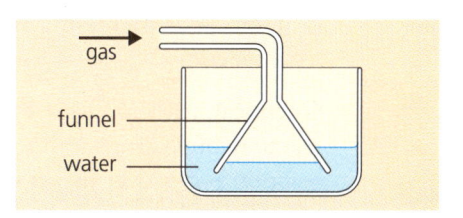

Test	Observations	Conclusions
Test pH with Universal Indicator	Red	pH 1
Add magnesium ribbon	Fizzes. Colourless gas burns with a squeaky pop	Gas is hydrogen
Add sodium carbonate	Fizzes. Colourless gas turns limewater milky	Carbon dioxide gas
Test conductivity of solution	Solution conducts electricity	Solution contains ions
Test for chloride ions – acidify with dilute nitric acid and add silver nitrate solution	White precipitate	Chloride present

The results of these tests confirm that the aqueous solution produced is hydrochloric acid.

Q2 A solution of dry hydrogen chloride in dry methylbenzene turns Universal Indicator green and gives no gas with magnesium ribbon or sodium carbonate. Suggest a reason for these observations.

Testing for chlorides, bromides and iodides

A solution suspected of containing chloride, bromide or iodide is acidified with dilute nitric acid, and silver nitrate solution is added. If a chloride is present a *white* precipitate of silver chloride is formed, e.g.

$Ag^+ (aq) + Cl^- (aq) \rightarrow AgCl (s)$ (white)

If bromide is present, a *cream* precipitate of silver bromide is formed. If an iodide is present, a *yellow* precipitate of silver iodide is formed.

Q3 Write ionic equations for the tests for bromide and iodide.

Uses of halogens

- **Fluorine** is used in the form of fluorides in toothpastes and drinking water, as it hardens the enamel on teeth and reduces tooth decay. Fluorine is used to make PTFE (Unit 17) for non-stick coatings on saucepans.
- **Chlorine** is used in making household bleaches. It is used to kill bacteria and viruses in drinking water and swimming pools. Chlorine is also used to make PVC (Unit 17) which is used in furniture etc.
- **Bromine** is used in making fire-retardant materials, disinfectants and medicines.
- **Iodine** is used in medicines, disinfectants and photographic chemicals. Radioactive iodine is used as a medical tracer.

38 Rates of chemical reactions – 1

In this unit you will learn the answers to these questions:
- What is meant by rate of reaction?
- What is the relationship between rate and time?
- How does increasing surface area (decreasing particle size) affect the rate of a reaction?

Chemical reactions can take place at different speeds. An explosion, such as the reaction of hydrogen and oxygen together to produce water vapour, is a very fast reaction – it is over in a tiny fraction of a second. The rusting of iron and the souring of milk are slow reactions.

A reaction which is over in a fraction of a second is a very fast reaction. We say it has a **high rate of reaction**. As the time taken for the reaction to be completed increases, the rate of reaction decreases. That is:

$$\text{rate of reaction} \propto \frac{1}{\text{time}}$$

Altering the rate of reaction

From everyday experience we know that changing the conditions can alter the time a reaction takes. For example, cooling milk in a refrigerator slows down the souring process. It is difficult to study very fast reactions or very slow reactions. It is better to study reactions which progress steadily and where changes in rate of reaction can be clearly seen. Then it is possible to identify factors which alter the rate of reaction and possibly try to explain why.

Effect of particle size on the rate of reaction

Calcium carbonate reacts with dilute hydrochloric acid as follows:

calcium carbonate + hydrochloric acid → calcium chloride + water + carbon dioxide

$$CaCO_3 (s) + 2HCl (aq) \rightarrow CaCl_2 (aq) + H_2O (l) + CO_2 (g)$$

Fig 1 shows a flask containing calcium carbonate and dilute hydrochloric acid. The progress of the reaction can be followed in several ways, including:

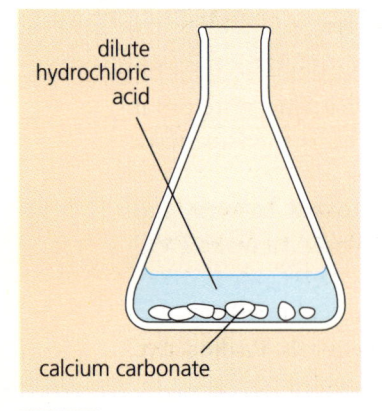

1. measuring the volume of carbon dioxide produced at regular intervals;

2. measuring the total mass of the container, calcium carbonate and hydrochloric acid at intervals. Remember that the carbon dioxide escapes from the container during the reaction.

Fig 1 Calcium carbonate and dilute hydrochloric acid

C Patterns of behaviour

Fig 2a shows how the gas can be collected in a gas syringe and its volume measured at intervals. Fig 2b shows how the loss of mass can be measured using a top-pan balance.

Q1 What is the job of the cotton wool in Fig 2b?

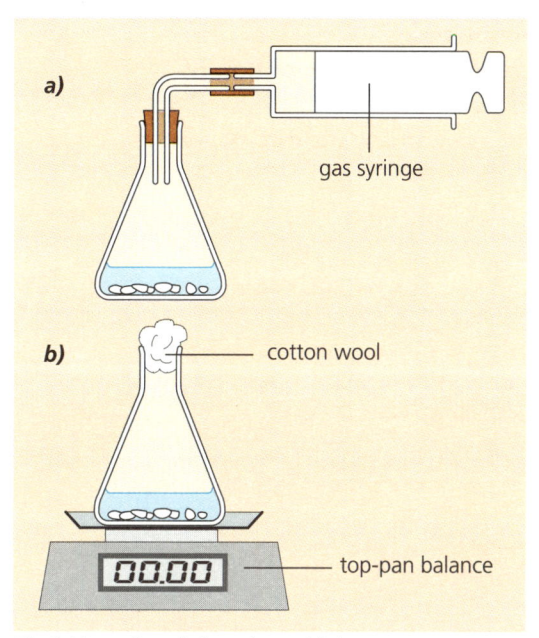

Fig 2 Measuring **a)** the volume, **b)** the mass

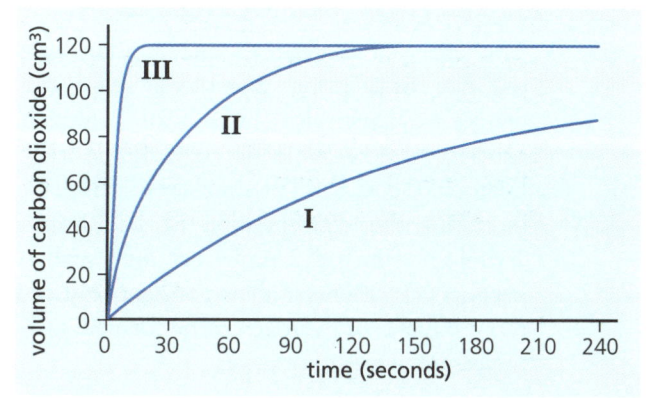

Fig 3 Reactions of different samples of calcium carbonate with dilute hydrochloric acid

Fig 3 shows graphs which were obtained when three samples of calcium carbonate reacted with the same volume of dilute hydrochloric acid of the same concentration and the same temperature. All possible variables were kept constant apart from the surface area. The three samples of calcium carbonate used were:

I 1.00 g of large lumps of marble (calcium carbonate);
II 1.00 g of small lumps of marble (calcium carbonate);
III 1.00 g of powdered calcium carbonate.

Powdered calcium carbonate has a much larger surface area than the small lumps which, in turn, have a much larger surface area than the large lumps.

Although lumps of coal do not react with oxygen in the air without heating, mixtures of coal dust and air can be explosive.

Q2 At the end of each experiment some calcium carbonate remains in the flask. What does this tell you about the contents of the flask at the end of the experiment?

Q3 Use Fig 3. After how many seconds is the reaction with small lumps complete?

Why decreasing particle size speeds up a reaction

Fig 4 shows the effect of particle size on the rate of the reaction. In Fig 4a the square represents a large lump of marble. In Fig 4b the small squares represent the same mass of marble in smaller pieces. There is a larger surface area with small lumps so the hydrochloric acid can come into contact with the marble more easily.

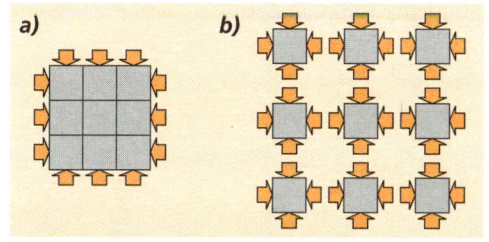

Fig 4 The effect of particle size on the rate of reaction

101

39 Rates of chemical reactions – 2

In this unit you will learn the answers to these questions:
- How is the rate of reaction affected by increasing the concentration of a reactant?
- How does increasing the pressure of reactant gases affect the rate of reaction?
- How does light affect some reactions?

Effect of concentration

The effect of increasing concentration on the rate of reaction is relatively easy to predict qualitatively. From the simple experiment between magnesium ribbon and hydrochloric acid in Fig 1 it can be seen that increasing the concentration of acid from 1 mole per dm^3 to 2 moles per dm^3, while keeping all other variables constant, causes more bubbles of hydrogen to be formed, i.e. increases the rate of reaction.

It is not possible to be sure of a quantitative relationship without carrying out experimental studies. In some cases, doubling the concentration of one of the reactants doubles the rate of reaction. However, it is possible to find reactions where increasing the concentration of one of the reactants has no effect at all on the rate of the reaction.

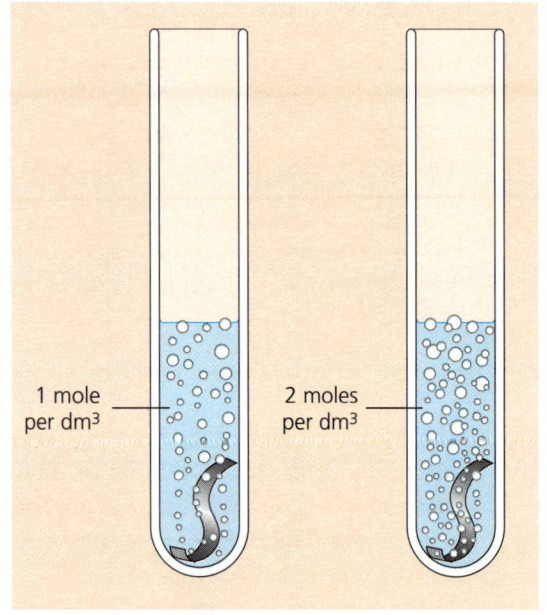

Fig 1 Increasing the concentration of acid causes more hydrogen to be formed

The reaction of magnesium and hydrochloric acid proceeds according to the equation:

magnesium + hydrochloric acid ➡ magnesium chloride + hydrogen
$Mg\ (s)$ + $2HCl\ (aq)$ ➡ $MgCl_2\ (aq)$ + $H_2\ (g)$

Equal lengths of magnesium ribbon, ensuring that equal masses were used, were added to 40 cm^3 hydrochloric acid of different concentrations. The length of time was measured for the magnesium to react with the hydrochloric acid and disappear. This is the end of the reaction because one of the reactants has been used up. The results are shown in the table.

Experiment	Concentration of acid/mole per dm^3	Time/seconds
A	0.5	500
B	0.7	250
C	0.8	160
D	1.0	100
E	1.5	30

Clearly, increasing the concentration of hydrochloric acid speeds up the reaction, i.e. increases the rate of reaction.

C Patterns of behaviour

Effect of pressure

Fig 2a shows a diagram of particles of two gases mixed together. They are going to react. The collisions between ● and ○ may lead to a reaction to form molecules ●○. Not all of the collisions will lead to a reaction, as only a fraction of the collisions will have sufficient energy. There will also be collisions between ○ and ○, and between ● and ●. Neither of these will lead to a reaction.

In Fig 2b there are more particles of the two gases, i.e. there is a greater concentration, and, as a result, there will be more collisions per second. With the same fraction of collisions leading to a reaction, the reaction between ● and ○ will be faster.

In the case of gases only, concentration and pressure are two ways of expressing similar things. When a gas is at a high pressure the molecules are close together, i.e. the concentration is high.

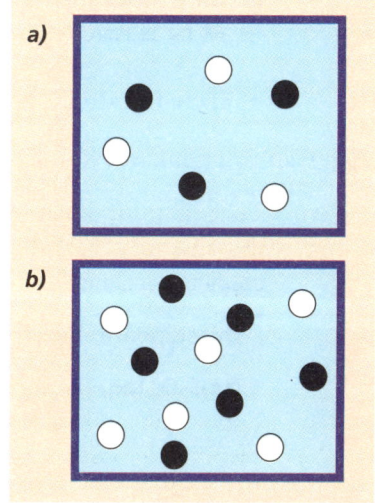

Fig 2 *Effect of pressure on the rate of reaction*

Effect of light

Some reactions are speeded up by light. For example, the reaction of hydrogen and chlorine is explosive in sunlight but only slow in the dark. In the case of this reaction, the sunlight breaks some of the chlorine molecules into **free atoms** and these react with hydrogen molecules. This is summarised in Fig 3.

Q1 Hydrogen molecules and chlorine molecules are represented by (H–H) and (Cl–Cl).

What do (H•) and (Cl•) represent?

Q2 Why is the reaction speeded up in sunlight?

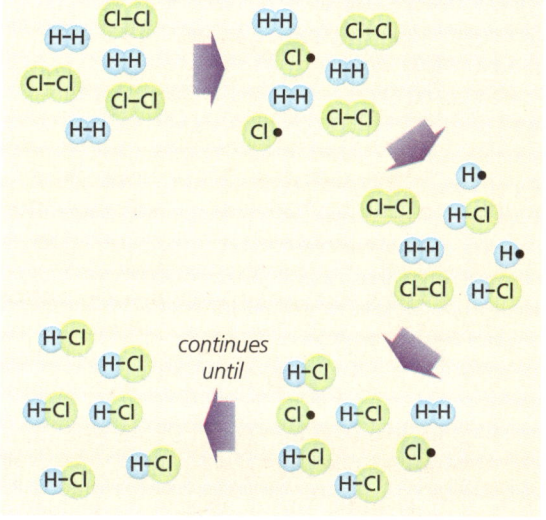

Fig 3 *Effect of sunlight on the reaction of hydrogen and chlorine*

Another reaction which is affected in a similar way is the decomposition of silver chloride or silver bromide. When silver chloride is freshly precipitated it is white in colour.

silver nitrate + sodium chloride ➡ silver chloride + sodium nitrate
$AgNO_3$ (aq) + NaCl (aq) ➡ AgCl (s) + $NaNO_3$ (aq)

When this is left to stand in sunlight, the precipitate partially decomposes into silver and chlorine and turns purplish. Silver bromide behaves in a similar way. This type of decomposition of silver compounds by light is the basis of photography.

103

40 Rates of chemical reactions – 3

In this unit you will learn the answers to these questions:
- How does increasing temperature affect the rate of reaction?
- Why is reaction rate affected in this way by increasing temperature?

Effect of temperature

Q1 Can you think of everyday examples where reactions are speeded up or slowed down by changing temperature?

The effect of temperature on the rate of a reaction can be studied using the reaction between sodium thiosulphate solution and dilute hydrochloric acid.

sodium thiosulphate + dilute hydrochloric acid → sodium chloride + water + sulphur + sulphur dioxide

$$Na_2S_2O_3 (aq) + 2HCl (aq) \rightarrow 2NaCl (aq) + H_2O (l) + S (s) + SO_2 (g)$$

When sodium thiosulphate solution and dilute hydrochloric acid are mixed, the solution goes cloudy. Eventually, it is not possible to see a cross through the beaker (Fig 1).

Q2 Why does the solution turn cloudy?

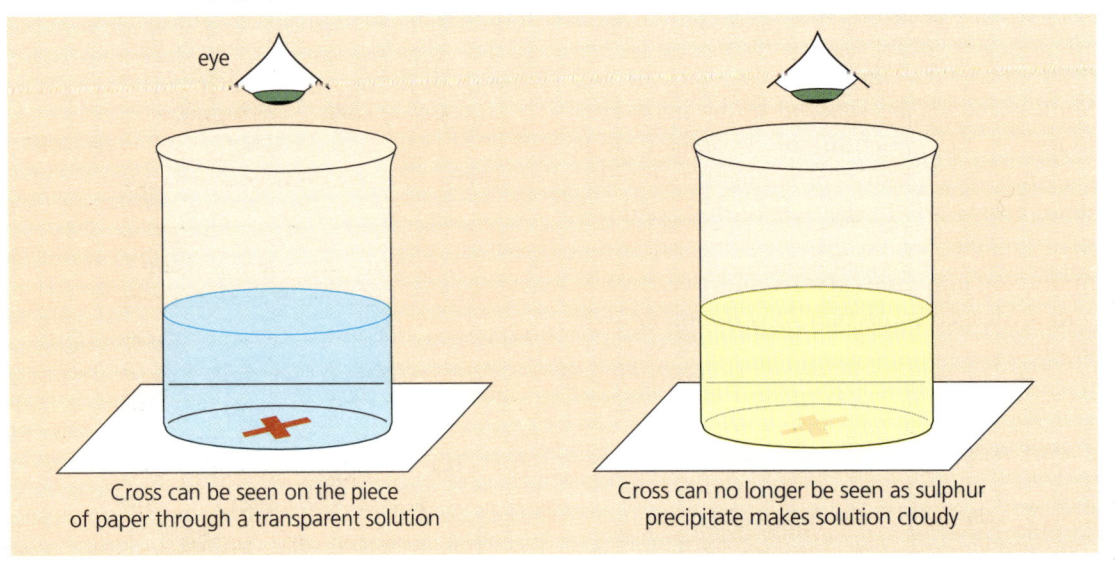

Cross can be seen on the piece of paper through a transparent solution

Cross can no longer be seen as sulphur precipitate makes solution cloudy

Fig 1 Reaction between sodium thiosulphate solution and dilute hydrochloric acid causes the solution to become cloudy

In an experiment to investigate the effect of temperature on the rate of reaction, the volumes and concentrations of the sodium thiosulphate solution and dilute hydrochloric acid are kept the same. Only the temperature is changed. The time is measured until the cross just disappears from view through the beaker.

Temperature/°C	Time for the cross to disappear/seconds
20	280
30	132
40	60
50	33
60	18

We can see from the results that the time taken for the cross to disappear decreases as the temperature of the solutions rises.

C Patterns of behaviour

Q3 A student carrying out this experiment recorded times as 4.40 min, 2.12 min, 1 min, 0.33 min and 0.18 min. Why are the results wrong?

Q4 It is often said that raising the temperature of a reaction by 10°C doubles the rate of reaction. Do these results support this general statement?

Why does raising the temperature speed up a reaction?

Fig 2 shows the particles of two gases mixed together. These particles are moving rapidly in all directions. Millions of collisions between particles will occur each second and some of these collisions will lead to a reaction. The 'successful' collisions are the ones where the particles hit 'head-on' and the particles contain high energy.

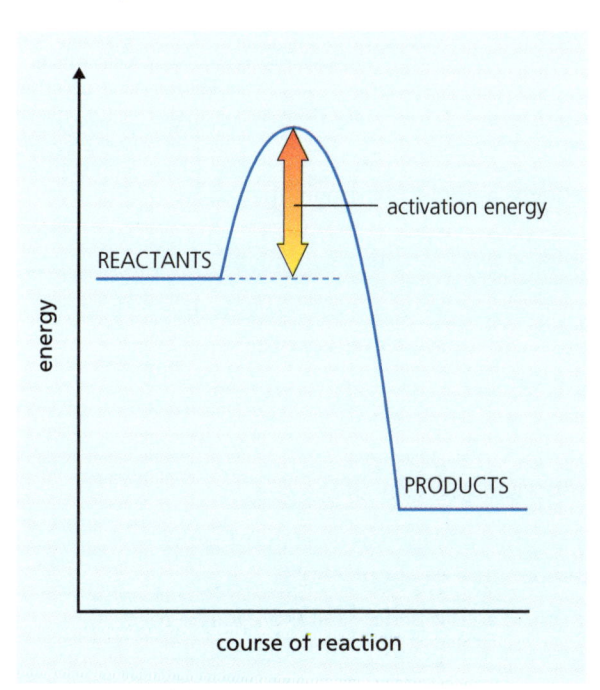

Fig 2 Raising the temperature speeds up a reaction

Fig 3 shows an energy level diagram which summarises the energy changes in a chemical reaction. The reaction is **exothermic** because the energy of the reactants is greater than the energy of the products. This extra energy is given out to the surroundings. There is an energy barrier, called the **activation energy**, which particles have to get over before a reaction can take place.

Fig 3 Energy level diagram

Raising the temperature of the mixture of gases will increase the average speed (and energy) of the particles in the mixture of gases. This has two effects.

1 If the particles are speeded up, there will be more collisions per second.

2 More of the collisions will possess the activation energy necessary for a reaction to take place.

41 Rates of chemical reactions – 4

In this unit you will learn the answers to these questions:
■ What is a catalyst?
■ How does a catalyst operate?

Catalysts

> A catalyst is a substance which alters the rate of a chemical reaction without being used up. The mass of catalyst remains unchanged throughout the reaction.

If a jet of hydrogen gas is directed at a piece of platinum gauze, a reaction takes place between the hydrogen and oxygen from the air, forming water. The gauze glows hot and acts as a **catalyst**.

Decomposition of hydrogen peroxide

Hydrogen peroxide decomposes very slowly at room temperature into water and oxygen.

hydrogen peroxide ➡ water + oxygen
$2H_2O_2 (aq)$ ➡ $2H_2O (l)$ + $O_2 (g)$

A wide variety of substances will speed up the decomposition of hydrogen peroxide. One of these substances is manganese(IV) oxide. Fig 1 shows the volume of gas collected at intervals when:

1. no manganese(IV) oxide is added to the hydrogen peroxide;
2. one spatula measure of manganese(IV) oxide is added to hydrogen peroxide.

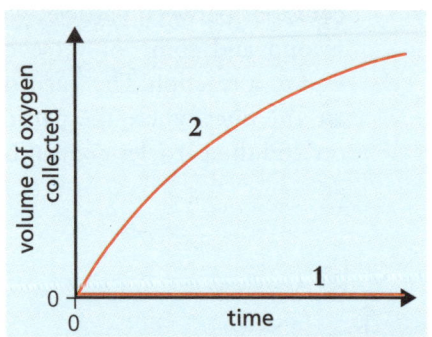

Fig 1 Volume of oxygen collected from hydrogen peroxide

> **Q1** Draw a diagram of apparatus which could be used for this experiment.
>
> **Q2** In order to be sure that the difference in the volume of gas produced is due only to the manganese(IV) oxide, various factors have to be kept the same. List the factors which should be kept the same.

Examples of catalysis

There are many examples of catalysis in industry and everyday life.

1. In the Haber process (Unit 44), finely divided iron is used as a catalyst for the reaction of nitrogen and hydrogen at a temperature of about 450°C.
2. In the Contact process (Unit 45), vanadium(V) oxide pellets act as a catalyst for the reaction of sulphur dioxide and oxygen at a temperature of about 450°C.
3. In the manufacture of nitric acid (Unit 50), a platinum–rhodium gauze acts as a catalyst in the first stage when ammonia and oxygen react together to form nitrogen monoxide and steam.
4. In the manufacture of margarine, a nickel catalyst is used to aid the reaction of hydrogen with unsaturated oils to form margarine. The temperature is about 140°C.
5. Long-chain hydrocarbons are cracked (Unit 16) when crude oil vapour is passed over a heated ceramic catalyst.

C Patterns of behaviour

6 Catalytic converters are included in car exhaust systems to reduce emissions of carbon monoxide and oxides of nitrogen. The converter contains finely divided platinum.

7 The filler used to make minor body repairs to a car consists of a resin which is hardened by adding a catalyst. This sets in a few minutes to make a material which is so hard it can be sandpapered.

Fig 2 *A catalytic converter from a car*

How a catalyst speeds up a chemical reaction

The following points about catalysts are important to remember.

1 A catalyst does not produce any more of the product, but only the same amount at a faster rate.

2 The mass of catalyst remains unchanged at the end of the reaction.

3 Catalysts are often finely divided powders, pellets and fine gauzes.

4 Catalysts are often transition metals or transition metal compounds.

> **Q3** Explain why usually only a small mass of catalyst is required to convert large masses of reactants into products.
>
> **Q4** Catalysts are often finely divided powders, pellets and fine gauzes. What does this suggest about the way that some catalysts work?

Many catalysts act via an **intermediate compound**, using the fact that transition metals can show variable oxidation states. Let us take the decomposition of hydrogen peroxide using manganese(IV) oxide as an example of the intermediate compound theory. The reaction takes place in two steps.

Step 1 Hydrogen peroxide oxidises manganese(IV) oxide to manganese(VII) oxide.

$$2H_2O_2 + 2MnO_2 + [O] \rightarrow Mn_2O_7 + 2H_2O$$

Step 2 The manganese(VII) oxide then decomposes into manganese(IV) oxide and oxygen.

$$Mn_2O_7 \rightarrow 2MnO_2 + O_2 + [O]$$

In Unit 40 the energy level diagram was given for an exothermic reaction. In order that the collisions could lead to a reaction, a certain minimum amount of energy was required – called the activation energy. A catalyst lowers this activation energy (Fig 3). This means that more collisions will now lead to a reaction and so the reaction will be faster.

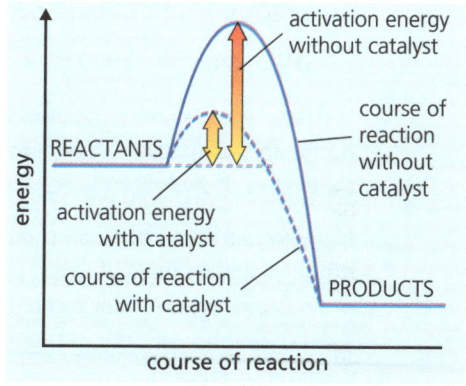

Fig 3 *Effect of a catalyst on the activation energy*

Inhibitors

Sometimes it is necessary to slow down reactions by adding negative catalysts or **inhibitors**. For example, sulphur dioxide is added to lemon juice to stop it oxidising and going bad. Phosphoric acid is added to hydrogen peroxide to slow down its decomposition.

42 Enzymes

In this unit you will learn the answers to these questions:
- What are enzymes?
- Under what conditions do enzymes operate?
- What are enzymes used for?

Enzymes are proteins that control vital biological processes. They often act as biological catalysts. In the human body enzymes control the breakdown of food and reactions which make chemicals such as fats, carbohydrates, proteins and DNA. Enzymes are used today in a wide range of industrial processes. These include fermentation (Unit 18), baking, cheese making, tenderising meat and treating leather. The table summarises some of the enzymes used in industrial processes.

Enzyme	Examples of use
α-amylase	stain removal, paper manufacture, making syrups
cellulases	making animal feed from straw
lipases	speeding up the ripening of cheese
proteases	stain removal, making leather pliable, making biscuit flour
catalase	preservative in soft drinks, rubber manufacture
glucose oxidase	preservative in soft drinks, detecting diabetes
pectinase	clearing fruit juices
streptokinase	treating blood clots and bruises

One of the most familiar household uses is in biological washing powders. Although the first biological washing powder was produced in 1913, only in the last twenty years have they been widely used.

Enzyme decomposition of hydrogen peroxide

The enzyme catalase is present in blood to prevent the build-up of dangerous peroxides. If a small piece of liver is added to hydrogen peroxide, a rapid evolution of oxygen is seen.

The catalase acts as a catalyst and speeds up the decomposition of hydrogen peroxide.

$$2H_2O_2 \ (aq) \rightarrow 2H_2O \ (l) + O_2 \ (g)$$

Catalase is an extremely effective catalyst. One molecule of catalase will decompose 40 000 molecules of hydrogen peroxide each second.

However, unlike chemical catalysts, which work under a wide range of conditions, enzymes are only able to work under limited conditions. Fig 1 shows graphs of the effectiveness of some enzymes under different conditions.

Q1 Which two conditions are being varied?

Q2 From the graphs, what conditions would be most effective for the operation of these enzymes?

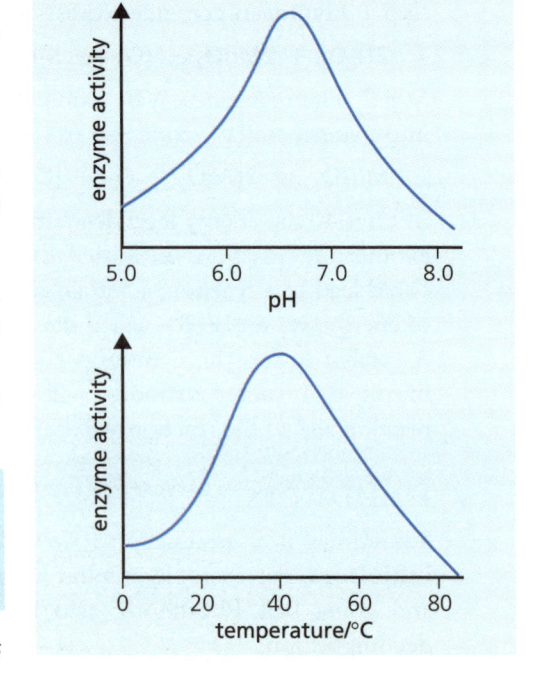

Fig 1 Effectiveness of some enzymes under different conditions

C Patterns of behaviour

How do enzymes work?

You can think of enzyme molecules as pieces of a jig-saw puzzle. In Fig 2, the enzyme molecule will fit together with reactant A but not with reactants B or C. When the enzyme molecule and reactant molecule fit together, a reaction can take place. This is summarised in Fig 3.

Fig 2 *Enzyme molecules are like pieces of a jig-saw puzzle*

Fig 3 *Summary of enzyme action*

enzyme + reactant   'complex'   reaction   enzyme + products

Biological washing powders

Fig 4 shows a label from a biological washing powder.

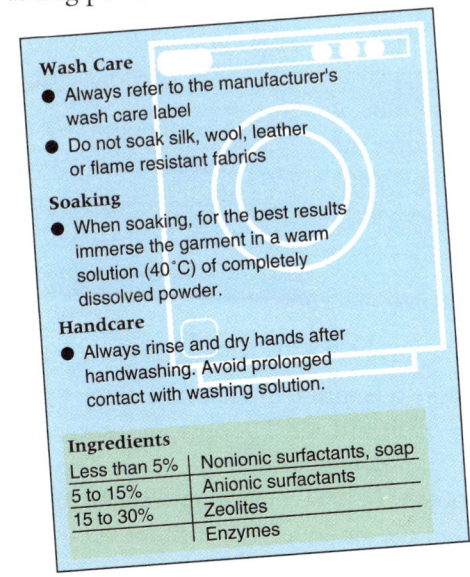

Wash Care
- Always refer to the manufacturer's wash care label
- Do not soak silk, wool, leather or flame resistant fabrics

Soaking
- When soaking, for the best results immerse the garment in a warm solution (40°C) of completely dissolved powder.

Handcare
- Always rinse and dry hands after handwashing. Avoid prolonged contact with washing solution.

Ingredients

Less than 5%	Nonionic surfactants, soap
5 to 15%	Anionic surfactants
15 to 30%	Zeolites
	Enzymes

Q3 Refer to the table (page 108). Which enzymes is the washing powder likely to contain?

Q4 Why should biological washing powders not be used with silk, wool and leather?

Q5 When soaking stains in biological washing powder, why is it better to use water at 40°C rather than hotter water?

Q6 Why should the powder be completely dissolved before the clothes are added?

Q7 Why should the clothes be thoroughly rinsed after washing?

Q8 What effect can biological washing powders have on the skin?

Fig 4 *Biological washing powder*

C1 Air

In this unit you will learn the answers to these questions:
- What is the approximate composition of air?
- How can you find, by experiment, the percentage of oxygen in air by volume?
- How can pure oxygen and nitrogen be obtained from air industrially?
- What are the uses of oxygen and nitrogen?
- What is the 'fire triangle'?

Composition of air

Air is a mixture of gases. Because it is a mixture its composition can vary. The table shows the composition of a typical sample of air, by volume.

Gas	Amount, by volume /%
nitrogen	78
oxygen	21
carbon dioxide	0.3
argon	0.9
helium	0.0005
neon	0.002
krypton	0.0001
xenon	0.00001

Q1 Which of the gases in the table is a compound?

Finding the percentage of oxygen in a sample of air

Oxygen is the reactive gas in the air. If a piece of copper is heated in air, the surface of the copper goes black due to the formation of black copper(II) oxide.

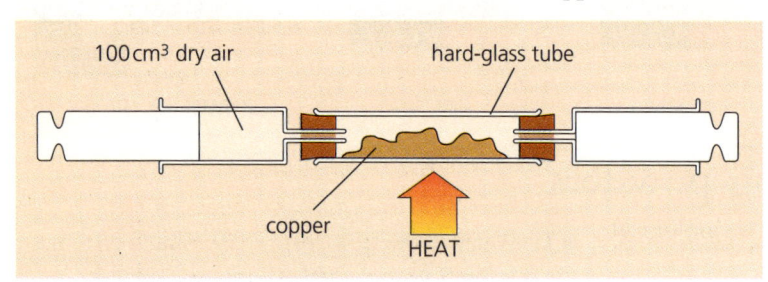

Fig 1 Apparatus used to demonstrate that the proportion of oxygen in air is 20%

In the apparatus in Fig 1, 100 cm³ of dry air is trapped in one gas syringe. The copper in the hard-glass tube is heated and air is passed backwards and forwards over the copper. The apparatus is left to cool to room temperature. If 80 cm³ of gas remain, this means that 20 cm³ have been removed. This is the oxygen removed by the copper. The percentage of oxygen in the air is 20%.

Q2 Write a balanced symbol equation for the reaction of copper with oxygen, O_2, to form copper(II) oxide.

Q3 Does the mass of the copper increase, decrease or stay the same when it reacts with oxygen in the air?

Q4 Why is the apparatus left to cool to room temperature?

Q5 Magnesium is more reactive than copper. Why should magnesium not be used in the experiment instead of copper?

Separating oxygen and nitrogen from air industrially

Oxygen and nitrogen are gases used in large quantities in industry. They can be separated from air by **fractional distillation of liquid air**. The air is first cooled in a refrigeration plant to remove water vapour and carbon dioxide as solids. The air is then compressed to about 150 atm and cooled, by allowing it to expand rapidly. Repeated cooling results in most of the gases in the air liquefying at about −200°C.

C Patterns of behaviour

The table gives the boiling points of the gases remaining in the air.

Gas	Boiling point / °C
nitrogen	–196
oxygen	–183
helium	–269
neon	–246
argon	–186
xenon	–107

Q6 Arrange the six gases in the table in order of increasing boiling point, i.e starting with the gas with the lowest boiling point.

Q7 Which gases in the table will not be liquefied if the air is cooled to –200°C?

The liquid air is then allowed to warm up slowly. Nitrogen boils off before oxygen because it has a lower boiling point. The gases can be separated and stored in cylinders. A fractional distillation factory can separate about 100 tonnes of air a day.

Q8 Why will the factory produce more nitrogen than oxygen?

Uses of oxygen and nitrogen

Oxygen

Pure oxygen (sometimes called Medical grade) is used to help people's breathing. It can revive a patient who has breathing problems after an accident, or during an operation. It is used by mountaineers, divers and pilots of high-flying aircraft.

Oxygen of lower purity is used in industry for steel-making to oxidise unwanted impurities in iron (see Unit 22). It is also used with ethyne (acetylene) in cutting and welding equipment. Ethyne burns in oxygen at a much higher temperature than in air. Oxygen is used to burn the fuel in rockets.

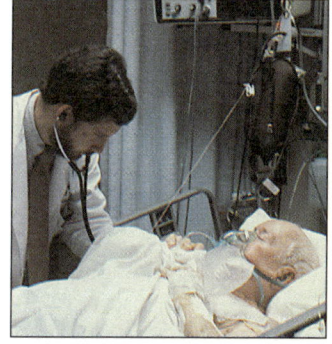

Fig 2 Oxygen being given in a medical emergency

Nitrogen

Much of the nitrogen is used to make ammonia, nitric acid and fertilisers (see Units 44 and 50). Unlike oxygen, which is a reactive gas, nitrogen is unreactive. Many of its uses depend upon its unreactivity. It is used to fill crisp bags. Crisps would spoil if oxygen was present. Liquid nitrogen is used as a refrigerant and for rapid cooling, e.g. freezing and storing embryos and rapid freezing of frozen foods.

The fire triangle

Fig 4 shows a fire triangle. Three things are necessary for a fire to continue to burn – fuel, oxygen (or air) and heat. If one of these is removed the fire will go out.

Fig 3 Human sperm stored in liquid nitrogen

Q9 Why will a fire go out if cold water is poured onto it?

Q10 Why will a fire go out if it is covered with a wet blanket?

Q11 In a forest fire, the firefighters cut down and clear an area of land in front of the fire. Why does this put out the fire?

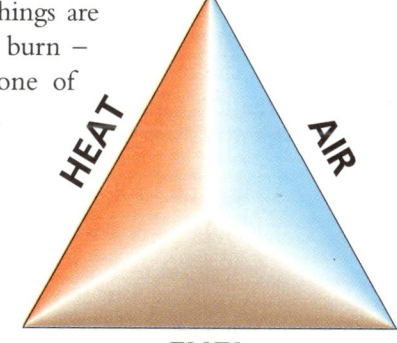

Fig 4

43 Reversible reactions and equilibrium

In this unit you will learn the answers to these questions:
- What are reversible reactions and how is an equilibrium established?
- How can the position of an equilibrium be moved?

Reversible reactions

When magnesium burns in oxygen, solid magnesium oxide is formed.

$$2Mg\,(s) + O_2\,(g) \rightarrow 2MgO\,(s)$$

This reaction cannot be reversed. Many reactions are like this and result in permanent change.

When blue copper(II) sulphate crystals are heated, steam is produced and white anhydrous copper(II) sulphate is formed. If cold water is added to anhydrous copper(II) sulphate, the mixture gets hot and blue copper(II) sulphate is re-formed. This reaction can be summarised by the equation:

copper(II) sulphate + heat $\rightleftharpoons$ anhydrous copper(II) sulphate + water
$CuSO_4.5H_2O\,(s)$ + heat $\rightleftharpoons$ $CuSO_4\,(s)$ + $5H_2O\,(g)$

The $\rightleftharpoons$ sign in the equation shows that the reaction is reversible. A **reversible reaction** is a reaction which can go from left to right or right to left, depending upon the conditions.

Q1 What other examples of reversible reactions can you find?

Reversible reaction of iron and steam

If steam is passed over heated iron, hydrogen and an oxide of iron are formed.

$$3Fe\,(s) + 4H_2O\,(g) \rightarrow Fe_3O_4\,(s) + 4H_2\,(g)$$

If hydrogen gas is passed over heated iron oxide, steam and iron are produced.

$$Fe_3O_4\,(s) + 4H_2\,(g) \rightarrow 3Fe\,(s) + 4H_2O\,(g)$$

Depending upon conditions, the reaction can go in either direction and can be represented by the equation:

$$3Fe\,(s) + 4H_2O\,(g) \rightleftharpoons Fe_3O_4\,(s) + 4H_2\,(g)$$

Equilibrium

If iron and steam are heated at 300°C in a closed metal globe so that the products of the reaction cannot escape, Fig 1 represents the situation inside the globe at the start and at one-day intervals for the first three days.

At first the iron reacts with steam to produce hydrogen and iron oxide. As the masses of hydrogen and iron oxide increase, the reverse reaction becomes possible and speeds up. After one day there is no further change in the masses of iron, iron oxide, steam and hydrogen in the globe, providing no change is made to the conditions.

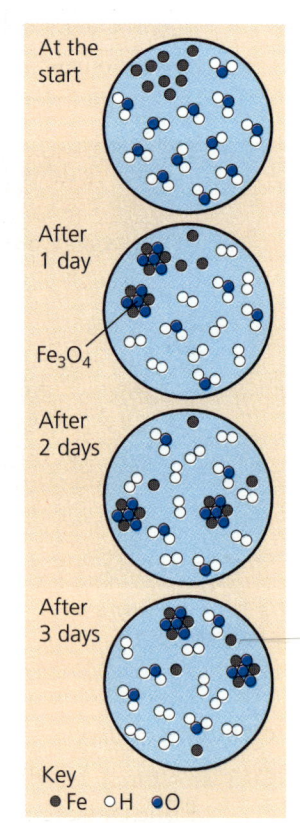

Fig 1 Iron and steam heated at 300°C. The system reaches equilibrium.

C Patterns of behaviour

The reaction has not, however, stopped but is in a system of **equilibrium**. When a system is in equilibrium the forward and reverse reactions are still continuing but both are taking place at the same rate so there is no change in any concentration of reacting substance or product.

Factors affecting an equilibrium

An equilibrium mixture of iron, iron oxide, hydrogen and steam with unchanging concentrations can be disturbed by altering a condition. If the equilibrium moves to produce more iron oxide and hydrogen (i.e. the forward reaction for a time becomes faster than the reverse reaction) the equilibrium is said to move to the right. The system is said to move to the left if the equilibrium changes to produce more iron and steam.

Consider a reaction where **A**, **B**, **C** and **D** represent reacting substances and products:

$$A + B \rightleftharpoons C + D + \text{heat}$$

The forward reaction is **exothermic**, that is, heat is evolved as the forward reaction proceeds. The table shows the changes which affect this equilibrium.

Factor	Type of equilibrium affected	Effect on equilibrium
increase in concentration of A and/or B	any	moves to the right
decrease in concentration of A and/or B	any	moves to the left
increase in concentration of C and/or D	any	moves to the left
decrease in concentration of C and/or D	any	moves to the right
increase in pressure	reactions involving gases	may move to the left, right or remain unchanged (see note 1)
catalyst added	certain reactions only	no change
increase in temperature	exothermic forward reaction endothermic forward reaction	moves to the left moves to the right (see note 2)
decrease in temperature	exothermic forward reaction endothermic forward reaction	moves to the right moves to the left

Notes

1 The resulting change in the equilibrium position when pressure is increased depends on the number of gas molecules on the left-hand side and on the right-hand side of the equation. If there are more molecules on the left-hand side, increasing the pressure moves the equilibrium to the right. For example:

$$2SO_2\,(g) + O_2\,(g) \rightleftharpoons 2SO_3\,(g)$$
3 gas molecules on the LHS   2 gas molecules on the RHS

If there are more gas molecules on the right-hand side, increasing the pressure moves the equilibrium to the left.

If there are equal numbers of gas molecules on both sides of the equation, increasing the pressure has no effect on the equilibrium.

$$3Fe\,(s) + 4H_2O\,(g) \rightleftharpoons Fe_3O_4\,(s) + 4H_2\,(g)$$
4 gas molecules on the LHS   4 gas molecules on the RHS

2 Increasing the temperature helps to establish the equilibrium more quickly. This is because it speeds up both the forward and reverse reactions.

44 The Haber process

In this unit you will learn the answers to these questions:
- What is the Haber process?
- What is the major use of ammonia?

Why is nitrogen important?

Nitrogen is absorbed by plants through the roots as a solution of nitrates. The nitrogen is used to build up proteins in the plants. When plants grow they use up nitrogen and so repeated agricultural use can reduce the yield of crops grown because there is not enough nitrogen in the soil.

> **Q1** When a protein, e.g. milk powder, is mixed with calcium hydroxide (an alkali) and heated, a strong-smelling gas is produced which turns damp red litmus paper blue. This gas is ammonia, NH_3. What does this tell us about the composition of proteins?

To overcome this, farmers used to rely on animal manure and crop rotation. To add to these sources of nitrogen, guano, a natural fertiliser from Chile, was imported. This consisted of the droppings of seabirds. However, these supplies were used up by the beginning of the twentieth century. The famous scientist Sir William Crookes warned that the exhaustion of these deposits rich in nitrogen would lead to worldwide starvation if an alternative could not be found.

A new source of nitrogen compounds was therefore needed for agriculture, and also to meet the demands of the dyeing and explosives industries.

The Haber process

In 1904 the German chemist Fritz Haber suggested that nitrogen from the air and hydrogen from water could be combined together to form ammonia. By 1908 he was able to demonstrate this in the laboratory using high pressures and a catalyst of osmium or uranium. With the help of Carl Bosch, but not without considerable problems of carrying out the process on an industrial scale, he was able to set up large-scale factories using a specially developed iron catalyst.

Ammonia is produced in very large amounts by the Haber process.

Hydrogen is obtained from the cracking of methane or naphtha (Unit 15). Methane and steam are passed over a nickel catalyst at high temperatures and pressures.

methane + steam ➡ carbon monoxide + hydrogen
$CH_4 (g)$ + $H_2O (g)$ ➡ $CO (g)$ + $3H_2 (g)$

Fig 1 Fritz Haber (1868 – 1934). Despite Haber's great scientific advances and his work for his home country, Germany, during the First World War, as a Jew he was forced to escape from Germany in 1933 and finished his life at Cambridge University. He was awarded the Nobel Prize for Chemistry in 1918.

Carbon monoxide is removed from the gas as this would poison the catalyst in the Haber process. The hydrogen is mixed with nitrogen from the air in the ratio of 3 parts of hydrogen to 1 part of nitrogen by volume.

The mixture of nitrogen and hydrogen is compressed and passed over a heated catalyst. The catalyst consists of finely divided iron with promoters to reduce the risk of catalyst poisoning. The catalyst is heated to about 450°C to start the reaction, and

C Patterns of behaviour

then this temperature is maintained because the forward reaction is exothermic. Depending upon the conditions, part of the mixture of nitrogen and hydrogen is converted into ammonia. The equation is:

nitrogen + hydrogen ⇌ ammonia
$N_2 (g)$ + $3H_2 (g)$ ⇌ $2NH_3 (g)$

The mixture of gases, containing ammonia, is cooled and ammonia liquefies and can be separated. The unreacted nitrogen and hydrogen mixture is recycled. The process is summarised in Fig 2.

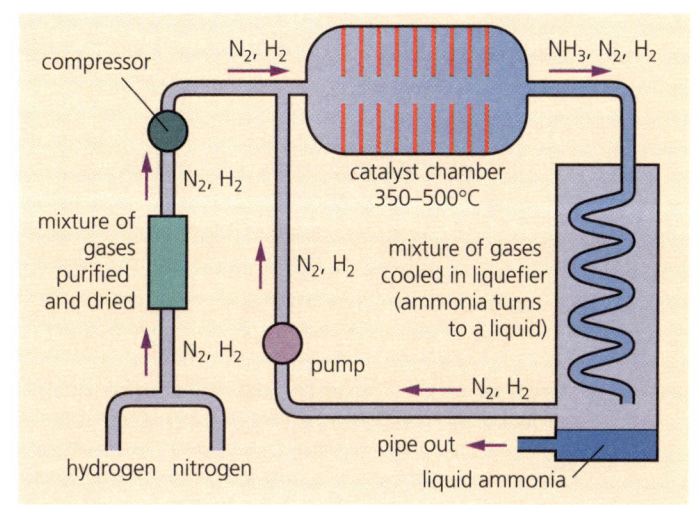

Getting the maximum yield of ammonia

In Unit 43 the conditions required to obtain the maximum yield of products from a system in equilibrium are discussed.

nitrogen + hydrogen ⇌ ammonia + heat
$N_2 (g)$ + $3H_2 (g)$ ⇌ $2NH_3 (g)$ + heat

Fig 2 The Haber process

In the above equilibrium, there are more molecules on the left-hand side than on the right-hand side. An increase in pressure will push the equilibrium to the right, increasing the yield of ammonia. Obviously, there are practical implications to increasing the pressure of the reactants. Increasing the pressure makes the cost of the plant (capital costs) much greater.

The reaction to produce ammonia is exothermic. If the temperature of the surroundings is lowered, the equilibrium will move to the right, evolving more heat to counteract the effect of the decrease in temperature of the surroundings. This produces more ammonia. Lowering the temperature slows down the reactions. It also increases the life of the catalyst.

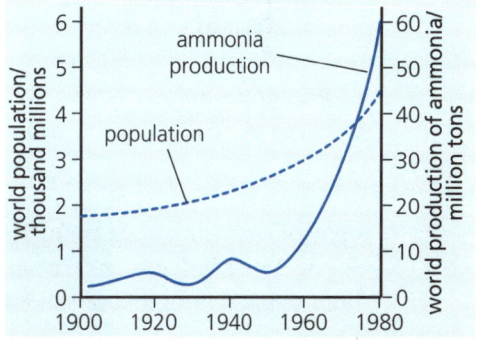

Fig 3 Ammonia production and the growth of population 1900 – 1980

Use of ammonia

Fig 3 shows a graph of the world ammonia production from 1900 to 1980, together with the growth of population. You will see the rapid growth in the mass of ammonia produced. This growth has been due to the development of the Haber process.

Fig 4 shows a pie diagram of the uses of ammonia. You will see that most of the ammonia is turned into fertilisers.

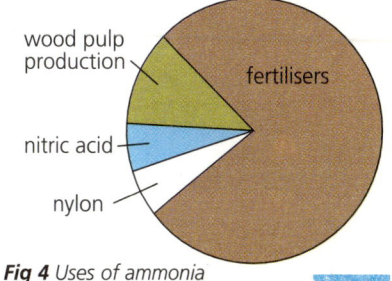

Fig 4 Uses of ammonia

45 The Contact process

In this unit you will learn the answers to these questions:
- What is the Contact process?
- What conditions will produce the best yield of sulphuric acid?
- What are the uses of sulphuric acid?

The Contact process is a process to produce sulphuric acid from sulphur or minerals rich in sulphur. It was first devised in 1831 by Peregrine Phillips and it replaced other processes which produced less pure acid. There are three stages to the process. The second stage involves a reversible reaction, and establishing suitable equilibrium conditions in this stage is a key to producing sulphuric acid economically.

Stage 1
Sulphur dioxide is formed from burning sulphur or minerals rich in sulphur.

sulphur + oxygen ➡ sulphur dioxide
$S(s) + O_2(g) \rightarrow SO_2(g)$

iron pyrites + oxygen ➡ iron oxide + sulphur dioxide
$4FeS_2(s) + 11O_2(g) \rightarrow 2Fe_2O_3(s) + 8SO_2(g)$

The sulphur dioxide produced is then purified to remove impurities such as arsenic which would poison the catalyst. The gas is passed through charged electrostatic plates in the dust precipitators to remove charged dust particles. It is then washed with water and dried.

Stage 2
Sulphur dioxide and air are passed over a heated catalyst in the catalyst chamber.

sulphur dioxide + oxygen (from the air) ⇌ sulphur trioxide + heat
$2SO_2(g) + O_2(g) \rightleftharpoons 2SO_3(g) + heat$

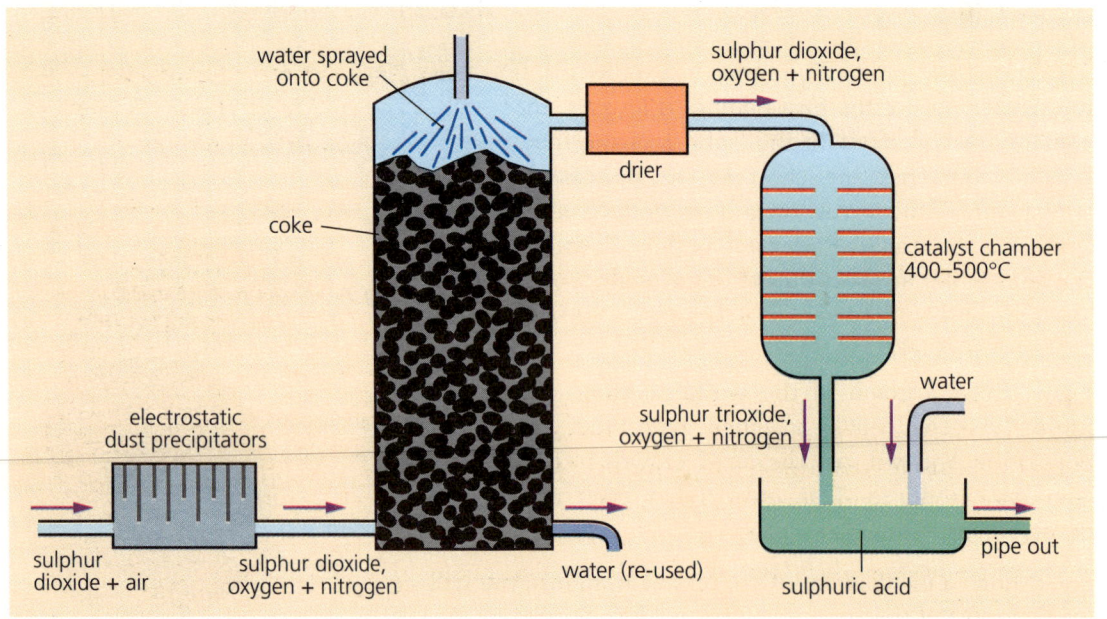

Fig 1 The Contact process

C Patterns of behaviour

A low temperature is suggested from a study of the equilibrium (Unit 43) because the forward reaction is exothermic. At a low temperature there would be a good yield of sulphur trioxide but the reaction would be very slow. A compromise of about 450°C is struck. The catalyst used now is vanadium(V) oxide in the form of pellets. An effective catalyst would be platinum. This is less easily poisoned but is no longer used because it is more expensive.

Increasing the pressure would also produce a larger yield of sulphur trioxide in the resulting equilibrium mixture but, in practice, the extra costs of increasing the pressure outweigh the benefits.

Fig 2 A sulphuric acid plant

Stage 3

The sulphur trioxide is removed from the mixture of gases and converted to sulphuric acid. The sulphur trioxide is not directly dissolved in water because this reaction is too violent on a large scale. Instead, it is dissolved in concentrated sulphuric acid to form oleum (fuming sulphuric acid). This is then diluted with the correct volume of water to make concentrated sulphuric acid.

sulphur trioxide + conc. sulphuric acid ➡ oleum
SO_3 (g) + H_2SO_4 (l) ➡ $H_2S_2O_7$ (l)

oleum + water ➡ conc. sulphuric acid
$H_2S_2O_7$ (l) + H_2O (l) ➡ $2H_2SO_4$ (l)

The overall reaction is:

sulphur trioxide + water ➡ conc. sulphuric acid
SO_3 (g) + H_2O (l) ➡ H_2SO_4 (l)

Because all of the impurities were removed from the gases before reaction, the acid produced is 99.5% pure. Fig 1 summarises the Contact process.

Q1 Why is it more important to control the conditions of stage 2 rather than stages 1 or 3?

Uses of sulphuric acid

Sulphuric acid has a wide range of uses and the amount of sulphuric acid used in a country is certainly a measure of that country's prosperity. Fig 3 shows a pie diagram of the uses of sulphuric acid.

Sulphuric acid is used to make fertilisers such as ammonium sulphate and calcium superphosphate. It is also used to make detergents. Soapless detergents are made by treating hydrocarbons from petroleum refining with concentrated sulphuric acid. Soapless detergents are preferable to soaps for many purposes because they lather well with water without forming any scum.

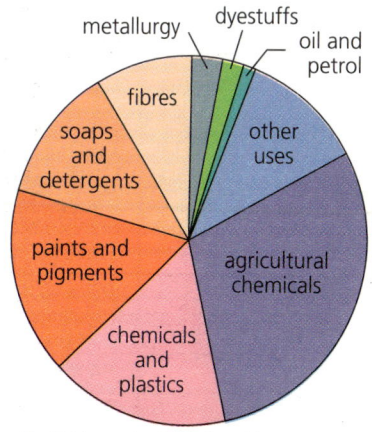

Fig 3 Uses of sulphuric acid

117

C2 Water

In this unit you will learn the answers to these questions:
- Why is it so difficult to keep water pure?
- How does water break down an ionic lattice?
- How does the solubility of gases in water change with increasing temperature and pressure?
- How can we test for water?
- How is water treated before being used in domestic water supplies?
- Why may fluorides be added to water supplies?

Keeping water pure

Water is a very good solvent. It dissolves a wide range of different substances. Most substances will dissolve even if it is only to a small extent. A sample of pure water will dissolve gases from the air and even sodium ions from a glass container. The very good solvent properties of water make it difficult to keep water pure.

Breaking down an ionic lattice

Fig 1 shows a water molecule. Within a water molecule there are slight positive (δ^+) and negative (δ^-) charges caused by a slight movement of electrons on the O—H bond towards the oxygen atom.

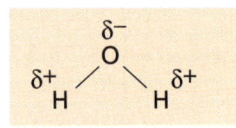

Fig 1 A water molecule

Fig 2 shows how water molecules break down the ionic sodium chloride lattice by pulling ions from the lattice. The negative end of the water molecule pulls on the positive ions in the lattice and the positive end of the water molecule pulls on the negative ions.

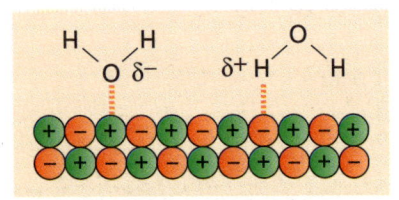

Fig 2 Water pulls ions from an ionic lattice causing the lattice to break up

When the ions are removed from the lattice, they are surrounded by water molecules (Fig 3). This process is called **solvation**.

Fig 3 The ions from the lattice are surrounded by water molecules – they are solvated

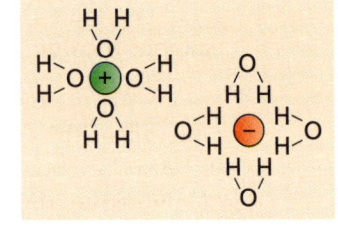

Q1 Breaking up a lattice requires energy. Where does this come from?

Solubility of gases in water

The table shows the solubilities of some gases in water at different temperatures. The figures refer to the mass of gas, in g, dissolving in 100 g of water at 1 atm pressure.

Gas	Temperature / °C				
	0	20	40	60	80
ammonia NH_3	89.5	53.1	30.7		
carbon dioxide CO_2	0.335	0.169	0.097	0.058	
hydrogen H_2	1.92×10^{-4}	1.60×10^{-4}	1.38×10^{-4}	1.18×10^{-4}	0.79×10^{-4}
hydrogen chloride HCl	82.3	72.1	63.3	56.1	
nitrogen N_2	2.94×10^{-3}	1.90×10^{-3}	1.39×10^{-3}	1.05×10^{-3}	
oxygen O_2	6.9×10^{-3}	4.34×10^{-3}	3.08×10^{-3}	2.27×10^{-3}	1.38×10^{-3}

Q2 Which of the gases in the table is least soluble at 20°C?

Q3 How does the solubility of each gas change with increasing temperature?

C Patterns of behaviour

Q4 When water is heated from 20°C to about 80°C, the gases dissolved in it are expelled. How would the composition of this gas differ from normal air?

The mass of a given gas dissolving in water depends upon pressure. The higher the pressure the more gas dissolves. This can be seen when the top is removed from a bottle of cola. Removing the top reduces the pressure and immediately a large number of bubbles of carbon dioxide escape. This carbon dioxide dissolves under pressure but does not dissolve at normal atmospheric pressure.

Tests for water

The presence of water in a liquid can be shown using either cobalt(II) chloride paper, or anhydrous copper(II) sulphate.

Cobalt(II) chloride paper
This is a piece of filter paper dipped into cobalt(II) chloride solution and dried. It is pale blue in colour. When this blue test paper is dipped into a liquid it will turn pink if water is present.

Anhydrous copper(II) sulphate
Anhydrous copper(II) sulphate is a white powder, formed when blue copper(II) sulphate crystals are heated.

$$CuSO_4.5H_2O(s) \rightleftharpoons CuSO_4(s) + 5H_2O(l)$$

When a liquid containing water is added to anhydrous copper(II) sulphate, the colour changes from white to blue.

These are only tests for the presence of water, not for pure water. To test for pure water, it is necessary to boil the liquid and confirm that it boils at exactly 100°C.

Water treatment

We all use vast amounts of water at home – about 120 litres per day per person – for washing, flushing toilets, cooking etc. Industry too uses a great deal of water. It takes 26 000 litres of water to make a tonne of newsprint and 45 500 litres of water to make a tonne of steel. How is a supply of safe water produced for houses and factories?

Fig 4 summarises the cycling of water. Water is taken from underground sources, unpolluted rivers and reservoirs and is treated before being released into the water system. The water is filtered through beds of sand to filter out solid materials.

In the final stage the water is disinfected. This is done by bubbling the highly poisonous gas chlorine through the water to kill germs.

In many areas fluoride is added to the water in the form of sodium fluoride. Research shows that the presence of natural fluorides in water hardens tooth enamel and reduces tooth decay. Fluorine gas is a highly reactive, poisonous gas.

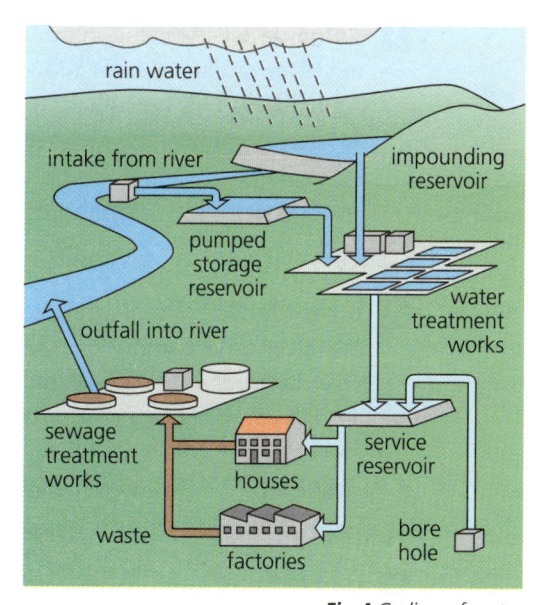

Fig 4 Cycling of water

Q5 Why do some people object to fluorides being added to water?

Q6 Suggest another way of providing fluorides without putting them into the water supply.

C3 Testing for ions

In this unit you will learn the answers to these questions:
- How can carbonate, sulphate, halide and nitrate ions be detected?
- How can flame tests be used to identify cations?
- How can ammonium ions be detected?
- How can cations be detected by precipitating hydroxides?

Carbonate, sulphate, halide and nitrate ions tests

1 Carbonate CO_3^{2-} When dilute hydrochloric acid is added to a carbonate, carbon dioxide gas is produced. No heat is required. Carbon dioxide turns limewater milky.
Example

$Na_2CO_3(s)$ + $2HCl(aq)$ ➡ $2NaCl(aq)$ + $H_2O(l)$ + $CO_2(g)$

sodium carbonate + hydrochloric acid ➡ sodium chloride + water + carbon dioxide

> **Q1** Write an ionic equation for the example given.

2 Sulphate SO_4^{2-} When dilute hydrochloric acid and barium chloride solution are added to a solution of a sulphate, a white precipitate of barium sulphate is formed immediately. *Example*

$Na_2SO_4(aq)$ + $BaCl_2(aq)$ ➡ $BaSO_4(s)$ + $2NaCl(aq)$

sodium sulphate + barium chloride ➡ barium sulphate + sodium chloride

> **Q2** Write an ionic equation for the example given.

3 Chloride Cl^- When a solution of a chloride is acidified with dilute nitric acid and silver nitrate solution added, a white precipitate of silver chloride is formed immediately. This precipitate turns purple in sunlight and dissolves completely in a concentrated ammonia solution.
Example

$NaCl(aq)$ + $AgNO_3(aq)$ ➡ $AgCl(s)$ + $NaNO_3(aq)$

sodium chloride + silver nitrate ➡ silver chloride + sodium nitrate

> **Q3** Write an ionic equation for the example given.

4 Bromide Br^- When a solution of a bromide is acidified with dilute nitric acid and silver nitrate solution added, a cream precipitate of silver bromide is formed immediately. This precipitate dissolves partially in a concentrated ammonia solution.
Example

$NaBr(aq)$ + $AgNO_3(aq)$ ➡ $AgBr(s)$ + $NaNO_3(aq)$

sodium bromide + silver nitrate ➡ silver bromide + sodium nitrate

> **Q4** Write an ionic equation for the example given.

5 Iodide I^- When a solution of an iodide is acidified with dilute nitric acid and silver nitrate solution added, a yellow precipitate of silver iodide is formed immediately. This precipitate is insoluble in a concentrated ammonia solution.
Example

$NaI(aq)$ + $AgNO_3(aq)$ ➡ $AgI(s)$ + $NaNO_3(aq)$

sodium iodide + silver nitrate ➡ silver iodide + sodium nitrate

> **Q5** Write an ionic equation for the example given.

C Patterns of behaviour

6 Nitrate NO_3^- Sodium hydroxide solution is added to a suspected nitrate and aluminium powder is added. The mixture is warmed and hydrogen gas is produced. If a nitrate is present, it will be reduced to ammonia gas. This gas will turn red litmus paper blue. *Example*

$$3NO_3^-(aq) + 8Al(s) + 5OH^-(aq) + 2H_2O(l) \rightarrow 3NH_3(g) + 8AlO_2^-(aq)$$

nitrate ions + aluminium + hydroxide ions + water ➡ ammonia + aluminate ions

> **Q6** Write a balanced symbol equation if the compound is sodium nitrate.

Flame tests to identify cations

A couple of drops of concentrated hydrochloric acid are added to a small quantity of compound. A clean piece of platinum (or nichrome) wire is dipped into the mixture and put into a hot Bunsen burner flame. Certain cations colour the flame, as in the table.

Flame colour	Cation
orange-yellow	sodium Na^+
lilac-pink	potassium K^+
brick red	calcium Ca^{2+}
pale green	barium Ba^{2+}
green	copper(II) Cu^{2+}
blue	lead Pb^{2+}

Testing for ammonium ions

Add sodium hydroxide solution to a suspected ammonium compound and heat. If an ammonium ion is present, ammonia gas is formed which turns red litmus blue. *Example*

$$NH_4Cl(s) + NaOH(aq) \rightarrow NH_3(g) + NaCl(aq) + H_2O(l)$$

ammonium chloride + sodium hydroxide ➡ ammonia + sodium chloride + water

> **Q7** Write an ionic equation for the example given.

Precipitating metal hydroxides to identify cations

Adding sodium hydroxide or ammonia solution (ammonium hydroxide) to a metal salt solution may precipitate a metal hydroxide as shown in the tables. This hydroxide may dissolve in excess of the reagent.

Addition of sodium hydroxide solution		
Cation	A couple of drops	Excess
potassium K^+	no precipitate	no precipitate
sodium Na^+	no precipitate	no precipitate
calcium Ca^+	white precipitate	insoluble precipitate
magnesium Mg^{2+}	white precipitate	insoluble precipitate
aluminium Al^{3+}	white precipitate	soluble precipitate – colourless solution
zinc Zn^{2+}	white precipitate	soluble precipitate – colourless solution
iron(II) Fe^{2+}	green precipitate	insoluble precipitate
iron(III) Fe^{3+}	red-brown precipitate	insoluble precipitate
lead Pb^{2+}	white precipitate	soluble precipitate – colourless solution
copper(II) Cu^{2+}	blue precipitate	insoluble precipitate
silver Ag^+	grey-brown precipitate	insoluble precipitate

Addition of ammonia solution		
Cation	A couple of drops	Excess
potassium K^+	no precipitate	no precipitate
sodium Na^+	no precipitate	no precipitate
calcium Ca^+	no precipitate	no precipitate
magnesium Mg^{2+}	white precipitate	insoluble precipitate
aluminium Al^{3+}	white precipitate	insoluble precipitate
zinc Zn^{2+}	white precipitate	soluble precipitate – colourless solution
iron(II) Fe^{2+}	green precipitate	insoluble precipitate
iron(III) Fe^{3+}	red-brown precipitate	insoluble precipitate
lead Pb^{2+}	white precipitate	insoluble precipitate
copper(II) Cu^{2+}	blue precipitate	soluble precipitate – deep blue solution
silver Ag^+	brown precipitate	soluble precipitate

C4 Calcium carbonate

In this unit you will learn the answers to these questions:
- How can we test to show that a rock contains calcium carbonate?
- What change occurs when calcium carbonate is heated?
- What is the difference between quicklime and slaked lime?
- Why does limewater turn milky and then clear when carbon dioxide is bubbled though it?
- How does rain water attack calcium carbonate?
- How can calcium carbonate be used to make mortar, cement and glass?

Identifying calcium carbonate in rock

Many rocks, including limestone, marble and chalk, contain calcium carbonate. Using the tests in Unit C3 it is possible to prove the presence of calcium carbonate in a rock.

> **Q1** What would you see when dilute hydrochloric acid is added to a rock containing calcium carbonate? Which gas would be produced?
>
> **Q2** What colour would you see in a flame test using calcium carbonate?

Action of heat on calcium carbonate

Calcium carbonate is decomposed when heated to about 900°C.

$$CaCO_3(s) \rightleftharpoons CaO(s) + CO_2(g)$$

calcium carbonate $\rightleftharpoons$ calcium oxide + carbon dioxide

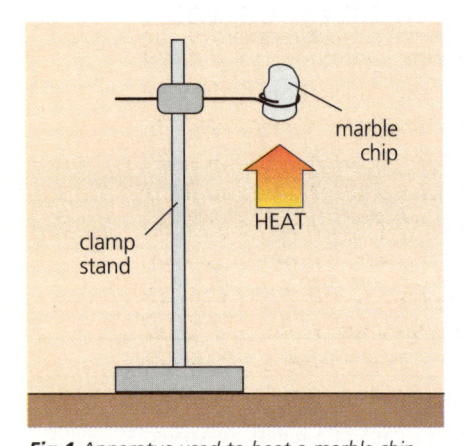

Fig 1 Apparatus used to heat a marble chip

If a marble chip is heated strongly in the apparatus in Fig 1, decomposition of the chip takes place. The chip glows with a dim white light during the decomposition.

Before electric lighting, theatres were lit by light from a lump of limestone heated on coal fires. This is the origin of the expression 'being in the limelight' when someone is prominent.

The lump of calcium oxide produced is called **quicklime**. If a piece of cold quicklime is added to cold water, a very exothermic reaction takes place and sufficient energy is given out to turn some water to steam.

$$CaO(s) + H_2O(l) \rightarrow Ca(OH)_2(s)$$

calcium oxide + water $\rightarrow$ calcium hydroxide

Solid calcium hydroxide is often called slaked lime. When calcium hydroxide solid is added to water it forms a creamy-coloured suspension called 'milk-of-lime'. If this suspension is filtered, a clear solution of calcium hydroxide is produced. This is called **limewater**.

> **Q3** Draw an energy level diagram for the reaction between calcium oxide and water.

C Patterns of behaviour

Action of carbon dioxide on limewater

Limewater is used as a test for carbon dioxide. If carbon dioxide is passed through calcium hydroxide solution, the limewater turns milky or cloudy. This milkiness is due to the formation of a fine suspension of calcium carbonate.

$$Ca(OH)_2(aq) + CO_2(g) \rightarrow CaCO_3(s) + H_2O(l)$$

calcium hydroxide + carbon dioxide → calcium carbonate + water

If the carbon dioxide gas continues to pass through the solution, the solution turns clear again. This is due to the formation of calcium hydrogencarbonate.

$$CaCO_3(s) + H_2O(l) + CO_2(g) \rightleftharpoons Ca(HCO_3)_2(aq)$$

calcium carbonate + water + carbon dioxide ⇌ calcium hydrogencarbonate

This reaction is reversible. Boiling a solution of calcium hydrogencarbonate will reverse the reaction and the solution will go cloudy again.

This reaction also takes place when rain water (containing water and carbon dioxide) attacks calcium carbonate rocks (see Unit 25).

Mortar, cement and glass

Mortar is a mixture of **slaked lime** (calcium hydroxide), sand and water. It is mixed into a thick paste and is used to fix bricks together when building. It sets by losing water and absorbing carbon dioxide from the air. Long dendritic crystals of calcium carbonate form which strengthen the mortar. Cement (see Unit 24) is a more advanced material. When it sets it produces a complicated mixture of calcium and aluminium silicates.

Ordinary glass is made by mixing calcium carbonate, silicon dioxide (sand) and sodium carbonate together and melting them. The resulting mixture of sodium and calcium silicates, on cooling, produces glass. This is the type of glass used to make windows. Hardened glass, such as *Pyrex*, contains boron compounds. This 'borosilicate' glass can be cooled quickly without cracking. Lead is added to glass to make it harder and suitable for 'cut-glass'.

Glass is coloured when certain metal oxides are present (Fig 2).

Q4 Why is glass collected for recycling put into different bins to keep the colours separate?

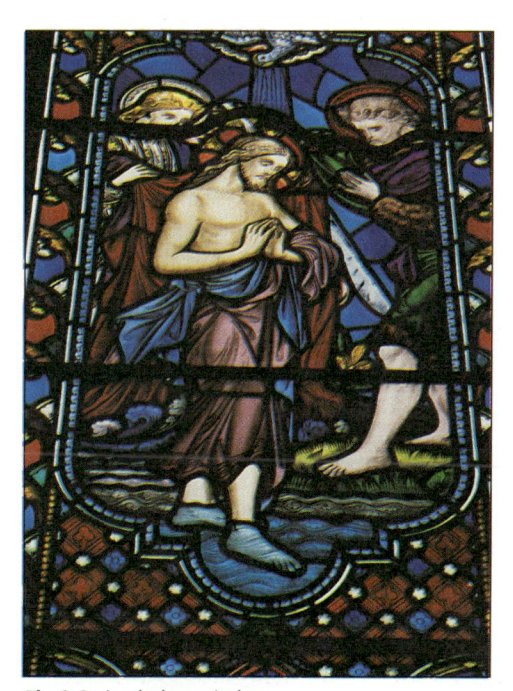

Fig 2 Stained-glass window

C5 Hard water

In this unit you will learn the answers to these questions:
- What is hard water and how is it caused?
- What are the advantages and disadvantages of hard water?
- What is the difference between temporary hardness and permanent hardness?
- How can hardness be removed?

Hard water

Hard water is water which does not lather well but forms scum or precipitate when used with soap. The hardness is due to certain impurities dissolved in the water.

Distilled water (pure water) contains no dissolved impurities. It is soft and lathers well with soap. Rain water is similar but contains dissolved gases such as carbon dioxide from the air. Rain water also lathers well with soap.

The hardness problem occurs when rain water trickles through the rocks in the Earth and dissolves certain minerals. Hardness is caused by dissolved calcium and magnesium compounds in the water.

Soap can be represented as sodium stearate, Na^+St^-. When water containing calcium or magnesium ions and soap are mixed, a precipitate of calcium stearate or magnesium stearate is formed. This is the scum and this uses up the soap which should be used for cleaning purposes.

$$Ca^{2+}(aq) + 2Na^+St^-(aq) \rightarrow CaSt_2(s) + 2Na^+(aq)$$
$$Mg^{2+}(aq) + 2Na^+St^-(aq) \rightarrow MgSt_2(s) + 2Na^+(aq)$$

Fig 1 shows a map of England and Wales. You will notice that hard water areas are associated with areas where the rocks are predominantly chalk and limestone, and soft water areas where the rocks are sandstone and granite.

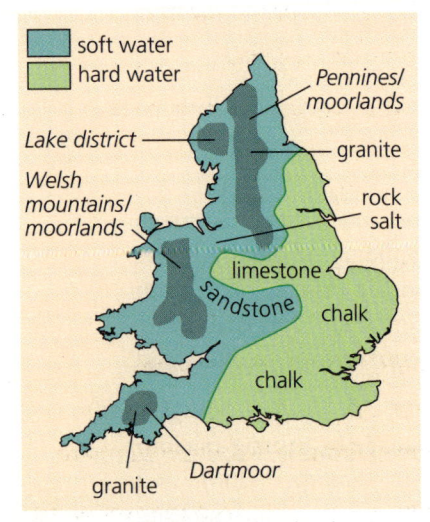

Fig 1 Map of England and Wales showing areas of hard water and soft water

The **advantages** and **disadvantages** of hard water are shown in the table.

Advantages	Disadvantages
Supplies calcium compounds required by the body for bones and teeth	Wastes soap because some of the soap forms scum with the impurities in the water
Has a better taste than soft water	Scum formed leaves marks on clothes and baths
Better for brewing beer	Causes a layer of 'fur' in kettles and scale in boilers and pipes. Scale in pipes may block pipes and make radiators less efficient
Lead compounds in pipes are less soluble in hard water	Can spoil special finishes on fabrics

Fig 2 shows a pipe from a central heating system which has a layer of scale inside it caused by the breakdown of hardness in water.

Fig 2 Hard water causes a build-up of scale in pipes

Q1 Beer brewing was brought to Burton on Trent because of the underground water was particularly suitable. What type of water would it be?

Q2 Why is poisoning by lead compounds in water less likely in hard water areas?

C Patterns of behaviour

Temporary and permanent hardness

Temporary hardness is caused by dissolved calcium hydrogencarbonate formed when rain water trickles through rocks containing calcium carbonate (see Unit 23).

$$CaCO_3(s) + H_2O(l) + CO_2(g) \rightarrow Ca(HCO_3)_2(aq)$$

When water containing temporary hardness is boiled, the calcium hydrogencarbonate decomposes and the hardness is removed. Permanent hardness is caused by dissolved calcium sulphate and magnesium sulphate. It is not destroyed by boiling. The water has to be softened (i.e. have the hardness removed) by chemical treatment.

Temporary hardness is removed by boiling because of the decomposition of calcium hydrogencarbonate to form calcium carbonate, which is insoluble.

$$Ca(HCO_3)_2(aq) \rightarrow CaCO_3(s) + H_2O(l) + CO_2(g)$$
calcium hydrogencarbonate $\rightarrow$ calcium carbonate + water + carbon dioxide

It is this deposit of calcium carbonate which forms the scale or 'fur' in a kettle.

Permanent hardness and temporary hardness can be removed by adding washing soda crystals (sodium carbonate crystals).

$$Ca(HCO_3)_2(aq) + Na_2CO_3(aq) \rightarrow CaCO_3(s) + 2NaHCO_3(aq)$$
calcium hydrogencarbonate + sodium carbonate $\rightarrow$ calcium carbonate + sodium hydrogencarbonate

$$CaSO_4(aq) + Na_2CO_3(aq) \rightarrow CaCO_3(s) + Na_2SO_4(aq)$$
calcium sulphate + sodium carbonate $\rightarrow$ calcium carbonate + sodium sulphate

$$MgSO_4(aq) + Na_2CO_3(aq) \rightarrow MgCO_3(s) + Na_2SO_4(aq)$$
magnesium sulphate + sodium carbonate $\rightarrow$ magnesium carbonate + sodium sulphate

In each case the calcium or magnesium ions in solution are precipitated and can no longer cause problems. Other substances, e.g. calcium hydroxide, 'Calgon' (sodium metaphosphate) and sodium sesquicarbonate, work in a similar way by precipitating the substances which cause hardness.

Hardness can also be removed by using an **ion-exchange column** (Fig 3). This is a column filled with a suitable ion-exchange resin in small granules. This resin contains an excess of sodium ions. When hard water passes through the column, the calcium and magnesium ions in the water (causing hardness) are exchanged for sodium ions. When all the sodium ions in the column have been replaced, the column is recharged. An ion-exchange column provides a solution where a continuous supply of soft water is required.

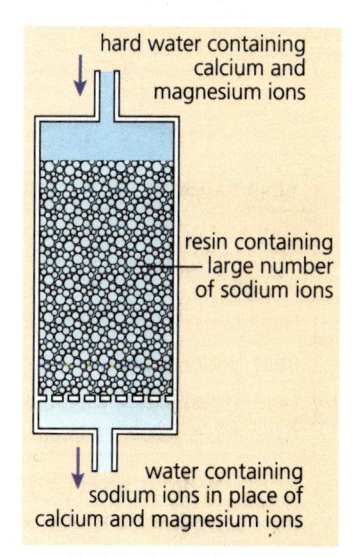

Fig 3 An ion-exchange column used to produce soft water from hard water

Q3 Write a balanced equation to show how temporary hardness can be removed by the addition of calcium hydroxide, $Ca(OH)_2$.

Q4 Why is it important that too much calcium hydroxide is not used?

C6 Soaps and soapless detergents

In this unit you will learn the answers to these questions:
- How does a detergent work?
- What is the difference between soaps and soapless detergents?
- How are soaps and soapless detergents manufactured?

Detergents

A **detergent** is a cleaning agent. Detergents can be classed as soaps and soapless detergents. Until about thirty years ago, most cleaning tasks were carried out by soaps. Today soapless detergents are used much more widely.

The actions of soaps and soapless detergents are similar. Both contain large molecules. In each molecule there is a long hydrocarbon chain (e.g. $C_{17}H_{35}-$) attached to an ionic group ($-CO_2^-$ in soap or $-SO_3^-$ in a soapless detergent). The molecule can be represented by the 'tadpole'-type structure shown in Fig 1.

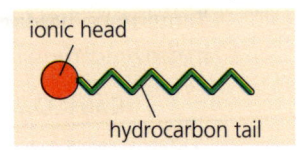

Fig 1 Detergent molecule

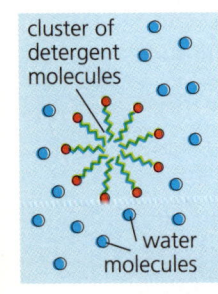

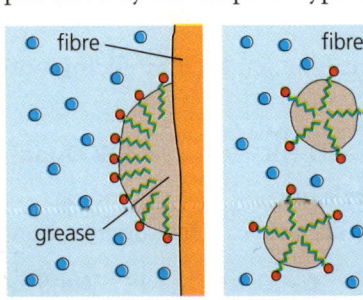

The hydrocarbon tail will dissolve in fats and grease and the ionic head will dissolve readily in water. The cleaning action of a soap or soapless detergent is summarised in Fig 2.

Fig 2 Steps in the cleaning action of a detergent

When the detergent (soap or soapless) is added to water the molecules are in clusters in the solution. The tails of the detergent molecules stick into the greasy dirt and attraction between the water molecules and the detergent molecules lifts the dirt from the fibre. Swirling the solution helps to lift the dirt. The grease is then suspended in the solution, with repulsive forces between detergent molecules preventing grease from returning to the material.

Soaps and soapless detergents

In Unit 18 you learnt about esterification reactions. *Example*

$$CH_3COOH(l) + C_2H_5OH(l) \rightleftharpoons CH_3COOC_2H_5(l) + H_2O(l)$$

ethanoic acid + ethanol $\rightleftharpoons$ ethyl ethanoate + water

This reaction is reversible. Soap making is the reverse of this reaction of esterification.

Natural fats and oils, e.g. olive oil, palm oil, are esters of an alcohol called **glycerol** and an acid called **stearic acid** (more correctly called octadecanoic acid). Glycerol is a **triol**, i.e. an alcohol with three –OH groups.

Soap is produced by splitting up these natural esters by boiling with an alkali such as sodium hydroxide. The process of hydrolysis of these esters to produce soap is called **saponification**. Salt is added to the solution to precipitate out the solid soap. The soap is filtered off.

Q1 How are natural fats and oils different chemically from crude oil (petroleum)?

Q2 What is the by-product in the manufacture of soap?

C Patterns of behaviour

Soapless detergents are made by the action of fuming sulphuric acid on alkyl benzene residues from crude oil.

Although soaps and soapless detergents are made in very different ways, they have a similarity in their structures. Soapless detergents have the big advantage that they lather equally well in hard or soft water and do not form scum.

Q3 A detergent manufacturer sells detergents throughout the world. What are the advantages of soapless detergents to the manufacturer?

Most detergents are sold as washing powders containing different ingredients, each with different jobs. Fig 3 shows the approximate composition of a soapless detergent washing powder. The alkylbenzene sulphonate is the active soapless detergent. Sodium sulphate and sodium silicate prevent the washing powder absorbing water from the atmosphere.

- alkylbenzene sulphonate (synthetic detergent): 30%
- sodium perborate (bleach): 15%
- sodium polyphosphate (to remove dirt): 35%
- anhydrous sodium silicate: 10% ⎫ to prevent
- anhydrous sodium sulphate: 10% ⎭ caking

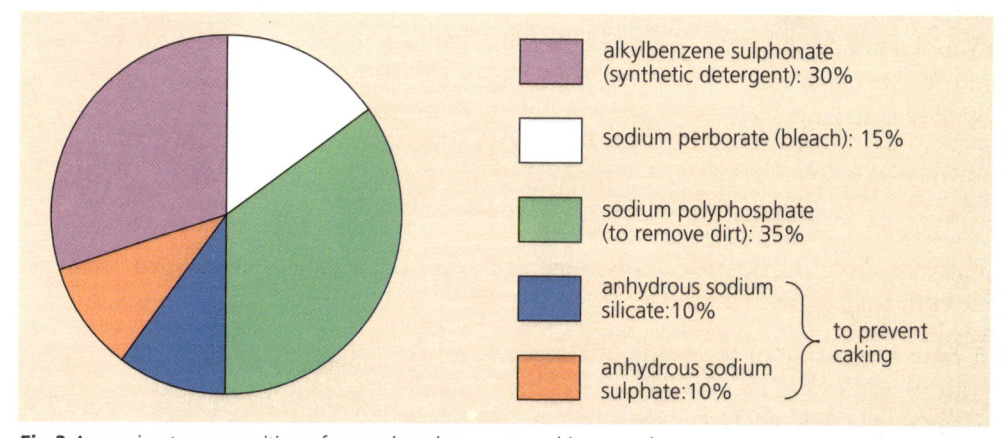

Fig 3 Approximate composition of a soapless detergent washing powder

Sodium perborate acts as a bleach to remove stains. In addition, the washing powder may contain enzymes (see Unit 42) to assist with stain removal, and fluorescent agents to help overcome the yellowing of clothes with age.

Fig 4 shows a spillage of crude oil into the sea. Detergent is used to help disperse the crude oil during clean-up processes. Detergent can also be used to clean the oil from sea birds (Fig 5).

Q4 What problems can oil spillages have for the environment?

Q5 Suggest how large amounts of detergent might affect the environment.

Fig 4 Clean-up after a spillage of crude oil

Fig 5 An oil-covered sea bird being cleaned using detergent

46 Acids and alkalis

In this unit you will learn the answers to these questions:
- What are acids, bases and alkalis?
- What are typical reactions of acids?
- How can acids and alkalis be detected?

There are many examples of acids and alkalis in everyday life.

Acid	Formula	Salt produced
sulphuric acid	H_2SO_4	Na_2SO_4
hydrochloric acid	HCl	NaCl
nitric acid	HNO_3	$NaNO_3$

Acids are compounds which contain hydrogen which can be replaced by a metal to form a salt. In the laboratory there are three common mineral acids, as shown in the table.

Q1 From your knowledge of apples, lemons and vinegar, suggest what kind of taste acids have?

Q2 Which element is present in all acids?

Q3 Hydrochloric acid and nitric acid are said to be **monobasic** acids and sulphuric acid is a **dibasic** acid. Suggest the meaning of the words monobasic and dibasic.

There are also many **organic acids** composed of carbon, hydrogen and oxygen. Examples are citric acid, tartaric acid and ethanoic acid. Many of these organic acids are solids.

A **base** is an oxide or hydroxide of a metal. It reacts with an acid to form a salt and water only. An **alkali** is a base which is soluble in water. A solution of an alkali contains an excess of hydroxide, OH^-, ions. The common laboratory alkalis are listed (right).

potassium hydroxide	KOH
sodium hydroxide	NaOH
calcium hydroxide	$Ca(OH)_2$
ammonia solution	NH_3 (aq)
(ammonium hydroxide)	or NH_4OH

Properties of acids

Apart from using indicators, acids have other properties in common:

1 Reaction with magnesium

Acids react with magnesium to produce hydrogen. This burns with a squeaky pop. For example:

magnesium + hydrochloric acid ➡ magnesium chloride + hydrogen

2 Reaction with sodium carbonate crystals

Acids react with sodium carbonate crystals to produce a colourless gas. This colourless gas, carbon dioxide, turns limewater milky. For example:

sodium carbonate + hydrochloric acid ➡ sodium chloride + carbon dioxide + water

3 Reaction with black copper(II) oxide

Acids react with copper(II) oxide to produce a blue or green solution. For example:

copper(II) oxide + hydrochloric acid ➡ copper(II) chloride + water

C Patterns of behaviour

Indicators

Acids and alkalis can be detected using indicators. Indicators are substances which change colour when acids and alkalis are added. Examples of good plant indicators are solutions from red cabbage, red roses, beetroot and elderberries.

In the laboratory the plant extract which is most commonly used to detect acids and alkalis is **litmus**. Litmus is extracted from a lichen. Litmus changes colour between red and blue.

in aci**d** solution – re**d**
in a**l**kali solution – **bl**ue

Solutions which are not acidic or alkaline are said to be **neutral**. Litmus is purple in neutral solutions.

Although litmus can detect acids and alkalis, it cannot compare the strengths of acids and alkalis. The comparative strengths of acids and alkalis is given by the **pH** scale. This is a scale from 1 to 14. A substance is an acid if it has a pH less than 7 or alkaline if it has a pH greater than 7. A neutral substance has a pH of exactly 7. The pH of a solution can be found in two ways.

1 Using mixtures of indicators called **Universal Indicator**. This changes to a number of colours rather than just the one of a simple indicator such as litmus. The table gives the colours for a simple form of Universal Indicator. For example, if Universal Indicator is added to a solution and the solution turns blue, the solution has a pH of 8 and is a very weak alkali.

	pH	Colour of Universal Indicator	Examples in the home	Examples in the laboratory
STRONG ACIDS	1		car battery acid	mineral acids
	2			
	3	red		
	4		lemon juice, vinegar	ethanoic acid
WEAK ACIDS	5	orange		
	6	yellow	soda water	carbonic acid
NEUTRAL	7	green	water, salt, ethanol	
WEAK ALKALIS	8	blue	soap, baking powder	sodium hydrogencarbonate
	9	blue-purple		
STRONG ALKALIS	10			ammonia solution
	11		washing soda	
	12	purple	oven cleaner	
	13			sodium and potassium hydroxides
	14			

Fig 1 The glass probe of a pH meter measuring the pH of a solution

2 Using a pH meter. A pH meter is an electrical device used to measure the pH accurately. A glass probe is put into the solution being tested and the pH can be read from a dial or a digital readout immediately.

47 Neutralisation

In this unit you will learn the answers to these questions:
- What is neutralisation?
- What examples of neutralisation are there in the world around us?

When an acid is mixed with an alkali, in the correct proportions, a neutral solution is formed. This process is called **neutralisation**.

One product of neutralisation is water. Any neutralisation can be represented by the equation:

$$H^+ (aq) + OH^- (aq) \rightarrow H_2O (l)$$

These reactions are exothermic. There is a temperature rise when the two solutions are mixed.

Uses of neutralisation

1 Soil testing

A soil with a pH value between 6.5 and 7.0 is suitable for growing most plants. If the pH falls below 6.0, the soil will become too acidic for growing some plants. If the pH rises to 8.0 it will again be poor for plant growth because very alkaline soil is short of vital minerals necessary for plant growth. The chemical **sequestrene** helps acid-loving plants to grow in alkaline soils. Sequestrene contains special iron compounds which plants cannot normally get from alkali soils.

The table shows plants which grow well in acidic and alkaline conditions.

You may be able to decide what the soil is like in your area by looking at the trees and plants which grow well in gardens around you. The pH of the soil can be found by mixing a sample of the soil with distilled water and adding pure, insoluble barium sulphate powder. The barium sulphate helps the solution to clear. Universal Indicator is then added and the colour of the solution compared with a Universal Indicator colour chart. Alternatively you could test the mixture of soil and distilled water with a pH meter.

Acidic conditions	Alkaline conditions
rhododendron	cherry
azalea	juniper
lavender	laburnum
wallflowers	lilac
stocks	birch
heather	broom
hydrangea	holly

Excess acidity of soils is an important cause of crop failure. It has been estimated that if this was always corrected properly there would be a one-fifth increase in food production.

Excess acidity of soils (or soil sourness) is caused by rainwater washing out alkalis from the soil and by rain containing acids. The excess acidity can be removed by neutralising it with alkalis.

Calcium oxide (or quicklime) and calcium hydroxide (or slaked lime) are frequently used to make the soil less acidic. They are made from limestone (calcium carbonate).

calcium carbonate $\xrightarrow{\text{heat strongly}}$ calcium oxide $\xrightarrow{\text{add water}}$ calcium hydroxide

$CaCO_3 \rightarrow CaO \rightarrow Ca(OH)_2$

C Patterns of behaviour

Calcium hydroxide and calcium oxide are quick-acting. In order to correct excess soil acidity, these alkalis should be used in autumn or winter. Calcium carbonate can also be used. It is less soluble and acts more slowly.

2 Acids in digestion

There is about $1000\,cm^3$ of dilute hydrochloric acid in your stomach. It is there to help you digest the food you eat. The food is broken down into simpler substances which can be used by your body. These substances are the vital supplies that your body needs for all kinds of jobs including building, repair and providing energy.

Indigestion is caused by too much acid in the stomach. It can be cured by taking antacids such as bicarbonate of soda (sodium hydrogencarbonate). These substances are weak alkalis and neutralise excess acidity.

3 Insect bites and stings

Insect bites or stings involve the injection of a small amount of chemical below the skin. This causes irritation. Nettle stings and ant bites inject acid into the skin. Bee stings also involve the injection of an acid. The sting or bite should be neutralised by using calamine lotion (a suspension of zinc carbonate) or sodium hydrogencarbonate. Both are weak alkalis. In neutralising the acid they reduce the irritation.

Wasp stings are different. They are best treated by applying vinegar (ethanoic acid) because the sting involves the injection of an alkali.

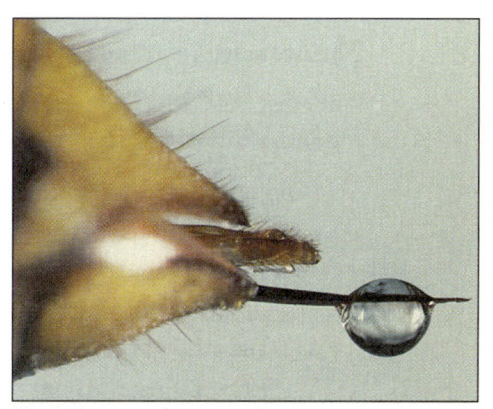

Fig 1 *Close up of a wasp sting*

4 Acidity in lakes

Many inland lakes are becoming too acidic because of acids in the atmosphere. This over-acidity can affect the life in the lake. Fish can die. The water in the lake can be neutralised by adding blocks of limestone.

5 Removing acidic gases from gases leaving power stations

Coal-fired power stations produce sulphur dioxide which can affect the environment. The sulphur dioxide can be removed by passing the gases over limestone. The limestone neutralises the acidic gases in the gases escaping from the factory. Calcium sulphate is produced and can be used in making plasterboards.

Fig 2 *Fish killed by acid in lakes*

Q1 Why is it important to remove acidic gases from power station gases?

48 Salt formation – 1

In this unit you will learn the answers to these questions:
- How can soluble salts be produced?
- What are the rules for the solubility of salts?

Salts

A **salt** is produced when hydrogen ions in an acid are replaced by metal or ammonium (NH_4^+) ions. For example:

hydrochloric acid ➡ sodium chloride
HCl ➡ NaCl

The hydrogen ion is replaced by a sodium ion.

nitric acid ➡ ammonium nitrate
HNO_3 ➡ NH_4NO_3

The hydrogen ion is replaced by an ammonium ion.

Sulphuric acid contains two replaceable hydrogen ions per molecule. For this reason it is called a **dibasic acid**.

sulphuric acid ➡ sodium hydrogensulphate ➡ sodium sulphate
H_2SO_4 ➡ $NaHSO_4$ ➡ Na_2SO_4

The salt formed when one of the hydrogen ions in sulphuric acid has been replaced is called sodium hydrogensulphate and is an **acid salt**. It has some of the properties of the acid and some of the properties of the salt.

Any metal carbonate, chloride, sulphate or nitrate will be a salt. In general, salts are solids with high melting points. Some salts crystallise, containing water of crystallisation. An example of this is hydrated copper(II) sulphate, $CuSO_4.5H_2O$. The method used to prepare a salt depends upon whether the salt is soluble in water or insoluble in water.

Solubility of salts

The table shows the solubility of a number of salts at room temperature.

Key: s soluble in water
ss slightly soluble in water
i insoluble in water

Metal	Chloride	Nitrate	Sulphate	Carbonate
sodium	s	s	s	s
calcium	s	s	ss	i
zinc	s	s	s	i
barium	s	s	i	i
magnesium	s	s	s	i
lead(II)	i	s	i	i
potassium	s	s	s	s
iron(II)	s	s	s	i
ammonium	s	s	s	s
copper(II)	s	s	s	i
silver	i	s	ss	i

C Patterns of behaviour

Q1 Copy and complete the following sentences by putting in the correct metals.
All salts of potassium, sodium and ammonium are soluble in water.
All nitrates are soluble in water.
All chlorides are soluble in water except _____ and _____.
All sulphates are soluble in water except _____ and _____.
All carbonates are insoluble in water except _____, _____ and _____.

These are the solubility of salt rules which you should know. You will then be able to decide which method you should use to prepare a particular salt.

Preparation of soluble salts

There are four possible starting materials for preparing each soluble salt:

1 the metal;

2 the metal oxide (a base);

3 the metal hydroxide (an alkali);

4 the carbonate.

The appropriate acid needs to be used:
- hydrochloric acid to prepare chlorides;
- nitric acid to prepare nitrates;
- sulphuric acid to prepare sulphates.

For example, magnesium sulphate can be prepared using dilute sulphuric acid and magnesium, magnesium oxide, magnesium hydroxide or magnesium carbonate (Fig 1). The choice of which one of these should be used depends upon:

1 price;

2 availability;

3 the speed of the reaction – not too fast nor too slow.

The following word equations summarise the possible reactions.

metal + acid ➡ salt + hydrogen
metal oxide + acid ➡ salt + water
metal hydoxide + acid ➡ salt + water
metal carbonate + acid ➡ salt + water + carbon dioxide

Fig 1 Preparation of magnesium sulphate – a soluble salt

49 Salt formation – 2

In this unit you will learn the answers to these questions:
- How can insoluble salts be prepared?
- How can electrical conductivity measurements be used to study the precipitation reaction?
- What can insoluble salts be used for?

Unit 48 listed the rules for solubility of salts at room temperature. These are:

> All salts of potassium, sodium and ammonium are soluble in water.
> All nitrates are soluble in water.
> All chlorides are soluble in water except lead and silver.
> All sulphates are soluble in water except barium and lead.
> All carbonates are insoluble in water except potassium, sodium and ammonium.

Preparation of insoluble salts

Insoluble salts are prepared by **precipitation**. Two suitable aqueous solutions are mixed together so that the insoluble salt precipitates.

For example, to prepare barium sulphate, choose a salt containing barium which is soluble in water to make one aqueous solution, e.g. barium nitrate (or barium chloride). (A useful tip here: remember that all nitrates are soluble in water and nitrates are often the best salt to use.) The other solution could be made using sodium sulphate or potassium sulphate.

The following equations summarise the reactions which take place:

barium nitrate + sodium **sulphate** ➡ **barium sulphate** + sodium nitrate
$Ba(NO_3)_2$ (aq) + Na_2SO_4 (aq) ➡ $BaSO_4$ (s) + $2NaNO_3$ (aq)

barium nitrate + potassium **sulphate** ➡ **barium sulphate** + potassium nitrate
$Ba(NO_3)_2$ (aq) + K_2SO_4 (aq) ➡ $BaSO_4$ (s) + $2KNO_3$ (aq)

barium chloride + sodium **sulphate** ➡ **barium sulphate** + sodium chloride
$BaCl_2$ (aq) + Na_2SO_4 (aq) ➡ $BaSO_4$ (s) + $2NaCl$ (aq)

barium chloride + potassium **sulphate** ➡ **barium sulphate** + potassium chloride
$BaCl_2$ (aq) + K_2SO_4 (aq) ➡ $BaSO_4$ (s) + $2KCl$ (aq)

All of these reactions could be summarised by one ionic equation:

Ba^{2+} (aq) + SO_4^{2-} (aq) ➡ $BaSO_4$ (s)

The method used to prepare barium sulphate is summarised in Fig 1. The barium sulphate produced is pure and dry.

The progress of a precipitation reaction

Barium sulphate can also be prepared by mixing solutions of barium hydroxide (containing barium ions) and sulphuric acid (containing sulphate ions).

barium hydroxide + sulphuric acid ➡ barium sulphate + water
$Ba(OH)_2$ (aq) + H_2SO_4 (aq) ➡ $BaSO_4$ (s) + $2H_2O$ (l)

A solution of barium hydroxide has a pH value of 13. It is a strong alkali.

C Patterns of behaviour

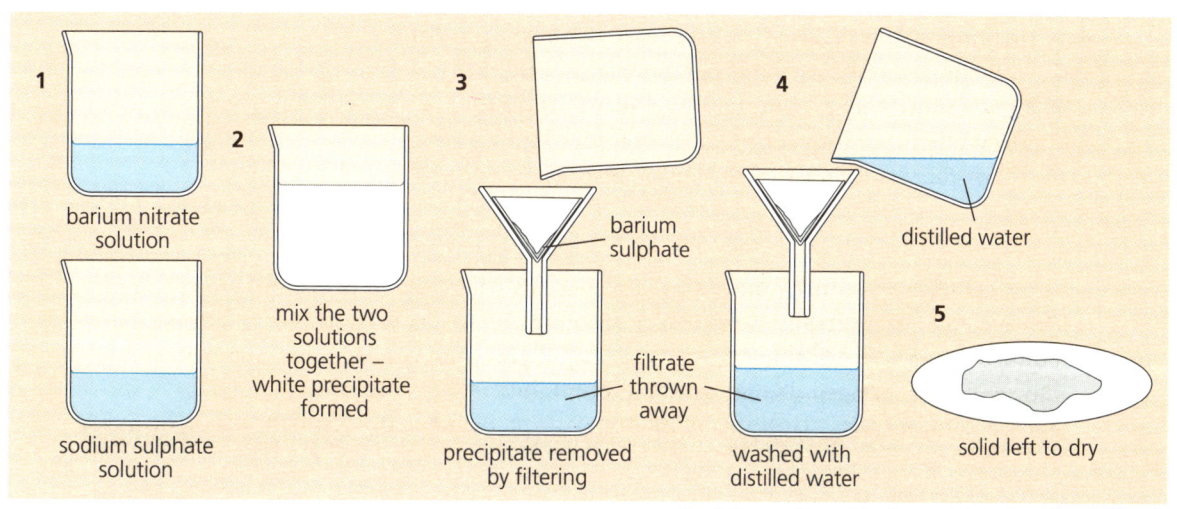

Fig 1 Preparation of barium sulphate – an insoluble salt

When sulphuric acid is added to the barium hydroxide solution, three things happen.

1 A white precipitate of barium sulphate is formed.

2 The pH of the solution is reduced from 13 down to 7 when all of the barium sulphate has been precipitated and all of the acid and alkali have been used up. Adding more acid will reduce the pH below 7 as excess acid will remain. The course of the reaction could be followed using indicators or, better, a pH meter.

3 The electrical conductivity of the solution could be followed during the reaction. As the barium sulphate is precipitated, barium ions and sulphate ions are removed and the electrical conductivity is reduced.

Fig 2 shows apparatus which could be used to follow the electrical conductivity of the solution during the experiment together with a graph of the results obtained.

Q1 Why is an alternating current used rather than a direct current?

Q2 Explain the shape of the graph obtained.

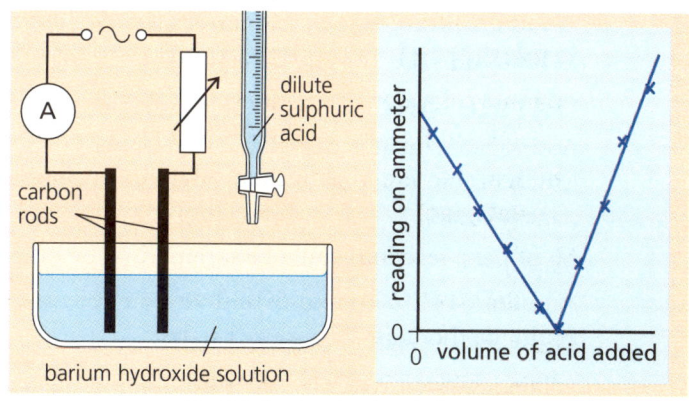

Fig 2 Following the electrical conductivity of the reaction between barium hydroxide solution and sulphuric acid

Uses of insoluble salts

Many insoluble salts are used in the paint industry as pigments. Pigments give the paint its colour. Many insoluble salts have characteristic colours, e.g. copper carbonate is green.

Toxic materials in waste water are removed by precipitation followed by filtration. Heavy metals such as lead and cadmium are removed by precipitating insoluble salts.

50 Fertilisers

In this unit you will learn the answers to these questions:
- Which elements are essential for plant growth?
- How is nitric acid manufactured from ammonia?
- How is ammonium nitrate manufactured?
- What factors affect the choice of fertiliser?

Essential elements for plant growth

For good plant growth, quantities of nitrogen, phosphorus and potassium are required. Other elements are required in smaller amounts. Elements such as boron and iron are required in very small amounts and are called **trace elements**. The table shows the importance of nitrogen, phosphorus and potassium.

Element	Importance of the element to a growing plant	Natural sources	Artificial fertilisers
nitrogen	necessary for the growth of stems and leaves	dried blood (14% N), hoof and horn (14% N)	sodium nitrate, calcium nitrate, ammonium sulphate, ammonium nitrate, urea
phosphorus	essential for root growth	slag, bone meal	ammonium phosphate, calcium superphosphate
potassium	for the production of flowers	wood ash	potassium sulphate

Q1 A fertiliser bag is labelled 'NPK 15:5:10'. What does this mean?

Q2 Which two substances in the 'Artificial fertilisers' column of the table could be mixed to produce a fertiliser which would provide nitrogen, phosphorus and potassium?

Industrial production of ammonium nitrate and ammonium sulphate

Ammonia is manufactured by the Haber process (Unit 44). Much of this ammonia is converted into nitric acid in a three-stage process.

Stage 1
A mixture of 10% ammonia and 90% air is passed over a heated platinum/rhodium alloy gauze catalyst.

ammonia + oxygen ➡ nitrogen monoxide + steam
$4NH_3(g) + 5O_2(g)$ ➡ $4NO(g) + 6H_2O(g)$

Stage 2
The mixture of gases is allowed to cool.

nitrogen monoxide + oxygen ➡ nitrogen dioxide
$2NO(g) + O_2(g)$ ➡ $2NO_2(g)$

Fig 1 Ammonia plant

C Patterns of behaviour

Stage 3
The mixture of gases dissolves in water to produce nitric acid.

nitrogen dioxide + water + oxygen ➡ nitric acid
$4NO_2 (g) + 2H_2O (l) + O_2 (g)$ ➡ $4HNO_3 (l)$

Manufacture of ammonium nitrate from ammonia and nitric acid

Ammonium nitrate is the most widely used fertiliser in Great Britain. It can be prepared by reacting ammonia solution and nitric acid.

ammonia + nitric acid ➡ ammonium nitrate
$NH_3 (aq) + HNO_3 (aq)$ ➡ $NH_4NO_3 (aq)$

In the final stage, the solution of ammonium nitrate is evaporated. Solid ammonium nitrate is melted and sprayed down a tall tower (Fig 2). As the droplets fall they meet an upward flow of air. The fertiliser solidifies and forms small, hard pellets called **prills**. These are easy to handle and to spread onto the fields.

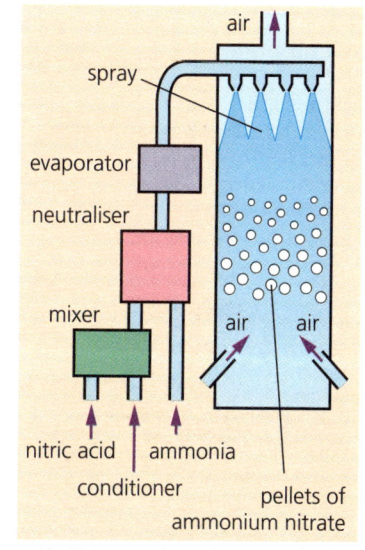

Fig 2 *Ammonium nitrate production*

Q3 Plan an experiment to prepare a sample of ammonium sulphate in the laboratory. Ammonium sulphate is a soluble salt.

Choosing the most suitable fertiliser

The factors which affect the choice of a nitrogen fertiliser include:

■ *Percentage of nitrogen in the fertiliser.*

Work out the percentage of nitrogen in ammonium nitrate, NH_4NO_3
Using the relative atomic masses (page 91):
Mass of 1 mole of ammonium nitrate = $14 + (4 \times 1) + 14 + (3 \times 16) = 80 g$
Mass of nitrogen in 1 mole of ammonium nitrate = $(2 \times 14) = 28 g$
Percentage of nitrogen
$= \frac{28}{80} \times 100 = 35\%$

Q4 Work out the percentage of nitrogen in ammonia, NH_3.

■ *Solubility in water.* Plants absorb fertilisers in solution through their roots. If a fertiliser is very soluble in water, it will be quick-acting. However, a very soluble fertiliser is quickly washed off the field and into drainage ditches, brooks and rivers. This will reduce the effectiveness of the fertiliser and will also cause water pollution. Ammonia is oxidised to nitrates by bacteria, using up dissolved oxygen in the river. The nitrogen fertiliser also makes the water plants grow better. When these die and decay they use up more oxygen in the water and the water becomes stagnant. Fish die and other river life is affected.

■ *Cost.* If two fertilisers have similar percentages of nitrogen and similar solubilities, the choice may be made on price.

Fig 3 *A tractor distributing solid fertiliser*

INDEX

A
acid lakes 131
acid rain 69
acid salt 132
acid-catalysed hydrolysis 50
acids 128–31
activation energy 105
addition polymerisation 44–5
addition polymers 44
addition reactions 41, 44
air 110–11
alkali metals 28–9, 92–3
alkalis 128–31
alkanes 37–9, 40, 41
alkenes 41, 44
allotropes 17
alloys 30–1
aluminium 60, 63
amino acids 27, 50–1
ammonia 7, 9, 114–15, 136
ammonium chloride 25
ammonium ions 121
ammonium nitrate 137
ammonium sulphate 136–7
anaerobic respiration 48
anodising 60
aqueous solutions 85
ascending paper chromatography 26
atomic number 11, 90
atoms 10–11, 16, 18
Avogadro's number 76

B
base 128
bauxite 63
bedding planes 67
body-centred cubic structure 29
bonding
    covalent 2, 14–15
    ionic 2, 12–13
brass 30, 31
bromides 99, 120
bromine 7, 41, 96–9
buckminsterfullerene 17

C
calcium carbonate 100–1, 122–3, 125
calculations 3, 80–1
carbohydrates 50
carbon 17, 30–1
carbon cycle 52–3
carbon dioxide 9, 52–3, 123
carbon fibre 5, 17
carbonate ions 120
catalase 108
catalysis 106–7
catalysts 106
catalytic decomposition 35

cations 121
cement 69, 123
changing materials 2, 32–87
chemical change 34
chemical properties 5
chlorides 99, 120
chlorine 9, 14, 93, 96–9
chromatograms 26–7
chromatography 26–7
classification 2, 4–31
coagulation 51
combustion 34, 35, 38–9, 42–3, 52
composite materials 5
compounds 19, 56–7
concentration 82–3, 102
concrete 69
condensation polymerisation 46–7
condensation polymers 46–7
condensation reactions 46
conglomerate 71
consolidation 66–7
constructive plate margins 73
Contact process 106, 116–17
copolymers 45
copper 30–1, 61, 65
copper oxides 79
corrosion, metals 58–61
covalent bonding 2, 14–15
cracking 40–1, 44, 106
crude oil 2, 24, 36–7, 40, 44
crystal structure 13
crystallisation 29

D
decomposition 19, 34–5, 84, 106, 108
dendrites 29
destructive plate margins 73
detergents 117, 126–7
diamond 17
diatomic gases 75
dibasic acid 132
diffusion 7
digestion 131
disaccharides 50
dislocations 29
displacement reactions 55, 98
distillate 22
distillation 22
double covalent bond 15
downward delivery 9
downward displacement of air 9

E
earthquakes 73
electrochemistry 84–7
electrolysis 65, 84–7, 163
electrolyte 84
electrolytic decomposition 35
electron microscopes 10

electrons 10–11, 60–1, 89
electroplating 59, 86
elements 18
emulsifying agent 23
emulsions 23, 51
endothermic reactions 3
energy changes 3, 105
energy content 43
enzyme-catalysed hydrolysis 50
enzymes 48, 108–9
equations 2, 74–5, 80–1
equilibrium 3, 112–13
erosion 70, 71
esters 49, 50, 126
ethanol 48–9
ethene 41, 44, 48
ethyl ethanoate 49
ethyne 15
exothermic reactions 3, 48, 105, 113
extrusive rocks 67

F
face-centred cubic structure 28–9
fats 49, 50
faults
    in ground 73
    metal structures 29
fermentation 25, 48
ferroxyl indicator 61
fertilisers 42, 114–15, 117, 136–7
fire triangle 111
flame tests 121
fluorine 96–9
food 2, 50–1
food additives 51
formulae 19, 74–5, 78–9
fossil fuels 42
fossils 67
fractional distillation 23, 24–5, 37, 40, 110–11
free atoms 103
free ions 16
fuels 38, 42–3, 49
fullerenes 17

G
galvanising 59, 61
gas syringe 8
gas–liquid chromatography 27
gaseous fuels 42
gases 6–9, 118–19
giant structures 16
glass 5, 123
global warming 53
glycerol 22–3, 50, 126
graphite 17
greenhouse effect 53

Index

H
Haber process 106, 114–15, 136
halide ions 99, 120
halogens 96–9
hard water 124–5
hexagonal close-packed structure 28
hydration 118
hydrocarbons 37, 38–9, 40–1, 106
hydrochloric acid 7
hydrogen 9, 14, 39, 97
hydrogen halides 98–9
hydrogen peroxide 106, 108
hydrolysis 50

I
igneous rocks 67, 73
immiscible liquids 22–3
indicators 129
inhibitors 107
insect bites/stings 131
insoluble salts 134–5
intermediate compounds 107
intrusive rocks 67
iodides 99, 120
iodine 16, 96–9
ion-exchange column 125
ionic bonding 2, 12–13
ionic equations 2, 75
ions 11, 16, 120–1
iron 16, 30–1, 58–9, 64, 112
iron sulphide 19
isotopes 11

L
lattice 13, 118
lead(II) bromide 84
light effects 103
limestone 68, 69, 70, 122
limewater 122–3
liquid fuels 42
liquid paraffin, cracking 41
liquids 6–7
    separation from a solid 22
    separation of mixtures 22–3
litmus 129

M
magnesium 34, 35, 74, 102, 112, 128
magnesium oxide 12, 78
margarine 51, 106
mashing 24
mass 77, 80
mass number 11
materials 2–5
mercury oxide 35
metal carbonates 57
metal hydroxides 121

metal nitrates 57
metals 18
    alloys 30–1
    corrosion 58–61
    extraction 62–5, 86
    extraction from ores 57, 62
    halogens reactions 97
    reactivity series 54–5, 56
    structure 28–9
metamorphic rocks 67, 71
methane 14, 38–9, 42–3
minerals 50
miscible liquids 22
missing atoms 29
mixtures 18, 19, 20–7
Moh's scale 66
molar concentrations 82
mole 76–7
molecular structures 16
monomers 44, 46
monosaccharides 50
mortar 123

N
naming of compounds 19
neutralisation 130–1
neutrons 10–11
nitrate ions 121
nitrogen 9, 15, 94, 110–11, 114–15, 136–7
noble gases 12, 94–5
nucleus 11, 29

O
oil-in-water emulsion 23, 51
ores 2, 57, 62
organic acids 128
organic compounds 36
organic solvents 21
oxidation 35, 85
oxidising agents 35
oxygen 9, 15, 92, 110–11

P
Pangaea 72
paper chromatography 26–7
particle size 100–1
particles 6–7
patterns of behaviour 3, 88–137
peptide link 51
percentage yield 81
Periodic Table 88–91
pH 129
phenylketonuria 27
phosphorus 136
photosynthesis 52
physical change 34
physical properties 5

plate tectonics 72–3
polyamide 46
polyester 46
polymerisation 44–7
polymers 2, 44–7
polysaccharides 50
potassium 136
potassium chlorate 33
precipitation 121, 134–5
pressure effects 103
products 74
proteins 50–1
protons 10–11
purity 20, 118

Q
quantitative electrolysis 87
quicklime 122

R
rates of reactions 3, 100–7
raw materials 4–5
reactants 74
reactivity series 54–5, 56
redox reactions 35
reducing agents 35
reduction 35, 85
refining 37
reforming 40
renewable fuels 42
reversible reactions 3, 112–13
rock cycle 70–1
rocks 2, 66–9, 122
rusting 58–9

S
salt formation 132–5
saponification 49, 126
saturated hydrocarbons 38, 40
saturated solutions 32
sedimentary rocks 36, 66–7, 71, 73
separating mixtures 20–7
silicon chloride 78–9
silicon(IV) oxide 16
slaked lime 123
soap 49, 124, 126–7
soapless detergents 117, 126–7
sodium 62
sodium chloride 25, 86–7
    bonding 12, 13
    giant structure 16
    purity 20–1
    sodium extraction 62–3
    solubility 32
soil testing 130–1
solid fuels 42
solids 6–7, 22

139

Index

solubility 32–3
    curves 33
    salts 132–3
soluble salts 133
solutes 32
solution mining 21
solvents 21, 32, 49
stability of compounds 56–7
starch 50
states of matter 6–7
steam reforming 39
stearic acid 126
steel 30, 31, 58
stills 25
stone 68–9
streak test 66
sublimation 25
sulphate ions 120
sulphuric acid 116–17
symbols 18
synthesis 19

T

temperature effects 104–5
thermal decomposition 34
Thermit reaction 55
thermoplastic 47
thermosetting polymers 47
tin-plating 61
titrations 83
trace elements 136
transition metals 90
triol 126
triple covalent bond 15

U

Universal Indicator 129
unsaturated hydrocarbons 40
upward delivery 9
upward displacement of air 9

V

vitamins 50
volumes
    of gases 80–1
    of solutions 83

W

washing powders 109, 127
water 3, 6, 22–3, 32, 118–19
    alkali metal reactions 92–3
    halogens reactions 96
    hard water 124–5
weathering 70, 71
whisky production 24–5

Z

zinc 30–1, 59, 61